Inside the
LSAT

Inside the
LSAT

Thomas O. White
Former President
Law School Admission Services

PETERSON'S Guides
Princeton, New Jersey

Copyright © 1992 by Thomas O. White

All rights reserved. No part of this book may be reproduced, stored in a retrieval system, or transmitted, in any form or by any means—electronic, mechanical, photocopying, recording, or otherwise—except for citations of data for scholarly or reference purposes with full acknowledgment of title, edition, and publisher and written notification to Peterson's Guides prior to such use.

Library of Congress Cataloging-in-Publication Data

White, Thomas O.
    Inside the LSAT / Thomas O. White.
      p.   cm.
    ISBN 1-56079-404-6
    1. Law schools—United States—Entrance examinations. 2. Law School Admission Test.
I. Title.
KF285.Z9W48 1991
340'.076—dc20   91-1881

Composition and design by Peterson's Guides

Printed in the United States of America

10 9 8 7 6 5 4 3

Contents

Introduction 1

Training Sessions

1. Warming Up for Your LSAT Training 5
2. Preparation Anxiety Brings Us Together 15
3. Academic Conditioning May Be Hazardous to Your LSAT Score 18
4. Getting to Know the LSAT 22
5. Test Preparation Strategy 30
6. The 9-12-18 Test Planning System 32
7. LSAT Questions 40
8. Relationships Problems 44
9. Relationships Problems in Depth 49
10. Relationships Pretests and the 9-12-18 System 62
11. Arguments and Passages Problems 71
12. Arguments Problems in Depth 78
13. Arguments Pretests and the 9-12-18 System 85
14. Passages Problems in Depth 94
15. Passages Pretests and the 9-12-18 System 102
16. The Writing Sample 116
17. Writing Sample Pretests 122
18. The Finishing Touches 131

Law School Admission Test Simulation 136

Answers to Pretests and LSAT Simulation

Pretest 6-1 Answer Key 166
Relationships Pretests Answer Key 166
Arguments Pretests Answer Key 167
Passages Pretests Answer Key 167
LSAT Simulation Answer Key 168

Introduction

The chances are good that you are reading this introduction, trying to decide whether to use this book or another as you prepare for the time of reckoning—your appointment with the dreaded Law School Admission Test. You must *do* something, and you will—you could follow the well-trodden path of your predecessors, repeating the rituals they have left behind and hoping that you can crack, beat, or bust the LSAT by taking a course, practicing endless questions, reviewing subject matter, or listening to tapes.

But just like thousands of others I have met during my twenty-five years' experience with the LSAT, you sense that there must be another way—a better way—of dealing with this problematic test. Unfortunately, it's difficult to think about changing as you bump along through daily life, and you may console yourself with the thought that perhaps there really isn't another way after all.

But there is. And you have it in your hands. *Whatever else you do to prepare for the LSAT, read this book first.*

What can I tell you about this unfamiliar test?

I have worked with standardized testing and the LSAT for twenty-five years. During that time, I have administered, criticized, designed, interpreted, justified, promoted, studied, taught, thought, and testified about the LSAT. I have been responsible for the administration of more than 1,500,000 tests—over half of all the LSATs ever given—and I have studied the results of over 2 million administrations. I have learned what there is to know about this generally unfamiliar test and the way test-takers respond to it. Now I have the opportunity to share a little of what I have learned with you.

Admission tests were first toyed with by law schools in the 1920s. Over the next three decades, a variety of tests were tried but attracted little interest or following in the field of legal education. But in 1947 the LSAT came along to change all of that. The first version of the LSAT did not build upon the previous experiments in law school admission testing. Rather, it was based upon the Pepsi-Cola Scholarship Test and a number of examinations that were developed for the U.S. Navy!

After two years, changes in the test's structure were introduced, and change has become the hallmark of the LSAT. Changes in content, structure, and timing were made fourteen times in the next forty-four years. Some of them were extensive, and others, like those of 1991, were more limited.

These frequent changes alone would serve to make the LSAT unfamiliar, and the fact that it is completely different from the well-known verbal-mathematical standardized tests makes it that much more obscure. Yet, out of my long experience with the test have emerged certain truths, and it is these truths upon which this book is based.

Among the more significant things experience has taught me is that, as Dostoevsky put it, "taking a new step, uttering a new word, is what people fear most." People will go to incredible lengths to convert an unfamiliar experience into something they can recognize and "get a handle on." That is how they have dealt with the unfamiliarity of the LSAT. Courses, books, and counselors expound all kinds of theories and strategies for converting the LSAT into something else, and test-takers become disciples of these theories and strategies. Although many of the books, courses, and counselors are well intentioned, virtually all of them fail to generate much more than the enthusiasm that is substituted for the test-taker's lack of confidence.

All of the failures share two root causes: one is conceptual and the other is tactical. The conceptual flaw is the common perception on the part of teachers, writers, and advisers that the LSAT is complicated—enigmatic, tangled, and formidable. The tactical flaw is in depicting the test and its makers as adversaries of the test-taker. Making an enemy of the test *always* succeeds, and this, combined with efforts at simplification, produces a body of vulnerable test-takers who find the whole process extremely counterproductive.

However, with proper training the test can be seen differently and the vulnerable test-taker become a thing of the past. By taking advantage of my experience and insights, mastering the new perspectives and techniques provided here, you can be transformed from a potential victim to an advantaged exploiter of the LSAT.

Do not misunderstand. The path to LSAT mastery is no cakewalk, but it's far easier and more rewarding than battling an adversary who has written the rules, the questions, and the answers and, for good measure, keeps the score. It's a contest that can't be won. Far better to have the test and test-maker working *for* you, and this guide is designed to help you achieve that objective.

What factors have the most impact on your test performance?

Certain factors have a high impact on LSAT performance, and others have little. There is no practical value in

1

fooling around with aspects of the test that have little impact. By learning techniques that put high-impact factors to work for you, you improve your LSAT performance.

ANXIETY

Anxiety centers on your unfamiliarity with the LSAT and your past experience with standardized tests. By confronting the factors that produce anxiety about the LSAT, you can have a substantial impact on your preparation and performance. By learning that your past experience with standardized tests is irrelevant to the LSAT and learning new, more appropriate techniques, you can remove another layer of anxiety. Anxiety-producing misinformation, contradiction, and exaggeration will be exposed and the apparent complexity of the LSAT shown to be an illusion.

✓ AS YOU GAIN CONTROL OVER YOUR ANXIETY, YOU TAKE CHARGE OF THE TEST AND YOUR RELATIONSHIP TO IT.

ACADEMIC CONDITIONING

Your past academic experience has taught you that a superior test performance results from attending lectures, taking and reviewing notes, reading, cramming, and memorizing everything you can. Naturally you conclude that the path to a superior LSAT score is the same—listening to lectures, taking and reviewing notes, reading, memorizing, and cramming into your head everything you can about the LSAT.

Wrong! *The LSAT is not an academic exercise and cannot be converted into one.* It is much more like athletics, business, or the military, in all of which a superior performance results from superior *training*, not learning. The training techniques you will learn in this book will permit you to sidestep the negative consequences of your academic training.

✓ FOR SUPERIOR PERFORMANCE ON THE LSAT, YOU MUST TRAIN.

REASONING

The LSAT tests your skill at being able to "think like a lawyer"—reasoning in the principal ways law schools and the legal system require. This way of thinking is generally unfamiliar to people who are considering a legal education, and the LSAT attempts to measure their aptitude for it. By providing you with techniques designed to respond to the reasoning requirements of the LSAT, this book will enable you to perform more successfully on every aspect of the test.

✓ TRAINING IN THE FUNDAMENTALS OF THIS UNFAMILIAR REASONING SKILL IS THE BEST WAY TO HAVE A HIGH IMPACT ON YOUR LSAT PERFORMANCE.

What is different about high-impact training?

In the academic or "sponge" method of test preparation, you soak up as much information as you can in the hope that you will be able to squeeze out important droplets of knowledge when the time comes.

If you are proficient at the sponge method, you may feel that a few hours of your time can be converted into effective preparation for the LSAT. Forget it. And forget the notion that you can achieve a superior performance by listening to lectures or practicing test questions and memorizing clever strategies without first getting a firm grip on the test basics. High-impact training is different from all the above.

✓ TRAINING IN TECHNIQUES FOR GRASPING TEST BASICS PRODUCES THE HIGHEST IMPACT.

When you acquire a new skill, the gains are often great. For example, after training in computer basics for a short time, you find you can get results you never could before. So it is with training in LSAT basics: if you use the techniques you will learn here to *train actively* for a short time, you will find you get big results. Then, and only then, will you be ready for practice with test questions and other theories of preparation.

What do the training sessions consist of?

Each of the eighteen training sessions is relatively short and deals with a discrete subject, guiding you in the training techniques relevant to that subject. Remember, sessions are not designed as academic exercises.

✓ YOU CAN USE EACH SESSION INDEPENDENTLY.

How do you use them?

Using these sessions, you can tailor your training program to make the best possible use of the time available to you. Seven programs are mapped out in the following paragraphs. They are designed to be completed in as many as seven weeks or as little as seven hours.

THE SEVEN–WEEK PROGRAM

The order of the eighteen sessions is designed to take you through the training process in the course of thirty-five days. If you complete one session or pretest assignment each day and work five days each week, you will complete the full program in seven weeks. This is a healthy but not demanding pace. (In this and the following lists, S indicates a training session and P a pretest.)

Day	Assignment	Day	Assignment
1	Intro	19	P 13-2
2	S 1	20	P 13-3
3	S 2	21	P 13-4
4	S 3	22	P 13-5
5	S 4	23	S 14
6	S 5	24	S 15, P 15-1
7	S 6	25	P 15-2
8	S 7	26	P 15-3
9	S 8	27	P 15-4
10	S 9	28	P 15-5
11	S 10, P 10-1	29	S 16
12	P 10-2	30	S 17, P 17-1
13	P 10-3	31	P 17-2
14	P 10-4	32	P 17-3
15	P 10-5	33	S 18
16	S 11	34	P 10-6, P 13-6, P 15-6, P 17-4
17	S 12		
18	S 13, P 13-1	35	Simulated LSAT

THE FIVE–WEEK PROGRAM

The five-week program is a variation of the seven-week program. It assumes that you complete one session or pretest assignment each day and work seven days each week. Again, you complete the training process over the course of thirty-five days. This program keeps you working each day at a reasonable pace.

THE FOUR–WEEK PROGRAM

The four-week program picks up the pace a bit. It assumes that you work six days each week, completing the program in twenty-four days. This further assumes that you will usually devote at least 1 hour of concentrated effort to the training each day—a little extra time in which to think through the exercise will help.

Day	Assignment	Day	Assignment
1	Intro	15	P 13-2, P 13-3
2	S 1	16	S 14
3	S 2	17	S 15, P 15-1
4	S 3	18	P 15-2, P 15-3
5	S 4, S 5	19	S 16, P 17-1, P 17-2
6	S 6	20	P 10-4, P 13-4, P 15-4
7	S 7		
8	S 8	21	P 10-5, P 13-5, P 15-5, P 17-3
9	S 9		
10	S 10, P 10-1	22	P 10-6, P 13-6, P 15-6, P 17-4
11	P 10-2, P 10-3		
12	S 11	23	S 18
13	S 12	24	Simulated LSAT
14	S 13, P 13-1		

THE THREE–WEEK PROGRAM

The three-week program requires you to work at an accelerated pace. It includes all of the sessions and assumes that you will be able to put in 1½–2 hours of concentrated effort each day. It also assumes that you work six days each week, so you complete the program in eighteen days.

Day	Assignment	Day	Assignment
1	Intro, S 1	12	S 14, S 15, P 15-1
2	S 2, S 3	13	P 15-2, P 15-3, P 15-4
3	S 4, S 5		
4	S 6	14	S 16, P 17-1, P 17-2
5	S 7	15	P 17-3, S 18
6	S 8, S 9	16	P 10-5, P 13-5, P 15-5
7	S 10, P 10-1, P 10-2		
8	P 10-3, P 10-4	17	P 10-6, P 13-6, P 15-6, P 17-4
9	S 11, S 12		
10	S 13, P 13-1, P 13-2	18	Simulated LSAT
11	P 13-3, P 13-4		

THE TWO–WEEK PROGRAM

The two-week program sets a demanding pace. It drops two sessions and some of the pretests. It assumes that you will be able to put in 1½–2 hours of concentrated effort each day, working thirteen days straight.

Day	Assignment	Day	Assignment
1	Intro, S 1	9	P 15-2, S 16, P 17-1
2	S 3, S 5, S 6	10	P 17-2, S 18
3	S 7, S 8	11	P 10-3, P 13-3, P 15-3
4	S 9		
5	S 10, P 10-1, P 10-2	12	P 10-4, P 13-4, P 15-4
6	S 11, S 12		
7	S 13, P 13-1, P 13-2	13	Simulated LSAT
8	S 14, S 15, P 15-1		

THE ONE–WEEK PROGRAM

This program is cutting it very fine. It goes directly to the sessions that will produce the greatest impact in seven days of some 1½–2 hours of concentrated effort each day.

Day	Assignment	Day	Assignment
1	Intro, S 1	6	P 10-1, P 13-1, P 15-1
2	S 3, S 5, S 6		
3	S 7, S 8, S 9, S 10	7	P 10-2, P 13-2, P 15-2
4	S 11, S 12, S 13, S 14		
5	S 15, S 16, S 17, S 18		

THE ONE–DAY PROGRAM

This program goes at warp speed. It assumes that you will spend 7 hours with the sessions in the order set out. This can make a meaningful difference in your performance, but don't expect a miracle.

Assignment	Assignment
Intro	S 14
S 3	S 18
S 7	S 6
S 8	S 10, S 13, S 15
S 9	P 10-1, P 13-1, P 15-1
S 11	P 10-2, P 13-2, P 15-2
S 12	P 10-3, P 13-3, P 15-3

What's next?

The next sessions deal with two critical factors in test performance that do not appear directly on the LSAT: anxiety and academic conditioning. After this, the sessions concentrate on elements of the LSAT and the type of reasoning required by law schools and the legal system. The final sessions discuss techniques for handling the LSAT Writing Sample and the test environment.

A number of sessions include sample LSAT questions; in fact, the guide includes the equivalent of nearly three LSATs'-worth of test questions. Yet it is not filled with practice questions. This is not to imply that you should not train with practice questions; it simply means that a limited number of practice questions are required to develop the techniques needed to train effectively for the LSAT. Once you develop the requisite skills, you can practice as much as you wish with questions that you can get from Law School Admission Services or other sources.

TRAINING SESSION 1

Warming Up for Your LSAT Training

You will warm up for your LSAT training by developing basic performance information to determine where you stand. In this session, you will complete three short exercises that give you data about your handling of critical aspects of the LSAT, getting a sense of your present state of test readiness as well as of those aspects of test performance that will benefit most from LSAT training.

What are these warm-up exercises?

The test-maker is interested in *results only*—that is, how many *best answers* the scoring machine finds on your answer sheet. (We will refer to "best" rather than "right" answers throughout. The reason will become clear later.) The route you take to the answer is of no interest to the test-maker: your score is the same whether you guess an answer or spend 20 minutes puzzling it out. But *your* interests are different from those of the test-maker. *How* you select answers is critical to your performance and its improvement, so the exercises in this session are structured to elicit basic information about the way you select answers as well as the answers you select.

The exercises are based on the three types of questions found on the LSAT. Each exercise involves a set of questions that you are to answer in *exactly 10 minutes*. Using more than 10 minutes, no matter how tempting, will corrupt the results and attenuate the value of the analysis.

How do you complete the exercises?

Before beginning, make certain that you will not be interrupted during the 30-plus minutes required to complete the exercises. Turn off the phone, hang out your Do Not Disturb sign, and secure the perimeter of your work area. Pencils with erasers and a watch, clock, or other precise timing device are essential. No reference materials, scratch paper, or outside help are permitted.

To reiterate, the LSAT score is determined only by the number of best answers marked on the answer sheet. Unlike similar standardized tests, *there is no penalty for guessing when you don't know the answer*. Omitted answers count as wrong answers. Selecting a wrong answer is no worse than omitting an answer, which means that you should never omit an answer, whether on the actual LSAT or in these introductory exercises.

✓ GUESS WHEN YOU DON'T KNOW THE ANSWER.

Follow the brief instructions that precede each set of questions. The time you take to read them is included in the 10 minutes allotted for each exercise.

How do you mark the answer sheet?

The format of the answer grid used with these exercises is different from that of typical standardized tests and of the actual LSAT. As usual, there are five bubbles that correspond to the answer options for each question, but there are two additional bubbles.

1. Ⓐ Ⓑ Ⓒ Ⓓ Ⓔ   Ⓖ Ⓣ

There are four possible situations that apply to every question you answer in the three exercises. Be sure you understand them fully.

SITUATION 1

Situation 1 involves the **certain answer** selection that you make when you are *sure* of the best answer to a question. You blacken the space on the answer sheet that corresponds to your answer selection for that question.

For example, suppose your answer selection for question 1 is E. You would mark the answer sheet as follows:

1. Ⓐ Ⓑ Ⓒ Ⓓ ●   Ⓖ Ⓣ

SITUATION 2

Situation 2 involves a **second answer** selection. If you have *any doubt* about the choice between two answer op-

5

tions, indicate both your first and second selections on the answer sheet by using two different marks in the spaces corresponding to your two choices for that question.

On question 1, suppose you determine that answer options B, D, and E are wrong, but you are uncertain of the choice between the two remaining options, A and C.

1. First, decide which of the two options is best, and blacken the space that corresponds to your first answer selection.
2. Next, place an X over the space that corresponds to your second answer selection.

Assume that your first answer selection is C and your second is A. The answer sheet would be marked as follows:

1. ⊗ Ⓑ ● Ⓓ Ⓔ   Ⓖ Ⓣ

SITUATION 3

Situation 3 involves **guessing after consideration** of the question and the answer options. When there are more than two answer options about which you are uncertain, you make three marks on your answer sheet.

For example, suppose you consider question 1 and determine that answer option B is wrong, but you cannot narrow the other options to two. In fact, you cannot decide among the four remaining options, A, C, D, and E.

1. First, decide which of the four options is best, and blacken the space that corresponds to this selection.
2. Next, place an X over the space corresponding to your second answer selection.
3. Finally, blacken the space designated G (for "guess") on the answer sheet.

Assume that, after considering the question and the answer options, your best guess is option D, and your second choice is A. The answer sheet would reflect your selections as follows:

1. ⊗ Ⓑ Ⓒ ● Ⓔ   ● Ⓣ

SITUATION 4

Situation 4 involves **insufficient time**. When you have had insufficient time to consider all questions on the exercise, you indicate this fact by making two marks on your answer sheet.

For example, suppose that you do not have time to consider question 7.

1. First, blacken the space that corresponds to your random selection or guess of an answer.
2. Next, blacken the space designated T (for "time") on the answer sheet.

Assume that your guess is C. The answer sheet would be marked as follows:

1. Ⓐ Ⓑ ● Ⓓ Ⓔ   Ⓖ ●

What is the exercise procedure?

Note the time, or set an alarm clock for 10 minutes. Begin Exercise 1. Allow only 10 minutes to complete it, and take a very short break. Proceed through Exercises 2 and 3 in the same fashion. Then complete the analyses that follow the exercises.

For your convenience, answer blanks are provided at the end of each exercise. In an actual test situation, you would be given an answer sheet. The marking possibilities are reiterated in the following chart.

Certain answer selection	1. Ⓐ Ⓑ Ⓒ Ⓓ ●	Ⓖ Ⓣ
Second answer selection	1. ⊗ Ⓑ ● Ⓓ Ⓔ	Ⓖ Ⓣ
Guessing after consideration	1. ⊗ Ⓑ Ⓒ ● Ⓔ	● Ⓣ
Insufficient time	1. Ⓐ Ⓑ ● Ⓓ Ⓔ	Ⓖ ●

EXERCISE 1. ARGUMENTS

Complete the following seven-question exercise. Evaluate the reasoning contained in the brief statements, and select the best answer. Do not make implausible, superfluous, or incompatible assumptions. Select the best answer to each question, and mark the corresponding space(s) on the answer grid at the end of the exercise. Follow the procedures described previously.

1. The alumni of Elmont think very highly of their college. The annual giving campaign of the school raised more than $10-million last year. This amount is much more than any other college of comparable size was able to raise.
   The above assumes which of the following?
   (A) Elmont has the largest fund-raising staff of any college of its size.
   (B) The per capita gift by Elmont alumni is larger than that of any other college of its size.
   (C) The contributions to the Elmont annual giving campaign reflect the esteem in which alumni hold the college.
   (D) The Elmont fund-raising staff is more able than the comparable staff of any other college of its size.
   (E) The annual giving tradition at Elmont is of longer standing than that of any other college of its size.

2. Cutting taxes results in more money being available to spend. The result of more spending is greater demand for goods and services. The result of greater demand is more production and higher employment. Therefore, cutting taxes is good for the economy.
   The above argument is NOT based upon which of the following assumptions?
   I. Cutting taxes will result in less government spending.
   II. High employment is good for the economy.
   III. Cutting taxes will result in increased savings.
   (A) I only
   (B) II only
   (C) III only
   (D) I and II only
   (E) I and III only

Questions 3-4
   Must you diet to lose weight? Or can you shed unwanted pounds just by taking four tiny pills daily? Never before has it been possible for you to easily and safely have a chance to be as slim as you once were. Try Waist Away today and find out.

3. The argument in this advertisement makes which of the following assumptions?
   I. The readers do not want to diet to lose weight.
   II. The readers have tried unsuccessfully to lose unwanted pounds in the past.
   III. The readers previously weighed more than they now do.
   (A) I only
   (B) II only
   (C) III only
   (D) I and II only
   (E) I and III only

4. Assuming that the representations in the preceding advertisement are true, they most reasonably lead to which of the following conclusions?
   (A) You will lose weight if you take Waist Away.
   (B) It is safer to lose weight by taking a pill than by dieting.
   (C) Taking Waist Away might help you lose weight.
   (D) You will become as slim as you once were if you take Waist Away.
   (E) It is difficult to lose weight by dieting.

5. Nicotine is a drug. Some drugs are harmful. All tobacco products contain nicotine.
   If the above statements are true, which of the following can be inferred?
   (A) All tobacco products are harmful.
   (B) Not all, but some, tobacco products are harmful.
   (C) Some tobacco products are harmful.
   (D) Not all, but some, tobacco products may be harmful.
   (E) All tobacco products may be harmful.

6. Blaming airline accidents on pilot error is a mistake. Pilots should not be held responsible for a lapse or confusion that results in an airplane's controls not being activated or being wrongly activated. All humans err in this way. Accidents occur because cockpit designers expect pilots to behave like automatons.
   Which of the following, if true, does NOT strengthen the above argument?
   (A) The familiar color convention of green for safe and red for danger is reversed for some cockpit controls.
   (B) Every surface in the cockpit is crammed with meters, gauges, and controls that look alike except for small labels.
   (C) Controls for dissimilar functions are located far apart in the cockpit.
   (D) Controls are located in the cockpit for ease of maintenance rather than ease of operation by the pilot.
   (E) In the cockpit, controls for dissimilar functions have the same shape.

GO ON TO THE NEXT PAGE.

7. A person is either an extrovert or an introvert. Since this woman is not an introvert, she is an extrovert.

Which of the following, if true, does NOT weaken the argument?

   I. There is no evidence that this woman is not an introvert.
   II. A person can be extroverted in some environments and introverted in others.
   III. It is hard to determine whether a person is an introvert or an extrovert.

(A) I only
(B) II only
(C) III only
(D) I and II only
(E) I, II, and III

EXERCISE 2. PASSAGES

Complete the following nine-question exercise. The questions are based on what is stated or implied in the passage. Select the best answer to each question, and mark the corresponding space(s) on the answer grid at the end of the exercise. Follow the procedures described previously.

Throughout the world, people concerned with the problem of drinking and driving have absorbed the impression that in Scandinavia—particularly in Sweden and Norway—the problem has been controlled by means
(5) of law. Swedish and Norwegian statutes are the world's first examples of *per se* drinking and driving laws. These statutes are distinguished from the laws of other nations by their use of prison and license deprivation as the routine penalties and by the prohibition, not of
(10) impairment while driving, but of attaining a specified level of blood-alcohol concentration as determined by scientific tests of bodily substances. To date, however, very little information other than personal experiences and anecdotes has been provided by the Scandinavians
(15) and their admirers to support the claim that the Swedish and Norwegian legal approach has deterred drinking drivers.
  This report presents the findings of a study of evidence concerning this deterrence hypothesis evaluated
(20) by the technique of interrupted time-series analysis. Under proper conditions, the interrupted time-series method provides a procedure for deciding between alternative hypotheses. These conditions are a sharp introduction of the legal change and valid measures of
(25) crashes over an extended time period surrounding the change. The study found that the widespread belief in the deterrent effect of the Swedish and Norwegian laws has little solid support. The arguments appearing in various research reports prepared by the Universities of Helsinki,
(30) Oslo, and Stockholm are inconclusive, and application of the interrupted time-series method to the available data does not furnish support for the deterrence hypothesis. The impression that there is strong and convincing evidence to believe that the Scandinavian laws have
(35) deterred drinking and driving is false. This impression may be fairly characterized as "the Scandinavian myth."
  The arguments that have been made in favor of the deterrence hypothesis are weak and unconvincing. When interrupted time-series analysis is applied to series of
(40) motor vehicle casualty data from Sweden and Norway, according to the deterrence hypothesis it would be expected to show changes corresponding to the initiation of the legal reforms in question. This expectation is not fulfilled. Failure to find support for the deterrence
(45) hypothesis does not disprove the hypothesis, which has the merit of common-sense plausibility, but it indicates that the current widespread faith is without firm grounding. From the practical viewpoint, it is suggested that the continuation of current policy in Sweden and
(50) Norway, and its adoption elsewhere, should be more tentative and subject to more scrutiny and critical evaluation. The search for systematic evidence of deterrence by the Norwegian and Swedish laws yielded only four arguments that alleged that deterrence was
(55) indicated by the stability of the violation rate, the low frequency of blood-alcohol concentrations found among motor vehicle fatalities, the strong public support for existing laws, and the prominence of alcohol problems among convicted drivers. None of these arguments is
(60) adequate or convincing, in part because their premises are suspect and in general because they fail to show that the asserted conditions are necessarily produced by the laws in question. A reasonable alternative explanation of all the data raised by the Scandinavian supporters of the
(65) deterrence hypothesis is that both the facts they cite and the laws purportedly explaining these facts are the product of attitudes and behavior patterns that differentiate Norway and Sweden from the countries with which they are compared.

1. The principal point of the passage is that
   (A) Scandinavians do not drink and drive less than others
   (B) drinking drivers are not deterred by Scandinavian laws
   (C) evidence that Scandinavian laws deter drinking and driving is weak
   (D) Scandinavian drinking and driving policies should not be continued
   (E) the strong support for Scandinavian drinking and driving laws is not justified

2. According to the passage, which of the following are features of the Scandinavian laws to deter drinking and driving?
   I. Violations are determined by driving impairment.
   II. Violations are routinely punished by imprisonment.
   III. Violations are decided by tested blood-alcohol levels.
   (A) I only
   (B) II only
   (C) III only
   (D) II and III only
   (E) I, II, and III

3. Which of the following does the author conclude best accounts for "the Scandinavian myth" (line 36)?
   (A) the general belief in the deterrence hypothesis
   (B) the common-sense plausibility of the arguments supporting it
   (C) the prominence of alcohol use among those convicted
   (D) the impression that the laws have discouraged drinking and driving
   (E) the strong public support for the existing laws

4. According to the passage, interrupted time-series analysis is a
   (A) technique used to support the deterrence hypothesis
   (B) scientific test used to measure legal change
   (C) system used to disprove claims made for legal reforms
   (D) process used to evaluate competing theories
   (E) method used to determine valid legal reform strategies

5. *Per se* laws (line 6) describe which of the following?
   (A) statutes that are expected to show changes in current policy
   (B) statutes that determine an offense by scientific tests
   (C) statutes that have deterrence of offensive behavior as their purpose
   (D) statutes that are distinguished by their requirement of strong evidence
   (E) statutes that punish impairment while driving

6. According to the passage, a low incidence of drinking and driving in Scandinavia is NOT explained by which of the following?
   I. attitudes of drivers in Norway and Sweden
   II. stable violation rates of drivers in Norway and Sweden
   III. behavior patterns of drivers in Norway and Sweden
   (A) I only
   (B) II only
   (C) III only
   (D) I and III only
   (E) I, II, and III

7. Which of the following, if true, would most weaken the conclusion the author reaches with respect to Scandinavian drinking and driving laws?
   (A) There is a low incidence of drinking and driving in France and Spain.
   (B) Blood-alcohol concentration does not measure driving impairment.
   (C) Motor vehicle fatalities in Scandinavia are higher than for most countries.
   (D) Alcohol problems in Scandinavia show little change over time.
   (E) Drinking and driving laws were enacted over a long period of time.

8. Which of the following, if true, would most strengthen the conclusion the author reaches with respect to Scandinavian drinking and driving laws?
   (A) The legal drinking age in Scandinavia was raised from 18 to 25 at the same time *per se* drinking and driving laws were enacted.
   (B) Driving impairment is not consistently the result of high blood-alcohol concentration.
   (C) Motor vehicle fatalities in France and Spain are higher than in Denmark.
   (D) Scandinavian countries have a higher incidence of alcoholism than any other developed country.
   (E) Scandinavian drinking and driving laws have been changed many times.

9. Which of the following accounts for the Scandinavian drinking and driving data, in the view of the statement's author?
   (A) The Scandinavians report only personal experiences and anecdotes.
   (B) The research producing the data was superficial and not rigorously performed.
   (C) The customs and temperament of Scandinavians are different from those of people in other countries.
   (D) The application of time-series analysis methods to compiled information produces valid measures.
   (E) The Scandinavians have faith in the plausibility of their approach to the problem.

EXERCISE 3. RELATIONSHIPS

Complete the following nine-question exercise. The questions are based on a set of conditions. Select the best answer to each question, and mark the corresponding space(s) on the answer grid at the end of the exercise. Follow the procedures described previously. Making a diagram may be helpful in the answer selection process.

Questions 1-9
Four fathers, Mr. Reed, Mr. Stark, Mr. Taylor, and Mr. Vine, each with one daughter, are seated at a square table at a father-daughter dinner in Greenville. There are two seats on each side of the table.

The Reeds sit next to each other on one side of the table.
Mr. Stark sits directly opposite Mr. Taylor.

1. If Ms. Stark sits on the same side of the table as Mr. Taylor, which of the following must be true?
   (A) One of the Reeds sits next to one of the Starks.
   (B) The Vines sit opposite the Reeds.
   (C) The Taylors sit together.
   (D) The Vines sit together.
   (E) One of the Taylors sits next to one of the Reeds.

2. If Mr. Vine sits next to Mr. Taylor, which of the following could be true?
   I. All fathers sit next to each other.
   II. Three daughters sit next to each other.
   III. Each father sits next to his daughter.
   (A) I only
   (B) II only
   (C) III only
   (D) I and II only
   (E) II and III only

3. If one of the Vines sits opposite the Reeds, which of the following CANNOT be true?
   (A) All fathers and daughters sit next to each other.
   (B) The Taylors sit next to each other.
   (C) One of the Starks sits opposite the Reeds.
   (D) One of the Taylors sits opposite the Reeds.
   (E) Both of the Starks sit opposite the Reeds.

4. If the Taylors sit next to each other, which of the following could be true?
   I. A Reed sits next to each Vine.
   II. The Starks sit opposite the Reeds.
   III. The Vines sit opposite the Reeds.
   (A) I only
   (B) II only
   (C) III only
   (D) I and II only
   (E) II and III only

5. If Mr. Taylor sits next to Mr. Reed, which of the following must be true?
   (A) Mr. Vine sits opposite the Reeds.
   (B) Ms. Vine sits next to Mr. Stark.
   (C) Mr. Stark sits next to Ms. Reed.
   (D) Ms. Taylor sits next to Mr. Vine.
   (E) Mr. Stark sits next to Ms. Vine.

6. If the Starks sit next to each other, which of the following CANNOT be true?
   (A) A Reed sits next to each Vine.
   (B) The Taylors sit next to each other.
   (C) The Reeds sit opposite the Starks.
   (D) Every father sits next to his daughter.
   (E) The Vines sit opposite the Reeds.

7. If Mr. Vine sits directly opposite Mr. Reed, which of the following CANNOT be true?
   (A) Three daughters sit next to each other.
   (B) Mr. Taylor sits next to Mr. Vine.
   (C) The Reeds sit opposite the Vines.
   (D) Every father sits next to his daughter.
   (E) The Starks sit opposite the Taylors.

8. If Ms. Stark and Ms. Taylor sit opposite the Reeds, which of the following must be true?
   (A) Three daughters sit next to each other.
   (B) Three fathers sit next to each other.
   (C) The Reeds sit next to the Vines.
   (D) Every father sits next to his daughter.
   (E) The Vines sit on opposite sides of the table.

9. If the Taylors sit next to each other on the same side of the table, which of the following CANNOT be true?
   (A) The Vines sit next to each other.
   (B) The Starks sit next to each other.
   (C) The Reeds sit opposite the Vines.
   (D) Every father sits next to his daughter.
   (E) The Vines sit opposite the Taylors.

EXERCISE ANSWER KEY

Question	Best Answer	Best Match (Y or N)	Second Answer	Second Match (Y or N)	Multi Match (Y or N)	Single Match (Y or N)	Negative Match (Y or N)	Positive Match (Y or N)	Guessing (Y or N)	G
Exercise 1. Arguments										
1.	C	___	D	___	___	___	___	___	___	___
2.	E	___	B	___	___	___	___	___	___	___
3.	A	___	E	___	___	___	___	___	___	___
4.	C	___	D	___	___	___	___	___	___	___
5.	E	___	A	___	___	___	___	___	___	___
6.	C	___	D	___	___	___	___	___	___	___
7.	C	___	D	___	___	___	___	___	___	___
Totals		Ys___		Ys___	Ys___	Ys___	Ys___	Ys___	Ys___	Gs___
		Ns___		Ns___	Ns___	Ns___	Ns___	Ns___	Ns___	
Exercise 2. Passages										
1.	C	___	E	___	___	___	___	___	___	___
2.	D	___	C	___	___	___	___	___	___	___
3.	D	___	A	___	___	___	___	___	___	___
4.	D	___	B	___	___	___	___	___	___	___
5.	B	___	C	___	___	___	___	___	___	___
6.	B	___	D	___	___	___	___	___	___	___
7.	E	___	B	___	___	___	___	___	___	___
8.	A	___	E	___	___	___	___	___	___	___
9.	C	___	A	___	___	___	___	___	___	___
Totals		Ys___		Ys___	Ys___	Ys___	Ys___	Ys___	Ys___	Gs___
		Ns___		Ns___	Ns___	Ns___	Ns___	Ns___	Ns___	
Exercise 3. Relationships										
1.	A	___	E	___	___	___	___	___	___	___
2.	E	___	B	___	___	___	___	___	___	___
3.	E	___	A	___	___	___	___	___	___	___
4.	C	___	D	___	___	___	___	___	___	___
5.	C	___	A	___	___	___	___	___	___	___
6.	C	___	A	___	___	___	___	___	___	___
7.	A	___	D	___	___	___	___	___	___	___
8.	E	___	C	___	___	___	___	___	___	___
9.	E	___	D	___	___	___	___	___	___	___
Totals		Ys___		Ys___	Ys___	Ys___	Ys___	Ys___	Ys___	Gs___
		Ns___		Ns___	Ns___	Ns___	Ns___	Ns___	Ns___	

What do the warm-up exercises tell you about your performance?

Use the Exercise Answer Key on page 11, and record your answer choices in the spaces provided.

RECORDING BEST ANSWERS

Recording the **best-answer** results is straightforward. If your blackened answer *matches* the Best Answer on the answer key, place a Y in the corresponding space in the Best Match column. If your blackened answer *does not match* the Best Answer, place an N in the corresponding space in the Best Match column.

Total the number of Ys and Ns for each exercise, and enter those numbers in the Totals spaces in the Best Match column for that exercise.

RECORDING SECOND ANSWERS

Look sharp now, because recording your **second-answer** results requires some agility and concentration. Wherever you used an X to mark an answer choice, and that choice *matches* the Best Answer to the question, place a Y in the corresponding space in the Second Match column.

For example, suppose that for question 1 in the Passages exercise you blackened answer E and marked C with an X:

1. Ⓐ Ⓑ ⊗ Ⓓ ● Ⓖ Ⓣ

When you consult the answer key, you find that the Best Answer to question 1 is option C. You record the result by placing a Y in the corresponding space in the Second Match column.

Now for the complicated part. Review every question for which you placed an N in the Best Match column. If your blackened answer choice *matches* the Second Answer for that question, place a Y in the corresponding space in the Second Match column.

For example, for question 1 in the Passages exercise suppose you blackened answer choice E:

1. Ⓐ Ⓑ Ⓒ Ⓓ ● Ⓖ Ⓣ

The Best Answer to the question is C, but the Second Answer is E, so you place a Y in the corresponding space in the Second Match column. For those questions that do not merit a Y in the Second Match column, you place an N in the corresponding space.

Total the number of Ys and Ns for each exercise, and enter those numbers in the Totals space in the Second Match column for that exercise.

RECORDING MULTIPLE– AND SINGLE–OPTION ANSWERS

Recording **multiple-option** and **single-option** answer results requires you to review the Best Match column for every question. For every Y or N in the Best Match column, place a Y or N on the blank line in the Multi Match or Single Match column. (Blanks are provided only where the answer format of a question corresponds to one or the other designation.)

Total the number of Ys for each exercise, and enter that number in the Totals space in the Multi Match or Single Match column for that exercise.

RECORDING NEGATIVE AND POSITIVE MATCHES

Recording **negative** and **positive** results also requires you to review the Best Match column for every question. For every Y or N found in the Best Match column, place a Y or N on the blank line in the Negative Match or Positive Match column. (Blanks are provided only where the answer format of a question corresponds to one or the other designation.)

Total the number of Ys for each exercise, and enter that number in the Totals space in the Negative Match or Positive Match column for that exercise.

RECORDING GUESSING RESULTS

Recording **guessing** results requires you to review both your original answers and the Best Match column. If you blackened a G on your answer sheet, place a Y in the corresponding space on the first of the two Guessing columns. Otherwise enter an N in that column. Only when you enter a Y in the first column do you refer to the Best Match column. If there is a matching Y for that question in the Best Match column, enter a G in the second Guessing column.

Total the number of Ys and Gs for each exercise, and enter those numbers in the Totals spaces in the Guessing columns for that exercise.

What happens next?

Now you have the raw materials. Analyzing the exercise results comes next. As you will have gathered from your work on the answer key, we are looking at nine different aspects of your performance—overall, question types, second answers, multiple-option answers, single-option answers, negative matches, positive matches, time, and guessing. You will need to refer to your original answers and the Exercise Answer Key.

As you work through the analysis, remember that the exercises are only samples. They are designed to provide preliminary information about your performance, *not to develop expectations for your performance*. It is only in the course of your training that performance expectations will be established. And, by training, your performance will improve on all aspects of the LSAT.

OVERALL TEST PROFICIENCY

On the corresponding lines below, enter the total Ys for each exercise from the Best Match column on the answer key. After you enter this data, complete the three calculations indicated and total the results.

Arguments Total Ys ____ x 6.8 = ____

Passages Total Ys ____ x 3.1 = ____

Relationships Total Ys ____ x 2.7 = ____

Total ____%

The final calculation expresses your overall performance as a percentage. Simply speaking, the LSAT is designed so that, in order to get an average score, the test-taker needs to select slightly more than 60 percent of the best answers. The nature of the LSAT scoring system is such that getting a small number of best answers above 60 percent results in a relatively large increase in percentile placement on the LSAT scale. The higher the percentage, the stronger the performance.

QUESTION–TYPE PROFICIENCY

Next, your performance is analyzed by type of question. As with the previous calculation, enter on the corresponding lines below the total Ys for each exercise from the Best Match column on the answer key. After you enter this data, complete the calculations indicated.

Arguments Total Ys ____ x 680 = $\frac{\_\_\_\_}{48}$ = ____%

Passages Total Ys ____ x 310 = $\frac{\_\_\_\_}{28}$ = ____%

Relationships Total Ys ____ x 270 = $\frac{\_\_\_\_}{24}$ = ____%

Most test-takers perform differently on the three exercises and three question types. Your performance is set out in percentages that represent your **question-type proficiency**. When compared, these percentages indicate your relative strengths and weaknesses in working with the question types. The higher the percentage, the stronger the performance.

This performance information is not reported to the law schools, but it is useful to you to determine the question types with which you are most and least proficient. Your training will have the greatest impact in those areas where you are weakest and the largest gains may be realized.

SECOND–ANSWER PROFICIENCY

To determine your **second-answer proficiency**, enter on the corresponding lines below the total Ys for each exercise from the Second Match column and the total Ns from the Best Match column. Then total the Ys and Ns, and complete the calculations indicated.

Second Match

Arguments Total Ys ____

Passages Total Ys ____

Relationships Total Ys ____

Total Ys ____

Best Match

Arguments Total Ns ____

Passages Total Ns ____

Relationships Total Ns ____

Total Ns ____

$\frac{\text{Total Ys}}{\text{Total Ns}}$ = ____ x 100 = ____%

As you know, there are five answer choices for every LSAT question, but, to the trained eye, two choices will appear to be better than the other three in nearly every case. One of those two is the best answer; the other is the second-best. The percentage of second-best answers that you identified as the best or second-best represents your second-answer proficiency. Training will improve your skill at isolating second answer choices and selecting the best answer.

MULTIPLE–OPTION PROFICIENCY

To determine your **multiple-option proficiency**, enter on the corresponding lines below the total Ys for each exercise from the Multi Match column. Then complete the calculations indicated.

Multi Match

Arguments Total Ys ____

Passages Total Ys ____

Relationships Total Ys ____

$\frac{\text{Total Ys} \_\_\_\_}{7}$ = ____ x 100 = ____%

LSAT answer options are presented in two formats. Of the two, most test-takers find the multiple-option format more difficult. By comparing your multiple-option and single-option proficiencies, you can determine the answer formats with which you are most and least proficient.

SINGLE–OPTION PROFICIENCY

To determine your **single-option proficiency**, enter on the corresponding lines the total Ys for each exercise from the Single Match column, and complete the necessary calculations.

Single Match

Arguments Total Ys ____

Passages Total Ys ____

Relationships Total Ys ____

$\frac{\text{Total Ys} \_\_\_\_}{18}$ = ____ x 100 = ____%

As noted, comparing your multiple-option and single-option proficiencies highlights the answer format with which you are most or least proficient.

NEGATIVE QUESTION PROFICIENCY

To determine your **negative question proficiency**, enter on the corresponding lines the total Ys for each exercise from the Negative Match column, and carry out the calculations indicated.

Negative Match

Arguments   Total Ys ____
Passages   Total Ys ____
Relationships Total Ys ____

$$\frac{\text{Total Ys} \_\_\_\_}{8} = \_\_\_\_ \times 100 = \_\_\_\_\%$$

Most LSAT questions ask you to select the answer option that satisfies the conditions of the problem. But some ask you to select a *negative* answer option—one that does not satisfy, cannot satisfy, or is the exception to the options that do satisfy the conditions of the problem. Test-takers frequently find these more difficult than their positive counterparts. Your negative question proficiency is expressed as a percentage that can be compared to your positive question proficiency to determine whether you respond differently to the two types of questions.

POSITIVE QUESTION PROFICIENCY

To determine your **positive question proficiency**, enter on the corresponding lines the total Ys for each exercise from the Positive Match column, and complete the calculations.

Positive Match

Arguments   Total Ys ____
Passages   Total Ys ____
Relationships Total Ys ____

$$\frac{\text{Total Ys} \_\_\_\_}{17} = \_\_\_\_ \times 100 = \_\_\_\_\%$$

TIME PROFICIENCY

On the answer blanks, you marked every question you did not have time to consider. To determine your **time proficiency**, enter on the corresponding lines the total Ts for each exercise. Then complete the calculations indicated.

Arguments   Total Ts ____ x 680 = ____/48 = ____%
Passages   Total Ts ____ x 310 = ____/28 = ____%
Relationships Total Ts ____ x 270 = ____/24 = ____%

It is likely that your proficiency will vary from one question type to another. The higher the percentage, the more certain you can be that, for you, time is a major score factor with respect to that question type. A comparison of percentages will reveal your relative proficiencies. For most people, time appears to be *the* critical score factor on the LSAT. Training will clearly identify for you what would be *your* optimal use of test time.

GUESSING PROFICIENCY

Most people do some guessing on the LSAT. You were asked to indicate every question for which you were unable to eliminate at least three wrong answers and were required to guess. To determine your **guessing factor**, enter on the corresponding lines below the total Ys for each exercise from the first Guessing column. Then complete the necessary calculations.

Arguments   Total Ys ____ x 680 = ____/48 = ____%
Passages   Total Ys ____ x 310 = ____/28 = ____%
Relationships Total Ys ____ x 270 = ____/24 = ____%

It is likely that the amount of guessing you have done varies from one question type to another. The higher the percentage, the more you were required to guess. By comparing percentages, you determine your relative need to guess.

The percentage of guessed answers that are best answers indicates your **guessing proficiency**. To determine this figure, enter on the corresponding lines the total Gs for each exercise from the second Guessing column. Then enter the total Ys for each exercise from the first Guessing column. Complete the calculations.

Arguments $\dfrac{\text{Total Gs}}{\text{Total Ys}}$ = ____ x 100 = ____%

Passages $\dfrac{\text{Total Gs}}{\text{Total Ys}}$ = ____ x 100 = ____%

Relationships $\dfrac{\text{Total Gs}}{\text{Total Ys}}$ = ____ x 100 = ____%

To the extent that any of these percentages exceeds 20 percent, your guessing is better than predicted by statistics. Your training will prepare you to guess best and to recognize when guessing will produce the highest score.

TRAINING SESSION 2

Preparation Anxiety Brings Us Together

Admit it. You're nervous. You are probably reading this guide because of anxiety. Although you say you are simply interested in doing well on the test, in fact you are apprehensive.

Most people facing the LSAT feel two different kinds of anxiety. The first, test anxiety, is familiar to you—by this time in your academic career, you have undoubtedly experienced symptoms of anxiety during a test. Research has shown that anxiety during a test rarely impairs performance, though occasionally a person will become so upset that performance suffers significantly. But, unless you have already experienced such extreme test anxiety, it is unlikely the LSAT will provoke a similar reaction.

What is preparation anxiety?

Preparation anxiety is an obstacle to superior performance for many, if not most, test-takers. It *does* impair LSAT performance.

Most people sense that the LSAT is different. They feel the test preparation strategies that have worked for them in the past may be of no value when it comes to the LSAT. However, they don't know what else to do, so they go through the familiar motions of preparation. Something tells them this is no preparation at all, and the anxiety grows as their date with the test draws near.

What are the symptoms of preparation anxiety?

High achievers and perfectionists are the most susceptible to preparation anxiety. Although their past achievements testify to the contrary, they often feel unsure of their ability to perform well and, as a consequence, become very anxious when facing a critical test. They know that perfection is almost impossible to achieve, and their efforts are doomed from the start. Mild symptoms of preparation anxiety include tension, restlessness, boredom, disorganization, and a sense of being overwhelmed. Those more seriously affected experience depression, physical complaints, insomnia, appetite change, and shifts in their interpersonal behavior.

In nearly all instances, preparation anxiety manifests itself in procrastination: the avoidance of meaningful preparation. If you have a severe case of preparation anxiety, you will be committed to the notion of preparation—starting tomorrow or maybe next week. If the anxiety is less severe, you are likely to resort to familiar preparation rituals. You will read books about the test. You may enroll in a prep course, where you take notes for future study. Although no effective preparation actually takes place, you will try to persuade yourself otherwise, while your anxiety grows. If any of this sounds familiar, be assured that you are not alone. The majority of those facing the LSAT will be suffering the same symptoms.

Some LSAT anxiety is appropriate. After all, the test *is* difficult, and the score *is* important. But a colossal case of LSAT anxiety makes no sense at all—it is like being home alone on a dark night when the floor creaks, a door squeaks, shadows seem to dance, and the wind whistles at the window. The hair stands up on the back of your neck, and your heart begins to race. You have haunted house syndrome. Imagination takes over and projects horrors of every description onto the LSAT, and you convince yourself the score will be a measure of your worth and reveal your inadequacy to the world.

You are in needless pain. Do not project your fears onto the LSAT and give the syndrome a chance to undermine your effective test training. Sure, the LSAT is the most important factor in law school admission, but it does not measure your worth or predict your success in life. It simply does not merit projecting any such meaning onto it.

What causes preparation anxiety?

Whatever form your anxiety takes, fear of loss of control is the root cause of preparation anxiety. A feeling of loss of control over LSAT performance has four principal factors: anticipation, mystification, misinformation, and overcomplication.

✓ MOST PEOPLE ANTICIPATE THAT THE LSAT WILL BE IMPOSSIBLE.

Most people who take the LSAT believe that they will not be able to perform well on the difficult tasks it requires. They anticipate a poor performance on the test and are convinced there is little or nothing they can do about it. They sense that they have no control over the LSAT, and a classic case of preparation anxiety follows.

Most people feel mystified about what the LSAT measures, how the score is determined, what use is made of the score, and a passel of similar puzzlements. This lack of certainty feeds their sense of being unable to control their test preparation or performance.

Misinformation on the LSAT abounds, usually taking the form of contradictions, exaggerations, and everything from gossip to gospel. It travels by the printed word and by word of mouth. Nearly everyone who has come into contact with the test becomes a source, and even the official word seems contradictory. For example, some time ago, in its information book, the test-maker stated, "The LSAT measures skills and knowledge that typically develop over a long period of time, so that you cannot prepare for the test by making a last-minute effort to master specific subject areas." Although the type of questions included on the LSAT have not changed, the test-maker currently sells a kit "with hints and explanations that help you improve your skills."

The seeming complexity of the LSAT also contributes to a feeling of anxiety and loss of control. Five sections, three types of questions, a writing sample, raw scores, scaled scores, cut scores, percentiles, and all the rest serve to intensify most test-takers' apprehensions.

Where does this leave you?

Perplexed? Resentful? Angry?

Whichever it is, *you will benefit most if you acknowledge your state of mind*. Do not deny it or try to rationalize it. Accept your feelings. Acceptance is essential to your overcoming the anxiety obstacle. You need to *use* your anxiety to power your LSAT training. Effective training will give you the control you need for superior performance. And the best way to begin your training is to gain control over your anxiety.

What is the key to anxiety reduction?

When you feel that you are in control of a situation, you have little or no anxiety. Therefore, the key to reducing preparation anxiety is control, and *the key to control is developing choice, familiarity, and positivity.*

When you are told that you *must* do something, you feel that you have no control over the situation, and your anxiety increases. However, if you *choose* to do the same thing, you put yourself in control. Thus, the first key to control over preparation anxiety is to *choose* the LSAT rather than have it imposed upon you.

While it is true that you *must* take the LSAT if you intend to go to law school in the United States or Canada, the *choice* to attend law school is yours. Deciding to take the LSAT puts you in control and consequently reduces preparation anxiety. You are doing what you want to do, not what you must.

Familiarity with the test enhances your sense of control and reduces preparation anxiety. Effective training for the LSAT will show you exactly what to expect of the test and how to respond to it. This knowledge will give you more of the control you need to overcome preparation anxiety.

Positive thoughts, feelings, images, and attitudes also contribute to a sense of control. If, during test training, you keep on thinking about an exam you failed three years ago and imagine that everyone registered for the LSAT will outperform you and picture questions full of long Latin phrases and are sure you will blacken the wrong spaces on the answer sheet, chances are good that you will experience significant loss of control and suffer a terminal case of preparation anxiety. But if you think that the LSAT is totally predictable (it is) and are confident that you can take advantage of its weaknesses (you can) and can visualize the question types that are always asked on the LSAT (they always are) and are convinced that one of the 12,000 scores in the top 10 percent is waiting for you (yes, it is), then you will be in control, and your test training will be both powerful and effective.

When you encounter a negative experience during training, convert it into a positive. For example, if you miss a question, recall that no one gets all the best answers and that it is possible to miss as many as eighteen questions and still score in the top 10 percent on the LSAT.

By deciding that it is you who wants to take the LSAT, by becoming fully informed about the test and the appropriate responses to it, and by developing a positive attitude toward the test and your training for it, you will take control and overcome your preparation anxiety.

Practice worrying?

Throughout your life, people have encouraged you over obstacles with the words "don't worry." As you face the LSAT, your parents, friends, spouse, and others assure you that "Everything will be OK. Don't worry, you always do well." Accept this as encouragement, but forget it as advice.

✓ WORRY ABOUT THE LSAT.

Irrespective of how often you are told not to, you *will* worry about the LSAT. And, ironically, it's a good idea. Worrying about it motivates you to explore test-taking techniques and install a plan, and it is through these things that you gain control over the test.

However, *how* you worry is very important if the experience is to be positive and not undermine your training. The essentials of effective worrying are: identifying the threat, exploring the options available for dealing with it, and installing a safety net.

How does worry practice work?

When you practice worrying, you gain control of what threatens you. You determine the worst that can happen and install a plan that takes that outcome into account.

Suppose that studying for a multiple-choice test has never resulted in good scores for you. Naturally, you worry about having the same experience with the LSAT. Factor in the cost of a prep course and the potential loss of support of your family and friends, and you can gauge the embarrassment that a low score will cause you. This is a *threat*.

What options are available to you? One option is not to prepare for the LSAT at all—just take the test without telling anyone, since you don't believe preparation will help your performance anyway. Then when you don't do well, no one will be the wiser. This may help you deal with your preparation anxiety, but it won't help you achieve your goal of a top test score. A wiser course is to work hard to prepare for the LSAT, even if this preparation should turn out to have little effect. Explain to your family and friends that the test is very tough and the outcome very uncertain, but you will work as hard as you can to do well. Then if you don't do well, they will be prepared.

Next you install your safety net. Even if you do not do well, the worst that can happen is that you have wasted a large amount of time and money preparing. If, after all this, you perform no better than you would have done without preparation, you are no further behind than you were, and your family and friends will know that you worked hard. While this would not be a happy circumstance, it can get no worse than this, and this is not all that bad. The status quo is your safety net.

Do relaxation and concentration help reduce anxiety?

There is much evidence that people perform best when they are relaxed and able to concentrate. Training that facilitates relaxation and concentration will enhance your performance and counter preparation anxiety.

There is a straightforward training process that encourages relaxation and concentration. If it seems hokey, let me assure you it is not. You can practice its three steps frequently during your training period. The first step involves breath control—when you begin to feel anxious or tense, pause in what you are doing and *take three deep breaths*. Inhale slowly and fully, then slowly and fully exhale. As you breath deeply, execute step two, which is to *dismiss all thoughts of the past and future*. Put recollections of past performance and speculation about future performance out of your mind. Such thoughts are distracting and have no relevance to the task at hand. Finally, *focus exclusively on the immediate training task*—nothing more and nothing less. Try it. You will be relaxed and your powers of concentration restored. You will be in control.

As you have learned in this session, *control is the key to managing preparation anxiety, and training is the key to control*. By following the training regimen in this and subsequent sessions, you will gain control over your preparation anxiety and improve your LSAT performance.

TRAINING SESSION 3

Academic Conditioning May Be Hazardous to Your LSAT Score

Academic conditioning can impede LSAT performance. Yes, it's true. The learning and testing techniques that have helped you in school can actually lower your LSAT score. Even worse, the greater your academic learning and testing proficiency, the greater the risk to your test score. The objective of this session is to train you to avoid the hazards that arise from your academic conditioning.

Can you rely upon academic prowess?

Academic success has probably encouraged your interest in law school and led you to the challenge of the LSAT. You probably have some confidence in your academic ability. You have learned that a superior academic performance depends upon superior conditioning and techniques. Therefore, you reason that the conditioning and techniques that have produced good academic results for you in the past should also produce a superior LSAT score. For this to be correct, the LSAT would have to require a strictly academic performance—but this is not the case.

✓ THE LSAT IS NOT AN ACADEMIC EXERCISE.

Relying upon academic conditioning and techniques may actually impair rather than enhance your LSAT performance. By training to circumvent your academic indoctrination when preparing for and taking the LSAT, you dramatically improve your score potential.

✓ AVOIDING EFFECTIVE ACADEMIC TECHNIQUES CAN ACTUALLY IMPROVE YOUR LSAT SCORE.

Skeptical?

Sure you are. Skepticism is one of those successful academic techniques. You have been conditioned to question, and you insist on being convinced. And unless I can convince you that your academic conditioning must be put aside, your test training and LSAT performance will suffer, so here we go.

Isn't the LSAT a test like any other test?

No, it is not—at least not the kind of test you are familiar with.

Your academic conditioning has provided you with a clear picture of a test. For example, you are supposed to have acquired certain information in Professor Smoot's course. To measure the extent to which you have succeeded in this, Smoot gives a test. You know the information, answer the questions, and do well. That's a test.

Because it is called Law School Admission *Test*, your conditioning leads you to expect the customary test. Even the format of the LSAT confirms this expectation—questions and answers, paper and pencils. But appearances are deceiving. What kind of information is measured by the LSAT? What are you expected to know? The meaning of carmagnole? The formula for determining the surface area of a basketball? Everything? Nothing?

Aha! Now you know why the LSAT is not a test like other tests. Your knowledge of vocabulary, grammar, mathematical formulae, computation, facts, opinions, and other such information is not measured by the LSAT. No substantive knowledge is required. The LSAT is not designed to measure what it asks about; it is designed to measure your ability to select the best answer from the options provided by the test-maker. Unless you can avoid associating the LSAT with a familiar test, your academic conditioning may lead you astray.

What learning techniques are hazardous to LSAT Performance?

CONVERSION

When faced with the unfamiliar, we conventionally respond by doing something familiar and comfortable. Thus the majority of those facing the LSAT enroll in a "course" that they believe will teach them the substantive information required for the test—but, as we have just seen, the LSAT requires no substantive information.

As a substitute for effective preparation, weeks are wasted in the familiar classroom context searching for a way to convert the LSAT into the familiar academic test. The search is futile and just generates more preparation anxiety. Those who recognize its futility practice their academic test-taking techniques by slogging through hundreds of LSAT questions. But their practice reinforces techniques that, when applied, constrain LSAT performance.

✓ DON'T TRY TO CONVERT THE LSAT INTO SOMETHING FAMILIAR.

STUDY, STUDY, STUDY

In an academic course, success is achieved by studying. Your academic conditioning dictates that study is the best way to learn the information needed to perform well on a test. Consequently, you have been conditioned to "study" LSAT questions that will not appear on the test. Such study wastes time and amplifies preparation anxiety because, if you're honest with yourself, you know that nothing of consequence is happening.

✓ DON'T SUBSTITUTE THE COMFORT OF APPARENT STUDY FOR EFFECTIVE LSAT PREPARATION.

EFFORT EQUALS EXCELLENCE

Academic lore has it that excellent performance is a function of effort—no pain, no gain. You believe that if you work hard, you will do well on tests. "Hard work" generally means committing information to memory, but since the "information" presented by the LSAT is only a measurement vehicle, the hard work with which you are familiar has no value in the context of this test. Studying hundreds of LSAT questions misses the point. LSAT excellence depends on consistent execution of a basic reasoning task, not grunt work.

✓ DON'T SUBSTITUTE "HARD WORK" FOR EFFECTIVE LSAT PREPARATION.

GENERALIZATION

Academic rewards come regularly to those who discover the general concept that explains many specific observations. Those who are academically proficient anticipate the presence of consistency in a test and look for answers that are consistent with ones that have gone before. The LSAT anticipates this anticipation. Don't anticipate consistency in LSAT questions and answers—the opposite is often the case. The only reward for such anticipation and generalization is a consistently low test score.

✓ EACH LSAT QUESTION IS INDEPENDENT OF EVERY OTHER LSAT QUESTION.

COMPLEX DRIVES OUT SIMPLE

Your academic conditioning discourages choosing the simple or superficial answer to a test question and encourages a quest for the complex and thorough. When this conditioning is projected onto the LSAT, the test-taker frequently selects a less-than-appropriate answer because the best answer seems "too simple." Don't bypass the simple LSAT answer just because it would not be an adequate response on an academic test.

✓ THE SIMPLE ANSWER IS OFTEN THE BEST ANSWER TO AN LSAT QUESTION.

READING FOR INFORMATION

In an academic context, reading is the primary way to acquire information. When the LSAT presents a reading passage, the conditioned reaction is to read it for the information it contains. But the passages are not there to present information that you must commit to memory for future use. This would only detract from the purpose of LSAT reading passages, which is to provide a vehicle to measure your reasoning skill.

✓ DO NOT READ LSAT MATERIAL FOR THE INFORMATION IT PRESENTS.

Remember that when you read for information there is a clear context and purpose for its acquisition. Information acquisition is not among the purposes of the LSAT.

PERSUADED BY LOGIC

Perhaps the most hazardous item of academic conditioning is the belief that the logical presentation is the most persuasive one. Confidence in your knowledge of reality can lead to many an incorrect answer on the LSAT. The logic employed in the LSAT involves structure rather than reality.

✓ THE BEST ANSWER TO AN LSAT QUESTION OFTEN DEFIES REALITY AS YOU KNOW IT.

What test-taking techniques are hazardous to LSAT Performance?

THE WELL–WORN PATH

People who are successful at academic test taking generally follow a clear path to good grades. They find a routine that leads them to a consistently strong test performance. For example, they apply the first-to-last strategy, answering the first question first and proceeding through the questions in the order presented. Many standardized tests anticipate this strategy—the SAT, for example, presents questions in the order of least to most difficult. The LSAT is *not* such a test. LSAT questions are designated by a number that corresponds to a number on the answer sheet. There is no other purpose for the order of questions. Generally, there is no benefit in answering LSAT questions in the order presented.

✓ CONSIDER QUESTIONS IN THE ORDER THAT WILL PRODUCE THE HIGHEST SCORE FOR YOU.

THE COMPLETION DELUSION

Academic conditioning promotes the delusion that you can enhance your performance by considering every question and completing the test. For virtually everyone who takes the LSAT, the opposite is true. *No points are gained by completing the entire LSAT.* Your score results exclusively from the number of correct answers you select. In fact, it is by *not* completing the test that most people will hit their top test score.

✓ RARELY WILL COMPLETING THE LSAT PRODUCE A SUPERIOR PERFORMANCE.

PERFECTLY IMPOSSIBLE

Academic conditioning encourages the belief that a flawless performance is the test-taker's objective. For the LSAT, this objective is virtually impossible to achieve. Instead of striving for impossible perfection, the well-trained LSAT test-taker will expect to get certain types of questions wrong and will concentrate on those that are most likely to produce a top score.

✓ PLAN FOR A TOP SCORE, NOT AN IMPOSSIBLE PERFECT PERFORMANCE.

THE QUESTION IS THE QUESTION

Academic conditioning suggests that the test question is the question; that is, the question is the sentence that ends with a question mark. This expectation is confusing to the LSAT test-taker, because, *on the LSAT, it is the answer choices that define the questions.* Most LSAT questions are vague. Only by careful consideration of the answer choices can you clarify the questions and select the best answer.

✓ ON THE LSAT, THE ANSWER IS THE QUESTION.

HARD QUESTIONS COUNT MORE

Academic tests often reward correct answers to difficult questions with more points than are awarded for less difficult ones. This custom does not apply on the LSAT. While LSAT questions vary considerably in difficulty, the scoring rule is *one question, one point.* Answering the ten least difficult questions yields exactly the same number of score points as would answering the ten most difficult questions.

✓ ANSWER THE LEAST DIFFICULT LSAT QUESTIONS BEFORE ANSWERING THE MOST DIFFICULT ONES.

BYO

Academic conditioning prompts a bring-your-own strategy in most test-takers. In other words, successful academic test-takers have preconceived notions about what the questions and answers will be, and they tend to find only what they're looking for. This test-taking strategy is of no value with the LSAT. The LSAT provides all questions *and* answers. Having your own questions or answers in mind can only lead to confusion.

✓ AVOID THE TEMPTATION TO BRING YOUR OWN QUESTIONS OR ANSWERS TO THE LSAT.

ASSUMPTIONS

A superior performance often results from making the invited assumptions on an academic test. Students know the subject matter, the professor, the text, and the context in which the test is being given. It is natural and justifiable to make assumptions about test questions when they are presented in these circumstances. The LSAT exploits this conditioning by inviting many assumptions. But the LSAT is different—there is no course, no subject matter, no professor, no text, and no context. Making assumptions about test questions or answers is not only inappropriate but is hazardous to your test score. The LSAT is context-free.

✓ MAKE NO ASSUMPTIONS WHEN TRYING TO SELECT THE BEST ANSWER TO AN LSAT QUESTION.

THE BINGO FALLACY

The combination of the multiple-choice format of the LSAT and the BYO strategy of test-takers generates the "bingo fallacy." Its mechanics are as follows: the test-taker reads the LSAT question and develops an answer before looking at the answer options. This mental answer is then compared to those on the test. If a match is found, bingo! If not, the test-taker is frustrated. In either event, the process is wasteful and unnecessary. It is based on the misconception that the best technique for selecting an LSAT answer is to match the answers provided by the test with the one the test-taker has developed. When selecting the best LSAT answer, you should use only the choices provided by the test itself. You are not trying to come up with the best answer you can, but the best that's provided.

✓ DO NOT APPLY THE "BINGO FALLACY" TO THE SELECTION OF LSAT ANSWERS.

THE CREAM OF THE CRAP

Academic conditioning prompts the test-taker to seek the optimal answer, the cream-of-the-crop answer, to every question. The LSAT, on the other hand, requires the test-taker to select the best answer, the cream-of-the-crap answer, from the five choices provided.

If the best possible, cream-of-the-crop answers were to appear among the five LSAT answer choices, they would usually be obvious, and the purpose of the test, to array test-takers according to certain abilities, would not be achieved. Instead, to guarantee that its purpose is achieved, the LSAT includes one answer choice that is far from optimal but is somewhat better than the others. This makes the task of selecting the best answer much more difficult for the test-taker and promotes the array. The cream-of-the-crap answer is the best of the five options; it is usually not the best possible answer. Remember, "best," by LSAT standards, means *best among the five choices.*

✓ THE BEST ANSWER TO AN LSAT QUESTION IS THE CREAM OF THE CRAP.

SUBSTANTIVITIS

Superior performance on most academic tests results from "substantivitis"—the test-taker's effective demonstration that substantive information has been acquired. Superior performance on the LSAT, on the other hand, results from the effective demonstration that the test-taker can consistently apply the reasoning process required by law schools.

✓ IN SELECTING LSAT ANSWERS, CONCENTRATE ON FORM, AND AVOID BECOMING INVOLVED WITH SUBSTANCE.

FAIR MEANS UNPREDICTABLE

Finally, your previous academic conditioning promotes the notion that a fair test is one that is unpredictable. If the LSAT is to be fair, as it must be to be used in deciding the admission of students to law school, it follows that it should also be unpredictable. The idea of its unpredictability is reinforced by the point made early in this session: that the LSAT does not measure the subjects customary to standardized tests, such as facts, vocabulary, grammar, and mathematical formulae. But, as you have seen elsewhere in this session, the truth about the LSAT is often the opposite of what you might expect, and the matter of its predictability is no exception. *The LSAT is totally predictable.* Each of the subsequent training sessions provides techniques that can be used to take advantage of this predictability.

✓ THE LSAT IS TOTALLY PREDICTABLE.

You cannot quickly change your academic conditioning and the attendant learning and test-taking techniques it has taken you many years to develop just for the very limited purpose of achieving a superior LSAT performance. A better course is to follow the training techniques found in this and subsequent sessions; with them you will avoid the major hazards created by your academic conditioning. Your LSAT score will benefit.

TRAINING SESSION

4

Getting to Know the LSAT

Is there a purpose in the LSAT?

The purpose of the LSAT is to differentiate among those who aspire to law school. This, in turn, provides law schools with a simple way of ranking applicants for admission.

As noted in the previous session, you have been conditioned to believe that a test is designed to measure information acquired during your academic or other experience. Your conditioning tempts you to project such a purpose onto the LSAT, and this temptation is reinforced by much of the rhetoric and rumor that surrounds it. Your conditioning clouds your view of the LSAT.

A clear view of the purpose of the LSAT will allow you to bypass your academic conditioning and related temptations. The LSAT is nothing more or less than a device for distributing people along the 61 points of its score scale.

✓ THE PURPOSE OF THE LSAT IS TO ARRAY TEST–TAKERS.

No matter how great the test-taker's abilities and knowledge, the LSAT will distribute all who take it across the 61 points of its score scale. For example, only 20 percent of all test-takers can score in the top 20 percent. Not all test-takers can achieve a high score; if they could, the LSAT would fail in its purpose. Consequently, the test is designed to ensure that scores are distributed, not concentrated.

Is this justified?

There are two basic justifications offered for the use of the LSAT. The first involves the alleged correlation between LSAT scores and law school performance; that is, students who earn the highest LSAT scores also will get the highest first-year examination grades in law school. The relationship of the average first-year grades of the school's students to their LSAT scores establishes the association for the law school as a whole; this is referred to as its correlation coefficient. The coefficient is expressed as a number between 0 and 1, with 0 indicating no relationship and 1 a perfect relationship. Law schools justify their use of the LSAT on the basis of correlation coefficients as low as .19 or as high as .64.

The second justification concerns the correlation of LSAT questions with basic law school activities. Specifically, the form of Passages questions reflects the form of the casebooks that law students must read and analyze. The forms of Arguments and Relationships questions reflect those found in the Socratic discussions and the examinations of law school. (See the comparisons given on the following pages.)

Whether you are persuaded by these justifications is of little consequence, since the law schools have accepted the LSAT as the predominant factor in the admission decision. Accept this reality and the LSAT's purpose as a ranking device, and you will be in the best position to take advantage of its attributes as you train.

How does the LSAT carry out its purpose?

To serve its purpose, the LSAT must be reliable—in the jargon, it must "measure" consistently. In fact, to do its job properly, it should perform consistently in all of its outcomes. If it did not perform consistently, the scores from one administration—say, October of one year—could not be compared meaningfully with those from another—say, December of the next year. How can the necessary consistency be ensured? There is only one way: only when every edition of the LSAT requires that the same things be done in the same way will the outcomes be consistent. And the consequence of this design requirement is that *the test is predictable*.

✓ BECAUSE THE LSAT MUST PERFORM CONSISTENTLY, IT MUST BE PREDICTABLE.

Its predictability is the principal advantage you have as you train for and take the LSAT. It is possible to know exactly what to train for and what you will face when you take the test. Anxiety about the unknown is limiting to your performance and unnecessary, as is the academic conditioning that tells you the test content cannot be predicted in specific terms.

The Correlation of LSAT Passages Questions with Law School Tasks

Law school casebooks require the student to read and interpret edited appellate court opinions that use difficult grammar and complex reasoning.

Excerpt from a Professional Responsibility Casebook

It is plain that reversal of convictions that are infected by improper and prejudicial newspaper publicity, though necessary to protect the right of a defendant to a fair trial, no matter how heinous his crime would seem to be, is an expedient and not a cure. Such reversals cast a heavy burden, financial and otherwise, on the public and the defendant. For example, in this case, even though the improper publicity has not resulted in a new trial, it imposed a substantial and otherwise unnecessary expense on the taxpayers of the County of Passaic. As has been indicated above, there was to be no sequestration of the jury until the full complement of 14 had been chosen. But, when the prejudicial matter appeared in the two local papers on successive days, the trial court felt obliged to abandon the plan and to order immediate sequestration as jurors were accepted. Empaneling of the jury took three weeks. Sequestration began on the second day of trial and after only one juror had been sworn. The cost to the public of maintaining the jurors during that long period before a single bit of evidence could be offered in support of the indictment was wholly unnecessary but for the newspaper articles. Many curative measures have been proposed to curb improper crime reporting and trial of defendants by newspaper. Among them are greater use of the contempt power, legislation making it a criminal offense to divulge or publish prejudicial material pending a criminal trial, and the recognition of such pretrial publicity as a violation of the federal civil rights statute, on the ground that it deprives the defendant of a fair trial.

In the excerpt from Justice Frankfurter's opinion quoted earlier, he suggested that frequently the improper pretrial stories are published with the prosecutor's collaboration. In our case such collaboration was not shown. But the news accounts suggest that the inflammatory factual material (which was never proved at the trial) was furnished by the police. If true, such conduct is censurable and worthy of discipline. Control of the matter is largely in the hands of the prosecutor and local police authorities.

Excerpt from an LSAT Passages Section

The conception of order in the news varies with each type of disorder. In news about natural disasters, order is defined as the preservation of life and property; despite the concern for nature, flood stories do not often worry
(5) about how the flood may harm the river. Among technological disasters, plane crashes are usually more newsworthy than the winter breakdowns of tenement furnaces, even if they result in the same number of deaths. Yet, here as elsewhere, disorder news is affected
(10) by whose order is being upset.
    Social disorder is generally defined as disorder in the public areas of the society. A protest march in which three people die would be headline national news, whereas a family murder that claimed three victims
(15) would be a local story. Disorders in affluent areas or elite institutions are more likely to be reported than their occurrence elsewhere. In the 1960s, the looting of a handful of stores on New York's Fifth Avenue received as much attention as a much larger looting spree taking
(20) place in a ghetto area that same day. Peaceful demonstrations on college campuses, especially elite ones, are usually more newsworthy than those in factories or prisons. But the major public area is the seat of government; thus, a trouble-free demonstration in front of
(25) a city hall or a police station is news, whereas that in front of a store is not. Ultimately, social disorder is equated with political disorder; similarly, social order is viewed as the absence of violent or potentially violent threats to the authority of public officials, particularly the president.
(30)   Beneath the concern for political order lies another, perhaps even deeper, concern for social cohesion, which reflects fears that not only the official rules of the political order but also the informal rules of the social order are in danger of being disobeyed. This is apparent in the
(35) nonpolitical stories that either become or do not become news. Hippies and college dropouts of the 1960s were newsworthy in part because they rejected the so-called Protestant work ethic; even now, drug use by the young, and its consequences, is in the news more than alcohol
(40) use because it signifies a rejection of traditional methods of seeking oblivion or mind expansion. The romanticization of the past as an era in which formal and informal rules were obeyed betrays the same fear of contemporary disintegration, and the frequent celebration
(45) of past ways in the news may reflect an implicit ideal of the future. As Eric Sevareid put it during the live television coverage of the marriage of Princess Anne of England: "A people needs the past to hold them together."

The Correlation of LSAT Arguments Questions with Law School Tasks

Law school examinations and in-class Socratic discussions require the student to consider and evaluate arguments in hypothetical situations.

This brief exchange is an excerpt from a first-year class in contracts.

> *Professor:* Ms. Jones, suppose you represent the dealer who sold a motorcycle to a 16-year-old who refuses to pay for it, saying she is a minor, and therefore her contract with the dealer is unenforceable by law. You find out that the 16-year-old lives 50 miles outside the city and works downtown. She commutes every day. She also lives in an apartment by herself. Do these facts give you any ideas?
>
> *Student:* Uh. . . .
>
> *Professor:* What argument could you make to stick this 16-year-old hoodlum, this reneging infant, with the contract she willingly entered?

This Arguments question appeared on a recent LSAT.

> 2. No law should restrict the use of alcohol to any particular age group. Americans think that alcohol causes problems like drunk driving. In fact, repressive attitudes toward alcohol cause drunk driving, because children who are prohibited from drinking develop the unhealthy notion that drinking is a symbol of maturity and adult freedom. In the United States, where alcohol use is discouraged and attitudes are repressive, there are twice as many alcohol-related traffic fatalities per capita as there are in France, where drinking is a normal, routine part of family life.
>
> The author's argument would be most greatly weakened if it were true that

The Correlation of LSAT Relationships Questions with Law School Tasks

The formats of law school examinations and class discussions require the determination of various relationships.

```
Torts—Section 3.
(Time: One hour and 30 minutes)

A, an inexperienced but licensed airplane pilot,
rents from X a small dual-control plane manufactured
by Y and invites B, a friend, and C, an experienced
pilot, to fly with him. At 2,000 feet, owing to a
defect, the control mechanism operated by A fails,
and A asks C to take over. C refuses until too late
to avert a crash on M's land. A, D, the plane, N, a
trespasser on M's land, and P, an employee of M, are
hurt. What are the liabilities?
```

This question from a first-year Torts examination poses a hypothetical fact scenario requiring the ordering of various persons, objects, events, and so on.

This LSAT problem requires the ordering of various persons, objects, and events.

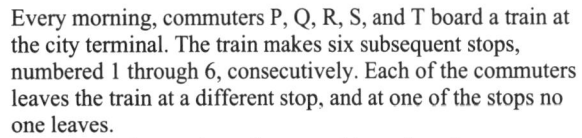

Every morning, commuters P, Q, R, S, and T board a train at the city terminal. The train makes six subsequent stops, numbered 1 through 6, consecutively. Each of the commuters leaves the train at a different stop, and at one of the stops no one leaves.
    P always leaves the train at an odd-numbered stop.
    Q is always the third of the five commuters to leave the train.
    S always leaves the train after R, and none of the other four commuters leaves the train at a stop that comes after R's stop but before S's stop.

What are the basic elements of the LSAT?

SECTIONS

In keeping with its predictability, every LSAT consists of the same basic units. These are commonly referred to as test sections, and these sections are, in fact, separate tests. Each LSAT consists of five of these sections or tests, as well as a Writing Sample.

A section is defined by time and by the type of questions it contains. Each test section is 35 minutes long. One section consists of questions about reading passages (sometimes referred to as reading comprehension questions). This is the **Passages** section. It is scored. One section consists of questions about relationships (sometimes referred to as analytical or logic-games questions). This is the **Relationships** section. It also is scored. Two sections consist of questions about arguments (sometimes referred to as logical reasoning questions). These are the **Arguments** sections. They too are scored.

There is one **experimental** section. This section is not scored. It is used to test questions for use on future editions of the LSAT. It consists of the same types of questions as are included in one of the scored sections.

Last and least, there is a **Writing Sample**. The Writing Sample is provided to law schools along with your test score, but it is not scored.

QUESTIONS AND ANSWERS

There are approximately one hundred scored questions on the LSAT. These questions generally are distributed across the separate test sections as follows, though any section may vary by one or two questions.

- Passages—28 questions
- Relationships—24 questions
- Arguments—24 questions in each of two Arguments sections

Each LSAT question is followed by five answer choices or options. This means that there are some 500 answer choices on every LSAT.

TIME

Of the many factors that determine the LSAT score, time is the most important one. While the test-maker states that time is not a factor in the design of the LSAT, the truth is that time accounts for test-takers' selection of greater numbers of wrong answers than any other factor involved in the test.

> ✓ FOR MOST PEOPLE, TIME IS THE PRINCIPAL FACTOR IN THEIR LSAT SCORE.

Most people find that the allotted 35 minutes is insufficient to consider each question in a test section carefully. Most respond to this time pressure by reducing the time they take to consider individual questions. As we will see in Session 6, reducing the time you take to consider individual questions may reduce your score. Thus, time becomes a significant performance factor.

Also important is the fact that each LSAT section is separately timed, and you cannot transfer time from one test section to another. For example, if you complete the Passages section in 30 minutes, you cannot use the 5 remaining minutes to start another test section, nor can you return to an earlier section you were unable to complete in the 35 minutes allotted. This means that you must treat every LSAT section as a separate test.

> ✓ THE LSAT IS ESSENTIALLY SIX SEPARATE TESTS.

How does the LSAT perform?

The LSAT has difficulty meeting its stated objective of ranking applicants to law schools so that the very skilled and superskilled are meaningfully differentiated for admission selection. In terms of actual performance, the LSAT does not meet its ranking objectives very well. For example, rather than distributing test-takers across the score scale, the LSAT tends to bunch test-takers at various places on the scale. The test-maker explains this phenomenon as "a sign that a test is too easy. . . ."

Whatever the explanation, you will design your LSAT performance strategy to take advantage of this tendency in the test. It is a strategy that will yield optimal test results for you.

What does the LSAT's performance mean to you?

Because the LSAT's sole purpose is to rank you in relation to others, it is only concerned with your performance in relation to that of others. And, in contrast to the academic conditioning that focuses on the number of questions you answer right, the LSAT's performance is based upon the number of wrong answers you and all other test-takers select. Where your number of wrong answers places you among all test-takers is the only information of interest to the test-maker and the law schools.

If all of you fail to select the necessary number of wrong answers, the test-maker concludes that the test is too easy. Since the LSAT is not an academic test, this cannot be solved by asking harder questions—seeking more obscure information or more complex calculations. What the test-maker must do is construct better wrong answers, and this is very difficult to do. What is difficult for the test-maker gives an advantage to the savvy test-taker, as you will find in future sessions.

✓ WRONG ANSWERS PROVIDE THE KEY
TO YOUR LSAT SCORE.

By training to control the number of wrong answers you select, you reduce performance anxiety and avoid academic conditioning that could limit your test score. You will train to take advantage of what might be called the "wrong-answer weakness" of the LSAT.

A review of past tests yields the following table. (Numbers will vary slightly, depending on the test form.) You would need to choose the specified number of wrong answers in order to be grouped with the percentage of test-takers indicated.

Number of Wrong Answers	% of Test-Takers with More Wrong Answers	% of Test-Takers with Fewer Wrong Answers
7	99.9	0.1
18	95	5
21	90	10
25	80	20
29	70	30
32	60	40
37	50	50

✓ YOU MUST SELECT AT LEAST TWENTY
WRONG ANSWERS TO SCORE IN THE
BOTTOM 90 PERCENT OF TEST–TAKERS.

To follow up on the significance of wrong answers, remember that you are not penalized for guessing on the LSAT. Whether you select a wrong answer or no answer, the impact on your score is the same, so there is no advantage to leaving any blanks on your answer sheet. Also, you can gain no advantage from knowing that some LSAT questions are more difficult than others. LSAT answers are not weighted, so each answer contributes equally to your score.

What does the LSAT's performance mean to law schools?

The least significant aspect of the LSAT's performance is its apparent similarity to the work law students do. However, the fact that its forms resemble those of law school texts and classroom and examination activities makes some in the law schools comfortable with its use.

The LSAT is a common denominator among law schools. With minor exceptions, every law school in the United States and Canada requires every applicant to present an LSAT score as part of the application process. This facilitates the comparison of applicants. Each applicant's test score can be compared with every other applicant's test score. Lines are easily drawn.

Scores over three years old are not routinely reported to law schools, so the LSAT score is current. Thus, when comparing applicants, law schools can minimize their dependence on evaluations or academic records reflecting work done at different times. The LSAT provides them with a comparison of applicants based upon a common recent experience.

The LSAT score is easily defensible. If you get a low score, it is attributable to you only—not to the law schools, admission officers, professors, counselors, or undergraduate schools. The score is a single "objective" number and not susceptible to interpretation.

As pointed out previously, the correlation between LSAT performance and first-year law school grades is offered as a justification for the use of the LSAT. Law schools routinely interpret this correlation as a prediction of first-year grades and of overall performance, operating on the assumption that the higher the LSAT score, the higher the law school grades and the better the law school performance.

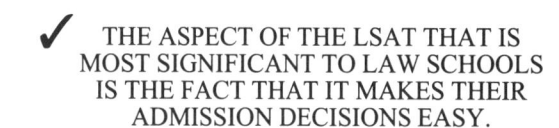

✓ THE ASPECT OF THE LSAT THAT IS
MOST SIGNIFICANT TO LAW SCHOOLS
IS THE FACT THAT IT MAKES THEIR
ADMISSION DECISIONS EASY.

Not only does the LSAT rank every applicant, but, because its score results are preset, law schools are able to predict the number and nature of test scores at any given point, knowing nothing more than the number of test-takers.

How does the LSAT influence the law school "rejection decision"?

The vast majority of applications for admission to law school are rejected. There are places in a law school class for some 60 percent of those who apply. For this and other reasons, the average law school aspirant applies to some five law schools. The result is that nearly 90 percent of all applications are wasted. Put another way, if the selection system worked perfectly, only about 10 percent of applicants would be accepted. Since the system is far from perfect, many more than 10 percent are accepted; however, the vast majority are rejected.

Virtually all of the law school rejection decisions made by directors of rejection (who prefer to be addressed as directors of admission) can be accounted for by the LSAT score and undergraduate grade point average (GPA). This does not mean that other factors are not taken into account, but that, after all is said and done, the LSAT and GPA usually can explain the decision to accept or reject, other factors notwithstanding.

To facilitate decision making, the vast majority of law schools combine the LSAT and GPA into an admission index. Each school determines the weight to be given to applicants' LSAT and GPA, and calculates each applicant's admission index.

✓ FOR EACH LAW SCHOOL TO WHICH YOU APPLY, YOUR ADMISSION INDEX IS A FUNCTION OF YOUR LSAT SCORE AND YOUR GPA.

All applicants can then be ranked by admission index and admitted or rejected according to the policies and practices of that law school. The facing page contains an illustration of this process.

The relative weight law schools assign to the LSAT score and GPA is all-important to the admission index. Assuming that all applicants have a GPA of at least 2 on a 4-point scale, a survey of the admission indices of 150 law schools shows that the effective weight of the LSAT is more than that of the GPA. For 45 percent of the schools, the LSAT score accounted for some 70 percent of the index. If you have a relatively strong GPA, you will want to apply to those schools that weigh the GPA most. If you have a relatively strong LSAT score, you will want to apply to those that weigh the LSAT most.

✓ KNOW HOW MUCH WEIGHT THE LSAT SCORE WILL BE GIVEN BY THE LAW SCHOOLS TO WHICH YOU APPLY.

What does the LSAT measure?

The test-maker says the LSAT measures the ability to "read and comprehend complex texts, manage and organize information, and process information to reach conclusions." This begs the question.

✓ IN ADDITION TO THE REQUIRED REASONING ABILITIES, THE LSAT MEASURES YOUR SPEED, ACCURACY AND SKILL AT PLANNING, DISCIPLINE, AND MECHANICS.

Your prior academic conditioning emphasizes speed over accuracy rather than the optimal balance between the two. The LSAT, however, indirectly measures your ability to break through the conditioning to find and consistently apply an optimal balance between speed and accuracy as you work your way through the test questions and answer choices.

Your academic conditioning suggests that you study for a test, and the test will measure your success at such study. But the total predictability of the LSAT suggests that you *plan* for the test, and the test will measure your success at such planning. Also indirectly, it measures your self-discipline in following a plan and avoiding the limitations that academic conditioning could impose on your LSAT score.

Its final measurement is of your skill at the mechanics of test taking. For example, transcription is a critical skill. LSAT test-takers often make errors in transcribing their answers from the test book to the answer sheet. By avoiding transcription errors and other mechanical mistakes, you can improve your score.

In constructing your test plan, we will consider both the selection of wrong answers and the factors that are measured indirectly by the LSAT.

UCS University Computer Services

Memorandum

To: Director of Rejection
University Law School

From: Computer Services

Re: Applicants Ranked by Index

Please find enclosed the list of applicants to University Law School, ranked according to the calculated index. If targeted entering class size is 75 (assuming 75% of those we accept will attend), you must reject all but about 100 applicants. The top 100 candidates on the enclosed list have index scores of 83.2 or above.

PAGE 5

Rank	Index	Name
83	84.4	EDWARDS, J. O.
84	84.3	ELLSWORTH, M. S.
85	84.2	CARDIN, L. P.
86	84.1	THOMAS, O. G.
87	84.1	BAKER, B. E.
88	84.1	SAUNDERS, H. J. M.
89	84.0	WILLETT, S. A.
90	84.0	BECKER, A. R.
91	83.9	DENNY, S. C.
92	83.7	SELIGMAN, S. A.
93	83.5	SCHLOSS, J. R.
94	83.5	MCELVEEN, E. E.
95	83.5	DEMEO, H. L.
96	83.4	GUTH, R.
97	83.4	GUZZO, M. A.
98	83.3	KOCHIS, N. M.
99	83.2	BROWN, A. T.
100	83.2	VANLOVEREN, S. A.
101	83.1	CORDERO, J. M.
102	83.0	BRIGLIN, R. V.
103	83.0	KETELTAS, T. C.
104	82.9	MCELROY, G. S.
105	82.8	BEVERSDORF, E. C.
106	82.8	HEDLUND, M. Q.
107	82.7	ENDERS, J. R.
108	82.6	EAMES, T. P.
109	82.5	COTT, M. A.
110	82.5	PECK, P. J.
111	82.3	HILL, F. X.

TRAINING SESSION 5

Test Preparation Strategy

What is the test-maker's preparation strategy?

The test-maker has a carefully prepared strategy to ensure that the expectations—yea, requirements—for the LSAT are met each time the test is administered. After all, if the LSAT does not perform consistently as expected, the value of the test is lost. So the test-maker spares nothing to make certain that the test results are those specified. The test-maker does not prepare the LSAT, administer it, and score it just to discover *how* it performed. *Au contraire.*

✓ THE TEST–MAKER'S STRATEGY IS TO KNOW HOW THE TEST WILL PERFORM BEFORE IT IS ADMINISTERED.

The adage of the trial lawyer applies equally to the LSAT: "Never ask a witness a question if you don't know what the answer will be." The LSAT is not improvised. It is fully scripted, planned in every detail. Long before the test is administered, test scores and their structure have already been determined. By the time it is administered, all that remains for the test-maker to do is assign the predetermined scores.

At the core of the test-maker's strategy is a plan. The test-maker's plan establishes objectives for the test, identifies the variables involved, determines the optimal mix of the variables needed to meet the objectives, and mixes the variables consistently. The test-maker has developed this planning process over a long period and at great expense. You have neither the time nor the resources to develop a competing process—nor should you try.

What is your preparation strategy?

As you know, most people's LSAT preparation strategy is to practice past or simulated LSAT questions and to review analyses of the questions and the answer choices. This means practicing test-taking habits, mechanics, and skills that are not appropriate to the LSAT, which further means little score improvement for most people. And for some, this practice strategy actually impairs rather than improves test performance.

Your strategy, on the other hand, is to take advantage of the test-maker's strategy. The test-maker has done the work, and that work provides the model for you.

✓ AT THE CORE OF YOUR TEST TRAINING STRATEGY IS YOUR PLAN.

You will follow the model of the test performance plan followed by the test-maker. You will begin, as does the model, by establishing your objectives for the test. Next you will identify the factors or activities that will be meaningful in achieving your objectives. Then you will determine the optimal mix of variables needed to meet the objectives. And finally, you will prosecute your plan consistently to ensure that your objectives are realized.

What are your objectives?

At this point, you have only one objective. You want a superior LSAT score. A score in the ninety-ninth percentile would do very nicely. In the context of your test plan and the purpose of the LSAT, this objective has little meaning. Put simply, it is too general. For practical purposes, the LSAT consists of six *separate* tests, only four of which contribute to your score.

The more specific your objectives, the better your plan will be. At the minimum, a good test plan will have an objective for each of the six separate tests that make up the LSAT. It will include the number of wrong answers planned for each test. It will also include a procedure to follow for achieving this wrong-answer objective. This procedure will take into account each of your test performance factors and the predictable attributes of the LSAT.

What is meant by test performance factors?

Your level of anxiety, test-taking habits and mechanics, reasoning skill, time use, and self-discipline are factors that influence performance on the LSAT. The training in this book is designed to minimize the impact that the factors of anxiety and entrenched academic test-taking habits and mechanics have on your performance. By learning and applying procedures that take advantage of the LSAT's non-academic nature, you will be able to avoid any negative impact these performance factors might have on your test score.

The reasoning skill required by law schools is a critical performance factor. Your training regimen will include regular monitoring of this skill as it develops and the adaptation of your test plan to take this development into account.

Self-discipline is the most difficult of all performance factors to build into your plan. Only you will know if you are strict or lax in following the test-taking procedures you have been trained to use. Avoid being over-optimistic in this regard—there is a great tendency to believe that each of us enjoys a generous measure of self-discipline, but the evidence consistently proves the contrary.

What is optimal mix?

The test-maker establishes an optimal mix of LSAT performance factors to ensure that the test results are precisely those desired; for example, that the proportion of test-takers assigned a score of 150 satisfies an objective for the test. Among other things, this effort leads to the structuring of the LSAT as six separate tests, the inclusion of a specific number of questions in each of the tests, the selection of certain types of questions, and the following of a particular presentation pattern. To achieve an optimal mix, the test-maker experiments with the variables, increasing this, decreasing that, changing something else.

As with the test-maker, your optimal mix of performance factors is the one that best ensures that your objectives are achieved. Just enough worry to make sure that you are in control of the training and testing process is best. Balancing your speed of working on the questions against the accuracy of your answers so that you select the expected number of wrong answers is crucial. Mechanics are important—the sequence in which you consider questions, the order in which you examine answer choices, the recording of your answers in the test book, the transcription of answer choices onto the answer sheet, and others.

How about consistent prosecution?

As you will understand better when you learn more about the structure of each of the question types on the LSAT, it is difficult for the test to perform consistently. It is also difficult for you to perform consistently over the course of the 205-minute LSAT. Yet your performance will depend on consistency.

✓ CONSISTENT EXECUTION OF YOUR TEST PLAN AND CONSISTENT PROSECUTION OF THE TASKS REQUIRED WILL CONTRIBUTE POSITIVELY TO YOUR PERFORMANCE AND TEST SCORE.

Where do you begin?

You will recall that the LSAT consists of five separately timed tests and a Writing Sample. Each of the five tests consists of four sets of questions and answer choices. The LSAT is made up of twenty of these question/answer sets.

✓ THE QUESTION/ANSWER SET IS THE FOCUS OF YOUR TEST PLAN.

A Passages question set consists of one reading passage and the questions and answer choices related to it. A Relationships question set consists of the facts and rules common to the problem and the questions and answer choices related to them. An Arguments question set consists of six questions and the related answer choices.

Your ability to handle these twenty sets will differ, so your test plan will reflect these differences. Also, your plan will be dynamic. It will change as you gain proficiency in the following:

- Leveraging the one basic reasoning task required by the LSAT
- Taking advantage of the LSAT's total predictability
- Exploiting your wrong-answer advantage
- Combating obfuscation, the test-maker's only tool
- Conquering the multiple-option trick
- Employing special mechanical and transcription techniques
- Mastering critical question-visualization techniques
- Preparing your Writing Sample in advance
- Avoiding the test habits that lower your score
- Using the 9-12-18 planning system

As you train, the optimal mix of your performance factors will change, and, as the optimal mix changes, so will your plan.

TRAINING SESSION

6

The 9-12-18 Test Planning System

What is the 9-12-18 system?

The 9-12-18 test planning system is based on the same process the test-maker uses in establishing the optimal mix of factors needed for the LSAT to meet its objectives. The process is well described by the proverb "The proof of the pudding is in the eating"—that is, the way to test whether something works as intended is to try it. Through the inclusion of a set of experimental questions on every LSAT, the test-maker learns exactly how these questions perform and exactly how test-takers perform with respect to these questions. This pretest process produces the information upon which the test-maker bases the performance plan for the LSAT.

The pretest process is effective for the test-maker because it avoids conjecture. This process can be equally effective for you, because it avoids the conditioning that leads you to aim your performance expectations away from what *is* toward what you *wish*. There is no ambiguity about your performance—what you see is what you get, and what you get is a function of what you base your test plan upon.

When you are presented with a set of LSAT questions, performance factors influence your approach, including the selection of answers. The only record of your consideration of test questions is your answer selection. Thus, you will base your test plan on the results of your answer selection activity. Through this pretest process, you will establish the optimal mix of factors required for you to establish and meet your LSAT performance objectives.

Each of the principal test performance factors—reasoning skill, speed, accuracy, planning, discipline, and mechanics—manifests itself in your selection of answers. Thus your plan, like that of the test-maker, takes advantage of this performance result.

The 9-12-18 test planning system is based on your selection of answers to a set of LSAT questions. You will be presented with a set of questions and will consider the questions and select answers for 9 minutes. The results of your performance will be recorded for later analysis. You will then give the same set of questions further consideration for an additional 3 minutes and record the results of your performance in those 3 minutes. Finally you will give the set of questions an additional 6 minutes' consideration and record the results of this performance as well. Following the pretest, you will analyze your performance results.

Would you like an example?

Suppose that you are working at selecting the best answers to a set of six Relationships questions. You calculate that there are about 9 minutes in which to complete all six questions in the set (four question sets into 35 minutes), so you decide to allocate 1½ minutes to each question. At the end of 9 minutes, you have completed the selection of six answers. Since you next have an additional 3 minutes to work, you follow the same strategy you used for the 9 minutes; you divide the time equally and spend an additional half minute on each question. After reconsidering each question, you change two answers. With the last 6 minutes you have available, you decide to concentrate on four questions about which you are unsure. As a result, you change three answers.

You next compare your answer choices to the key. Of the six answers you selected during the first 9 minutes, you find that only two were best answers. Of the answer choices you selected after the 3 additional minutes (for a total of 12 minutes), three were best. Of the answer choices you selected after the additional 6-minute period (for a total of 18 minutes), all six were best.

Summarized, your performance on this question set was as follows:

9 minutes	2 x 4 + 0 = 8
12 minutes	3 x 3 + 1 = 10
18 minutes	6 x 2 + 2 = 14

How are these results analyzed?

The first number in each formula represents the number of best answers selected in that period of time. When you considered the question set for 9 minutes, you selected only two best answers. When you spent 12 minutes you selected 3 best answers, and when you spent 18 minutes you selected 6 best answers.

The second number in the calculation represents the projection of your one-set performance onto the entire 35-minute Relationships section-test, were you to perform with the same accuracy as you did on the one set. Thus, in the first formula, the number of best answers (2) is multiplied by 4 (the full four question sets in the section-test).

The second formula shows what happens if you decide to work on just three question sets during the time allocated for the separate section-test. This means that there is an average of about 12 minutes (12 x 3 = 36) available for each set. The number of best answers (3) is multiplied by 3 (the three sets you intend to complete) to project your one-set performance onto the entire section-test, were you to perform on three question sets with the same accuracy as you did on the one.

The third formula shows what happens if you decide to work on only two question sets during the time allocated for the section-test. This means that there is an average of about 18 minutes (18 x 2 = 36) available for each set. The number of best answers (6) is multiplied by 2 to project your one-set performance onto the entire section-test, were you to perform on two question sets with the same accuracy as you did on the one set.

The third number in the formula represents the best answers that will result from guessing on question sets that you do not otherwise consider. Recall that you should always guess on an LSAT question, even when you have not considered it. Since there are five answer choices to every question, a guess has a one-in-five chance of being the best answer. There are six questions per set on the Relationships section-test; consequently, over a six-question set, chance alone will result in your selecting one best answer, even though you give that question no other consideration. Obviously, if you consider all four question sets in the section-test, you get no guessing bonus. If you consider three of the four question sets, you get a guessing bonus of one. If you consider two of the four question sets, you get a guessing bonus of two. This results from the fact that, even though you have not considered a particular six-question set, you have arbitrarily selected (guessed) an answer for each of those questions.

The total of best answers, the fourth number in the formula, shows how you would perform on the whole section-test, were you to consider four, three, or two question sets. In the example, you can see that you will select the fewest wrong answers on the section-test if you consider only two question sets and guess your answers for the other two.

This pretest process produces your optimal balance between speed and accuracy on the Relationships section-test of the LSAT. The example shows that by considering all four question sets (a total of 24 answers), you can plan on selecting 16 (24 total answers minus 8 best answers) wrong answers. By considering just three question sets, you can plan on selecting 14 wrong answers—not a large difference. However, by considering only two question sets, you can plan on selecting 10 wrong answers, an improvement of 75 percent over your performance on all four sets.

The 9-12-18 system uses your pretest performance to establish the optimal balance between speed and accuracy for you. In the example, this performance produces your basic test plan for the Relationships section-test. On the Relationships section-test, you will select the fewest wrong answers if you stress accuracy over speed.

This may not apply to the other section-tests on the LSAT. Following is an example that expands this pretest strategy to a full four-section-test LSAT. Hypothetical results on each of the four section-tests are summarized in the same way as in the preceding example.

Relationships Section-Test
9 minutes   2 x 4 + 0 = 8
12 minutes   3 x 3 + 1 = 10
18 minutes   6 x 2 + 2 = **14**

Arguments Section-Tests (remember, there are two)
9 minutes   3 x 4 + 0 = 12 x 2 = 24
12 minutes   6 x 3 + 1 = 19 x 2 = **38**
18 minutes   6 x 2 + 2 = 14 x 2 = 28

Passages Section-Test
9 minutes   3 x 4 + 0 = 12
12 minutes   5 x 3 + 1 = **16**
18 minutes   5 x 2 + 2 = 12

These calculations result in the following sample test plan:

Relationships section-test   2 sets at 18 minutes each
Arguments section-test   3 sets at 12 minutes each
Arguments section-test   3 sets at 12 minutes each
Passages section-test   3 sets at 12 minutes each

The total score of 68 that results from this plan contrasts with the total of 44 that would result if every question were given consideration. By focusing on the optimal balance between speed and accuracy, an increase of more than 50 percent in performance results.

How do you develop your own plan?

The 9-12-18 system of test-plan development starts on page 35 with three pretests. Each pretest measures and evaluates your test performance factors through a single experimental question set. The first pretest involves a Relationships set, the second an Arguments set, and the last a Passages set. The results of these pretests are used to establish the optimal mix of the principal test performance factors for you as they apply to the different question types found on the LSAT.

Use a watch, clock, alarm, or timer on each pretest. The three pretests can be completed at different times or in a 1-hour period. Try to take the pretests in a quiet place, under reasonably relaxed circumstances, and at a time when you will not be interrupted.

You will have 18 minutes to complete each pretest. Your objective is to select as many best answers as you can in the first 9 minutes, then to select as many best answers as you can in an additional 3 minutes, and finally to select as many best answers as you can in an additional 6 minutes.

The pretest process will be unfamiliar and may, at first, appear to be somewhat complicated. Review the directions carefully, and you will have no problems.

How do you take the pretests?

There are five steps to completing each of the pretests.

STEP 1

Set your timer for 9 minutes. Read the directions at the top of the set of questions. Then answer as many questions in the set as you can in 9 minutes. *Circle* your answers. Do not be concerned if you do not complete all of the questions. At the end of 9 minutes, stop. These answers become your 9-minute set.

STEP 2

Next give yourself an additional 3 minutes. Go back to the set, and answer any questions you did not get to in the first 9 minutes, or review the questions you answered in the first 9 minutes and change your answers if you wish. This brings the total minutes expired to 12.

Place a *box* beside each of the answers you selected during this 3-minute period. If you did not change an answer, place a box beside the circled answer. If you changed the answer, place a box beside the new selection. The boxed answers represent your 12-minute set. Do not erase or change the circles you placed beside questions during the first 9 minutes.

STEP 3

Finally, give yourself an additional 6 minutes. Go back to the set, and answer any questions you did not get to in the first 12 minutes, or review the questions and change answers if you wish. This brings the total minutes used to 18.

Place an *asterisk* beside each of the answers you selected during this 6-minute period. If you did not change an answer, place an asterisk beside the boxed answer. If you changed the answer, place an asterisk beside the new selection. The answers identified with asterisks are your 12-minute set. Do not erase or change the circles or boxes you placed beside questions during the first 12 minutes.

STEP 4

Turn to the Pretest Answer Key for this session at the back of the book. For each set, determine the number of best answers you selected in the 9-minute set (circled), 12-minute set (boxed), and 18-minute set (asterisked). Enter those numbers on the Pretest Performance Tracking Worksheet on page 39. Alternatively, you can use the following calculation form.

STEP 5

Complete the calculations indicated.

Relationships Set
Circles   _____ x 4 + 0 = _____
Boxes   _____ x 3 + 1 = _____
Asterisks   _____ x 2 + 2 = _____

Largest total _____

Arguments Set
Circles   _____ x 4 + 0 = _____
Boxes   _____ x 3 + 1 = _____
Asterisks   _____ x 2 + 2 = _____

Largest total _____

Passages Set
Circles   _____ x 4 + 0 = _____
Boxes   _____ x 3 + 1 = _____
Asterisks   _____ x 2 + 2 = _____

Largest total _____

What's next?

To develop your first test plan, enter in the blanks below the number of sets that corresponds to the largest total for each of the four section-tests.

Relationships section-test   _____ sets
Arguments section-tests (2)   _____ sets
Passages section-test   _____ sets

As your training progresses, you will monitor your performance on question sets by updating your Performance Tracking Worksheet as you complete additional pretest cycles. As your training results in more consistent and improved use of time, your optimal balance between speed and accuracy will change. The changes will be reflected in your test plan.

There are two major components to your test plan. One is your question-set performance, and the other is your section-test strategy. Your performance on each pretest question set determines whether your section-test strategy is to complete 4, 3, or 2 question sets in each. You want to produce the optimal balance between speed and accuracy for each of the three different types of section-test (five tests in all). Your combined strategies for the five section-tests will constitute your test plan.

PRETEST 6-1. RELATIONSHIPS

Directions: The questions are based on a set of conditions. A diagram may be helpful in the answer selection process. Select the best answer to each question, and mark your answers as described in the text.

Questions 1-6
Six building contractors, L, M, N, O, P, and Q, bid on the construction of a new school. Each submits one bid stating the total price for constructing the building. The school board must award the job to the lowest bidder.
   P bids less than N but more than Q.
   O bids less than P but more than M.
   Q bids less than N but more than L.
   No two bids are equal to each other.

1. Which of the following could be the ranking of the contractors' bids?
   (A) M, Q, O, P, L, N
   (B) M, L, O, Q, P, N
   (C) L, Q, M, P, O, N
   (D) Q, M, O, L, P, N
   (E) L, M, Q, N, P, O

2. If O submits the third-highest bid, which of the following contractors could get the job?
   (A) M only
   (B) L only
   (C) Q or M
   (D) M or L
   (E) Q or L

3. If O submits one of the lowest two bids, which of the following must be true?
   I. M submits the lowest bid.
   II. L submits the third-lowest bid.
   III. P submits the second-highest bid.
   (A) I only
   (B) II only
   (C) I and II only
   (D) II and III only
   (E) I, II, and III

4. If L submits the lowest bid, all of the following must be true EXCEPT
   (A) M submits a lower bid than P
   (B) Q submits a higher bid than M
   (C) Q submits a lower bid than P
   (D) P submits a higher bid than Q
   (E) M submits a lower bid than O

5. If M submits the second-lowest bid, which of the following could be a ranking of the contractors' bids?
   (A) L, M, Q, O, P, N
   (B) Q, M, L, O, P, N
   (C) O, M, L, Q, P, N
   (D) L, M, Q, P, O, N
   (E) L, M, P, O, Q, N

6. Which of the following contractors could submit the lowest bid and the second-lowest bid, respectively?
   I. L and O
   II. M and Q
   III. L and Q
   (A) I only
   (B) II only
   (C) III only
   (D) II and III only
   (E) I, II, and III

PRETEST 6-1. ARGUMENTS

Directions: Evaluate the reasoning contained in the brief statements and select the best answer. Do not make implausible, superfluous, or incompatible assumptions. Select the best answer to the question, and mark your answers as described in the text.

1. If Amelia's airplane was manufactured after 1980, it included a transponder.
   Which of the following dictates the above conclusion?
   (A) Only if an airplane was manufactured after 1980 would it include a transponder.
   (B) All airplanes manufactured after 1980 included a transponder.
   (C) All transponders are included in airplanes manufactured after 1980.
   (D) It was not required that airplanes include transponders before 1980.
   (E) No airplanes manufactured before 1980 included transponders.

Questions 2-3
Professor Tanner's review of her students' research showed that there was no observed theft in societies that always shared food resources among members. Thus, she concluded that sharing food resources would prevent theft in other societies.

2. If the following were true of societies in which theft was known to occur, which would weaken Professor Tanner's conclusion?
   I. Theft is not a crime in some of the societies.
   II. Some of the societies shared food resources.
   III. Food resources were not shared with thieves in some of the societies.
   (A) I only
   (B) II only
   (C) III only
   (D) I and II only
   (E) II and III only

3. Upon which of the following assumptions is Professor Tanner's conclusion based?
   I. Food resources should be shared by societies.
   II. There were no unobserved thefts.
   III. Theft is an unknown concept in societies that share food resources.
   (A) I only
   (B) II only
   (C) III only
   (D) I and III only
   (E) II and III only

4. Beauty exists only in the eye of the beholder.
   If true, which of the following most weakens the above statement?
   (A) Each beautiful remembrance is perfectly recorded.
   (B) Everyone agrees that a sunset is beautiful and that a hurricane is not.
   (C) Some people find beauty in an iceberg melting.
   (D) A sunrise is beautiful even when there is no one to appreciate it.
   (E) Beauty pageant judges generally agree on a winner.

5. Some of the accident witnesses who agreed that Will was at fault were acquaintances of Will's cousins. But none of the witnesses who agreed that Will was at fault was related to the victim, Angel.
   Thus, any of the following may be true EXCEPT
   (A) no accident witness is related to Angel
   (B) some of Will's relatives are acquainted with accident witnesses who agreed that he was at fault
   (C) no accident witnesses agreed about who was at fault in the accident
   (D) some of Will's relatives agreed that he was at fault in the accident
   (E) no accident witness who did not blame Will is acquainted with Angel's relatives

Questions 6-7
The law school faculty report finds that college graduates are less able than they were in the past, because law students' examination papers in the last three years were illegible, ungrammatical, and badly written.

6. Which of the following is an assumption upon which the faculty finding is based?
   I. Colleges do not train students to write.
   II. Previously students wrote better than they now do.
   III. Writing is a measure of student ability.
   (A) I only
   (B) II only
   (C) III only
   (D) I and III only
   (E) II and III only

7. If true, which of the following most weakens the law faculty's finding?
   (A) Law students are not representative of college graduates in general.
   (B) Law students' examinations are always badly written.
   (C) Examinations are an inaccurate measure of writing ability.
   (D) Fewer college graduates attended law school in the past three years.
   (E) Illegible handwriting does not reflect writing ability.

PRETEST 6-1. PASSAGES

Directions: The questions are based on what is stated or implied in the passage. Select the best answer to each question, and mark your answers as described in the text.

Political influence shapes the behavior of the Pittsburgh and Minneapolis judges in criminal court. Studies have also suggested that judges' social or ethnic backgrounds significantly shape their decisions. Thus it is
(5) possible that the Pittsburgh judges are lenient primarily because of their predominantly minority ethnic backgrounds and the Minneapolis judges more severe primarily because of their Northern European Protestant backgrounds. However, data show that while both the
(10) judges' pre-judicial career experiences and social backgrounds influence decision making in both cities, the former seem to be the more important characteristics, and their impact on decisions seems to be indirect. The crucial intervening variable is the city's political system; judges
(15) with a particular social and career background that may affect their decisions are recruited by the city's political and judicial selection systems. Significantly, that composition is more reflective of the influence of particular groups in the city's political system than it is of
(20) the ethnic composition of the city's population. The ethnic composition of the bench in each city can serve as a partial test of the intervening impact of the judicial selection system on judicial decision making.
The character of the Pittsburgh and Minneapolis
(25) judges' decision making in criminal court can be seen through consideration of recidivism. Offenders who have received probation generally have lower rates of recidivism than those who have been incarcerated. And, of those incarcerated, the offenders who have received a
(30) shorter term of incarceration generally have a somewhat lower recidivism rate than those who receive longer terms. One might infer that the Pittsburgh judges' decisions contribute more effectively to reduced recidivism because these judges grant probation more
(35) frequently. However, their frequent grants of probation for individuals with a high probability of recidivating probably do not. In contrast, the Minneapolis judges' sentencing decisions for such individuals may help to reduce recidivism. However, there are other goals of the
(40) criminal court in addition to reducing recidivism, and there is considerable tension among them.
The tension between the style of criminal court that may be preferable in an ideal context and that which may be necessary because of the actual context, and the
(45) difficulties inherent in the latter style, seem to be a product of a more general tension. According to notions of the rule of law and democratic theory, we ought to ignore class differences. But urban realities make this difficult. "Two cultures" exist in our large cities—a large
(50) lower class as well as the dominant middle class—but our theory of democracy assumes that we are able and willing to live together under a single set of rules or standards. The Minneapolis judges adhere to the rule of law but fail to consider the two cultures. The Pittsburgh judges often
(55) tend to base their decisions on the existence of the two cultures but usually fail to adhere to the rule of law. These shortcomings in both courts are largely a function of the two cultures, a factor external to the court systems. Any prescription for remedying these inadequacies must be
(60) directed primarily at this external factor and more basic cause.

1. The passage is primarily concerned with
   (A) the identification of influences on the decisions of criminal court judges
   (B) a comparison of the criminal courts of Minneapolis and Pittsburgh
   (C) recidivism as a method of evaluating court performance
   (D) the selection of criminal court judges in Minneapolis and Pittsburgh
   (E) tension between the rule-of-law and two-cultures styles of criminal courts

2. According to the passage, all of the following appear to significantly influence judges' decisions EXCEPT
   (A) the judicial selection system
   (B) rates of criminal recidivism
   (C) pre-judicial career experience
   (D) the city political system
   (E) ethnic background

3. According to the passage, which of the following contributes to lower rates of recidivism?
   I. shorter terms of incarceration
   II. the style of criminal court
   III. placing offenders on probation
   (A) I only
   (B) II only
   (C) III only
   (D) I and II only
   (E) I and III only

4. The author's evaluation of the two court systems can be summarized best by which of the following?
   (A) The tension between the rule of law and two cultures leads to bad judicial decision making.
   (B) The failures of both court systems is due primarily to the two-cultures urban reality.
   (C) The judges in each court system are not well chosen for their functions.
   (D) The problems of both court systems are the result of a large urban underclass.
   (E) The judges in both court systems deal with recidivism badly.

5. It can be inferred from the passage that the author prefers that selection of judges
   I. reflect the ethnic composition of the city's population
   II. reflect the influence of the city's political system
   III. reflect the social backgrounds of the city's population
   (A) I only
   (B) II only
   (C) III only
   (D) I and II only
   (E) I and III only

GO ON TO THE NEXT PAGE.

6. According to the passage, which of the following decisions would be most likely to reduce recidivism?
   (A) sentencing a repeat offender to probation
   (B) sentencing a first-time offender to probation
   (C) sentencing a first-time offender to a short jail term
   (D) sentencing a repeat offender to a short jail term
   (E) sentencing a first-time offender to a long jail term

7. Which of the following is implied by the passage?
   (A) There are fewer members of the lower class than middle class that live in urban Pittsburgh.
   (B) There are fewer members of the lower class than upper class that live in urban Minneapolis.
   (C) There are fewer members of the upper class than middle class that live in urban Pittsburgh.
   (D) There are fewer members of the middle class than upper class that live in urban Minneapolis.
   (E) There are fewer members of the middle class than lower class that live in urban Minneapolis.

NOTE: Answers to the preceding pretests will be found in the Answers section at the back of the book.

Pretest Performance Tracking Worksheet

Relationships

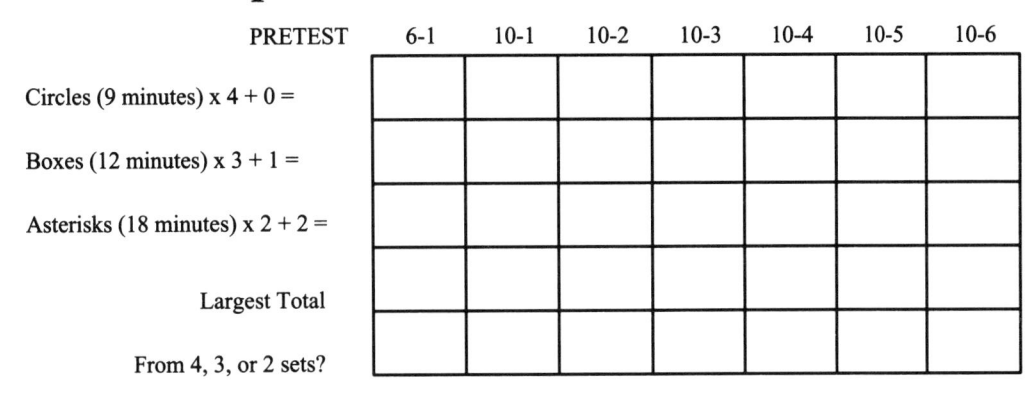

	PRETEST	6-1	10-1	10-2	10-3	10-4	10-5	10-6
Circles (9 minutes) x 4 + 0 =								
Boxes (12 minutes) x 3 + 1 =								
Asterisks (18 minutes) x 2 + 2 =								
Largest Total								
From 4, 3, or 2 sets?								

Arguments

	PRETEST	6-1	13-1	13-2	13-3	13-4	13-5	13-6
Circles (9 minutes) x 4 + 0 =								
Boxes (12 minutes) x 3 + 1 =								
Asterisks (18 minutes) x 2 + 2 =								
Largest Total								
From 4, 3, or 2 sets?								

Passages

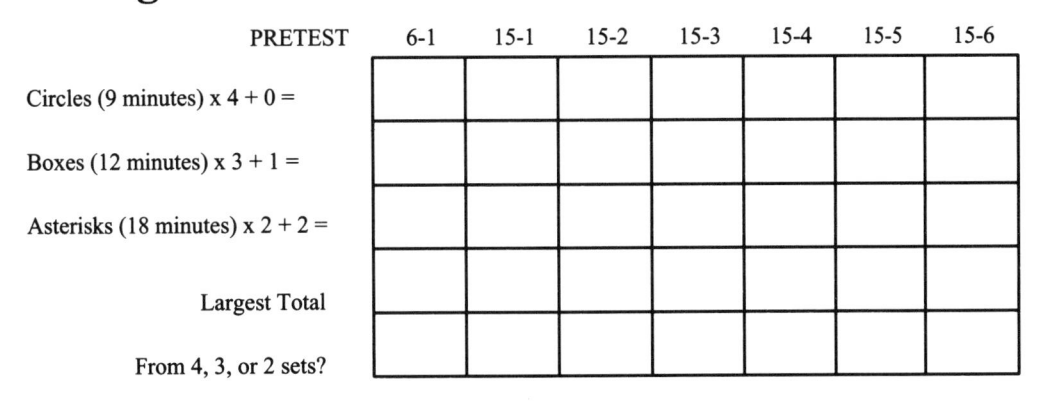

	PRETEST	6-1	15-1	15-2	15-3	15-4	15-5	15-6
Circles (9 minutes) x 4 + 0 =								
Boxes (12 minutes) x 3 + 1 =								
Asterisks (18 minutes) x 2 + 2 =								
Largest Total								
From 4, 3, or 2 sets?								

TRAINING SESSION 7

LSAT Questions

The question set is a critical component of the test plan: it facilitates your management of time, maximizes your sense of control, and avoids much of your academic conditioning. And the basic component of the set is the LSAT question. While generally referred to as a single question, in fact this component presents a multi-element profile.

What is the LSAT question profile?

The LSAT question profile is simple, and every question fits it. The profile has four elements. First are the **directions**, which make three important points. They tell you that every section-test is separately timed, that you are to select the best answer to each question, and that notes must be made in the test book, not on scratch paper, the work surface, or a shirt sleeve.

The second element is a **statement**. The statement provides the context for the questions. It varies in both length and structure. For a Relationships question, the statement presents a small number of facts and rules. The statement for an Arguments question is also short and consists of a small number of facts and/or conclusions. In contrast, Passages statements are lengthy extracts from journals and similar sources.

Following the statement is the **question**. LSAT questions are short. Each can be viewed as a variation on one of three basic types—that which *must*, *could*, or *cannot* be true given the information presented in the statement and question.

The fourth element of the profile is the **answer choice**, the most important element of the profile for the test-taker. Answer choices give meaning to the question and effectively *become* the question. For example, the question "Which of the following must be true?" can only derive meaning in the context of the five answer choices.

How can the answer choices be described?

LSAT answer choices appear in two formats: the single-option format and the multiple-option format.

THE SINGLE–OPTION ANSWER CHOICE

The single-option format presents five answer choices following a brief question. Your objective is to select the best answer choice from among the five options presented.

The question is identified by its number, which, as is conventional, corresponds to one on the LSAT answer sheet. The answer choices are identified by letters.

1. If Ms. Stark sits next to Mr. Taylor, which of the following must be true?

    (A) One of the Reeds sits next to one of the Starks.
    (B) The Vines sit opposite the Reeds.
    (C) The Taylors sit together.
    (D) The Vines sit together.
    (E) One of the Taylors sits next to one of the Reeds.

THE MULTIPLE–OPTION ANSWER CHOICE

The multiple-option answer choice is the second format found on the LSAT. It has a number of benefits for the test-maker, among them that more than one of the answer choices can be best and that five answer options are effectively expanded into seven. (This is illustrated in the diagram on the next page. Note that only five of the possible seven are actually used.) Because there can be more than one best answer, the test-maker doesn't have to work so hard to produce wrong answer choices. The complexity of the answer structure makes the selection of the best answer more difficult for the test-taker. So, with less effort than is required by the single-option format, the test-maker can produce a more difficult question. Following is an example.

2. If Mr. Vine sits next to Mr. Taylor, which of the following must be true?

    I. All fathers sit next to each other.
    II. Three daughters sit next to each other.
    III. Each father sits next to his daughter.

    (A) I only
    (B) II only
    (C) I and II only
    (D) II and III only
    (E) I, II, and III

40

I. All fathers sit next to each other.
II. Three daughters sit next to each other.
III. Each father sits next to his daughter.

(A) I only
(B) II only
(C) I and II only
(D) II and III only
(E) I, II, and III

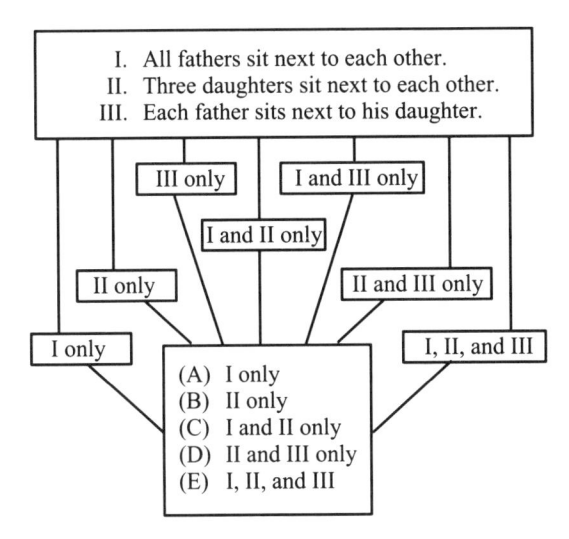

As you can see, the multiple-option format initially presents only three choices, any or all of which may meet the conditions set by the question. The answer-choice structure then presents five lettered single or multiple options from which to select one best answer.

When first encountering the complexities of the multiple-option format, many test-takers believe they are the victims of an insidious plot. They find the format problematic and confusing. However, this response is not called for; in fact, in most circumstances the format provides you with an advantage I call the multiple-option trick.

✓ THE MULTIPLE–OPTION TRICK IS A SHORTCUT TO THE BEST ANSWER.

Looking at the preceding example, review the five letter-designated answer choices. You will notice that II appears in answer choices B, C, D, and E. If you could determine the status of choice II, you would be able to eliminate four answers and identify the best answer. Suppose that you study the facts and determine that choice II cannot be true. If choice II cannot be true, neither can answers B, C, D, and E. The only answer not discarded is A, which thus must be the best selection.

Presto, you have selected the best answer by having to consider only choice II! The example shows the multiple-option trick at peak power. Usually the test-maker makes application of the trick helpful but not determinative, as here. Since using the trick has no downside risk for you, you can apply it every time you encounter the multiple-option format.

WHERE IS "NONE OF THE ABOVE"?

"None of the above" is another answer choice that test-makers frequently use to make their work easier by not having to produce a best answer. All answers can be bad. There is no "none of the above" answer choice on the LSAT.

What is the basic reasoning task required by the LSAT?

In addition to the four-element profile, all LSAT questions also have a reasoning task in common. The primary reason that the LSAT is useful to law schools is that it measures applicants' skill at reasoning in the principal way the schools and the legal system require.

However, the best information a single question can contribute to the measurement is very limited. Only after accumulating information from many test questions does the LSAT provide sufficiently precise results to be useful to the law schools. To get a reasonably accurate result, many individual measurements have to be taken, so the LSAT involves some 100 questions. If these questions measured a variety of skills, the test would be unable to give reasonably reliable information about each one, but because it measures a single skill, the results are reasonably consistent.

The single skill measured by the LSAT is difficult to describe in precise or familiar terms, though it can be relatively easily understood in terms of the task it requires. A good analogy is to aspirin, whose workings scientists have been unable to explain precisely despite vast amounts of research, although they *can* observe the results of its operation and understand its nature in terms of those results. By observing the basic LSAT task in operation, the test-maker can understand it in terms of the results produced.

✓ FOR OUR PURPOSES, THE BASIC REASONING TASK THE LSAT DEMANDS CAN BE CALLED "CONDITIONAL REASONING," THOUGH THIS IS NOT TO SUGGEST A FORMAL LOGICAL CONCEPT OR ANYTHING FORBIDDING.

Can the basic task be illustrated?

Following is an LSAT problem, with the elements of the question profile singled out.

DIRECTIONS
Answer the following question as quickly as you can. Circle the best answer choice.

STATEMENT
The oak is a deciduous, hardwood tree known for the fact that it always produces a nut commonly called an acorn.

QUESTION
1. If it has been determined that a specific tree produces acorns, which of the following descriptions of the tree must be true?

ANSWER CHOICES
(A) It is a deciduous tree.
(B) It is an acorn tree.
(C) It is a hardwood tree.
(D) It is an oak tree.
(E) It is an unknown species of tree.

The statement tells you that a tree called an oak has certain attributes or conditions. Among them are that it is deciduous, is a hardwood, and always produces acorns. The question, which involves a tree that produces acorns, is designed to exploit the statement that precedes it.

The statement uses the words "always produces . . . an acorn" to suggest more than it actually tells you, encouraging the assumption that a tree that produces acorns must be an oak. However, the statement only tells you that in order for a tree to be an oak it must produce acorns—*it does not tell you that a tree that produces acorns must always be an oak.*

In the spirit of the LSAT, the question also exploits what the statement does *not* tell you. The question asks you to identify a tree by providing you with only one of the three conditions that the statement says are necessary for a tree to be an oak. No matter what that condition (acorn), its existence does not identify the object (oak) to a certainty. For the acorn to be sufficient to establish the tree as an oak, the statement would have had to say that a tree that produces an acorn is *always* an oak, and the statement said no such thing.

However, you remember from your basic botany course that acorns are only produced by an oak tree. Besides, your own experience tells you this is so. No matter how certain you are about acorns and oaks, that is information from outside the test; it is not in the statement and has no relevance in the context of the test question. Such outside information can clearly be detrimental under certain test circumstances. Avoid it.

✓ NO EXTERNAL INFORMATION IS REQUIRED FOR YOU TO BE ABLE TO SELECT THE BEST ANSWER TO AN LSAT QUESTION.

While the test does not go out of its way to set traps of the acorn type, it often sets them. Using only the information you are given is the most effective way to avoid the BYO conditioning that has been so helpful to you in previous test situations.

Now you know why answer choice E is the best choice. It is the only one of the five that *must* be true. The other choices *could* be true, but, based on the information provided, they also could be untrue. You just don't know, and since the question asks you what you know to a certainty—what must be true—answer choice E is your only option. You are certain that you don't know.

✓ THE BASIC REASONING TASK IS FOUND IN EVERY LSAT QUESTION.

Unfortunately, the task is seldom presented as obviously as it is in the oak-acorn example. If it were, the test would be even more predictable than it is. It would be too easy and would not be able to rank people very well. The law schools would have little use for it, and the test-maker would have to find some other application for the many questions in its inventory. To make certain that this scenario is not realized, the test-maker goes to great pains to mask the basic reasoning task. This could be called camouflage, concealment, disguise, or—my personal favorite—"obfuscation."

What is obfuscation?

Obfuscation is the test-maker's primary tool. Obfuscation makes it difficult for the test-taker to see the basic reasoning task in most LSAT questions. The greater the degree of obfuscation, the more difficult the question becomes for the test-taker. Nevertheless, the basic reasoning task is there—it is the essence of every LSAT question. The task must be there if the test is to measure your skill with it. With some training, you can become effective at locating the basic task, avoiding the conditioning the problem sets out to exploit, and selecting the best answers.

In this next example you are asked to answer a question about cards. Give it a try, and see if you can notice how the test-maker obfuscates your route to the best answer. Once again, the basic elements of the problem have been identified—just remember, they won't always be spelled out in this way.

DIRECTIONS
Answer the following question as quickly as you can. Circle the best answer choice.

STATEMENT
The card-master holds four cards in a stack. Each card has a single letter on the front side and a single number on the back side. The master states that if a card has a vowel on one side it will have an even number on the other side. The master places the four cards on a table with the visible sides showing A, B, 1, and 2, respectively.

QUESTION
2. Of the following, which names only the cards that must be turned over to determine whether what the master said is true?

ANSWER CHOICES
(A) the cards showing A and B
(B) the cards showing A and 1
(C) the cards showing A and 2
(D) the cards showing A, B, and 1
(E) all four of the cards

The four cards on the table can be depicted as follows:

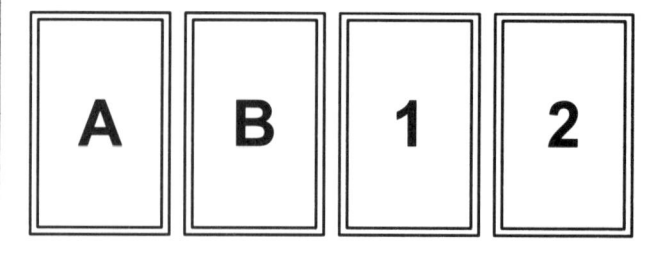

| A | B | 1 | 2 |

Remember that each card has a number on one side and a letter on the other. The card-master has said that if a card has a vowel on one side, it has an even number on the other. Circle only those cards that you have to turn over to determine if the card-master's statement is true.

The object is a card with a vowel on one side (front); the condition is an even number on the other side (back). There are four cards. As with the previous example, this question is designed to exploit your conditioning.

Remember, *no outside information.* You are not being asked about all possible cards. It may appear to you that the question seeks some universal proof, but the question only deals with four cards. Review the question carefully—it asks you to do what you can to establish the truth of the card-master's statement. In this context, what technique is available to you to establish that which is true? There is only one—to locate evidence that *disproves* the statement.

In your quest for such evidence, you consider each card. The first one has an A on the side you can see. A is a vowel. (Note that you do need this outside information.) This card is the object of the statement. By turning it over, you will determine if the condition is met. If the card has an even number on the reverse side, you will have learned no more than what the statement told you. But if an odd number appears on the reverse side, you will establish that the card-master's statement is untrue. Thus, you must turn the A-card over.

The second card has a B on the side you can see. B is not a vowel. It is not the object of the statement. In fact, it is irrelevant to your problem, whatever is on the back. Neither the statement nor the question says anything about consonants. This card is no help to you, and you need not turn it over.

The third card shows a 1, an odd number. If you turn it over and a consonant appears, you will gain no evidence concerning the question. But if you turn it and a vowel appears, you will establish that the card-master's statement is untrue. Thus, you must turn this card over.

The fourth card has a 2, an even number. If you turn this card over and find a consonant on the other side, you will gain no evidence concerning the question. Remember that there is nothing in the statement or question that would preclude there being an even number on a card with a consonant on its reverse side. Should you turn this card and find a vowel, you have no more evidence about the truth of the card-master's statement than you had before. Thus, there is no reason to turn the 2-card.

After consideration, you deduce that the best answer choice is B. Only B involves the object of the question and the relevant condition. The basic reasoning task is complete.

Obfuscation tactics make this example of the cards more difficult than the oak tree question. By inviting you to assume that even numbers cannot appear on cards with a consonant, the test-maker obfuscates the basic reasoning task. Then, by inviting you to read the question as if your task were the opposite of what you are actually asked to do (that is, to confirm the card-master's statement rather than disaffirm it), the test-maker further obfuscates the basic reasoning task. Such obfuscation tactics maintain the effectiveness of LSAT questions, and some work better than others.

What are the types of obfuscation tactics?

Three of the five general types of obfuscation tactics used on the LSAT involve **varying the presentation** of the basic task. First, the context in which the basic task is presented is varied. For example, three seemingly different section-tests are used—Arguments, Passages, and Relationships. Within each of these section-tests, the appearance of the questions is varied to add to the impression that many different tasks are required. The question structure is emphasized in the mind of the test-taker, who tends to concentrate on differences in form and overlook the essential similarity of LSAT questions. Varying the presentation of the basic task causes the test's focus to seem different from what it really is.

Related to the obfuscation-by-variation tactic is the use of **excessive information**. Although it is employed elsewhere on the test, this tactic is seen best in the Passages statements, which give the test-taker much more information than is needed to respond to the questions. The test-taker concentrates on the information presented, trying to understand and retain the data by using processes that have proven effective in the past. Thus, the test-taker becomes absorbed in processes that detract from work on the real task.

The third obfuscation tactic involves the **omission of information** in the statement and question. The test-taker gets the impression that there is insufficient information to respond to the question, and this "missing" data grabs and keeps the test-taker's attention away from the reasoning task involved. While it often may appear otherwise, the information needed to respond to the question is always given—what is *not* said is often as informative as what *is* said.

These three tactics generally result in difficulties of question location for the test-taker, who uses limited test time seeking rather than responding to the question. You can minimize the impact of these tactics by remembering that the basic task of reasoning with objects (including non-material ones) and conditions is always the same and avoiding activities that do not involve this basic task.

The last two obfuscation tactics are less obvious than the first three and pose greater difficulties for test-takers. You experienced the **invited assumption** tactic in both the oak-tree and card-master examples. In the oak-tree example, you were invited to assume that every tree that produces acorns is an oak. In the card-master example, you were invited to assume that cards with even numbers on one side had to have vowels on the other. You were also invited to assume that cards with consonants on one side had odd numbers on the other. Each of these assumptions was invited by a familiar or probable pattern (vowel = even, consonant = odd) or by external knowledge (acorns occur only on oak trees). The invited assumption usually involves such familiar patterns or external knowledge. Avoid it by identifying and using only the patterns and knowledge presented in the problem.

The **invited question** is also very difficult for the well-conditioned test-taker to resist. The invited question often shows up on television quiz shows—the host reads only a few words of the question and a contestant blurts out an answer. A more subtle form of the same thing was involved in the card-master example. Although the question invited you to identify cards that might confirm the truth of the card-master's statement, the *operative* question required you to identify only those cards that could *disprove* the truth of the statement. LSAT questions are generic and unclear. Consequently they invite interpretation. Effective interpretation of the questions results from a review of the answer choices.

> ✓ BY CONSIDERING ONLY THE FIVE ANSWER CHOICES, YOU CAN RESIST THE INVITATION TO ANSWER A QUESTION THAT WAS NOT ASKED.

TRAINING SESSION 8

Relationships Problems

Of the three LSAT question formats, Relationships questions present the basic task most clearly. This clarity can assist you in developing the skills and procedures you need for handling the basic task in the other two LSAT problem formats. Of the three question formats, Relationships is also the most difficult to master. Working on it first gives you plenty of time to get it under control and thus maximize your test performance.

Why are Relationships questions so difficult?

In short, the reason Relationships questions are difficult is that they are unfamiliar. Most test-takers are familiar with and relatively proficient at test questions that require recall or are based upon contexts with which they have experience. Questions about definitions, formulas, and facts require the test-taker to recall memorized information and perhaps apply it. Questions about the concepts, procedures, and theories presented in lectures, texts, and class discussions depend on the test-taker's assimilation of teachers' and writers' perspectives. These experiences and acquired perspectives permit the test-taker to consider points of view, arguments, and the like when responding to a question.

✓ RELATIONSHIPS QUESTIONS REQUIRE VERY LITTLE RECALL, NOR DO THEY INVOLVE LEARNED PERSPECTIVES, POINTS OF VIEW, OR ARGUMENTS. CONSEQUENTLY, THEY ARE UNFAMILIAR, DISCOMFITING, AND DIFFICULT.

How many questions are there in a Relationships section-test?

There are four sets of Relationships questions in each 35-minute section-test. Generally there are six questions in each of the four sets, though, occasionally, you will find as few as five or as many as seven questions in a set when the test-maker has had to deviate from the norm to get the test performance required. Thus, there are usually twenty-four questions in a Relationships section-test.

✓ THE FOUR SETS OF QUESTIONS IN THE SECTION–TEST ARE CRITICAL TO YOUR TEST PLAN.

What are the components of a Relationships question?

As you will recall, the LSAT problem profile has four components—directions, a statement, questions, and answers.

The directions for Relationships questions are brief. What they do say, however, is pertinent: "each group of questions is based on a number of conditions. You are to choose the best answer to each question." Interpreted, this means that the best answer is the only one of the five options that satisfies all the relevant conditions for the question.

This gives you an advantage. For example, if you are finding it difficult to select between two answer options to a Relationships question, you *know* that only one meets all of the conditions. You should be able to resolve your dilemma quickly by finding the condition that differentiates between the answer options. In this way you avoid a trap that captures many test-takers, who repeatedly review the same answers in the same way in the futile hope that the best answer will eventually reveal itself.

How do Relationships questions work?

THE DIRECTIONS

The directions for Relationships questions are brief and not very enlightening. The test-maker tells you that questions are based on a set of conditions and that you are to select the response that most accurately and completely answers the question. And that's it! The important thing you are not told is that the conditions that appear in the statement apply to all questions, and the conditions that appear in a question apply *to that question only*. As you will soon learn, the response that most accurately and completely answers a question will be the only answer option that satisfies all of the conditions applicable to that question.

THE STATEMENT

Relationships statements usually consist of two parts, designated here as facts and rules. Although they are short and seemingly simple, there is a possible complication unique to Relationships questions. While each question in a set shares the common statement, some problems include an additional statement embedded in the question itself. In general, about two thirds of Relationships questions include one of these supplemental statements.

The facts and rules in the common statement apply to all questions in the set. The facts and rules in a supplemental statement apply only to the questions in which they appear.

✓ WHEN THE TEST–MAKER PLACES A SUPPLEMENTAL STATEMENT WITHIN A QUESTION, THE ADDED STATEMENT APPLIES ONLY TO THAT QUESTION.

Not only does the supplemental statement apply solely to the question in which it is found, but it may contradict another such statement placed in a different question in the set.

In the facts portion of the statement, the test-maker presents the variables involved in the question set. By including many variables in the statement, the test-maker obfuscates the fact that only a few are actually relevant to the set of questions. Test-takers become confused by the presence of many variables, with their potential for vast numbers of combinations. They then spend much time trying to sort through the variables and their combinations, or they move to another question set in the hope that it will be less forbidding. You can avoid these detrimental reactions by looking to the rules and questions to render the facts manageable.

✓ CONCENTRATING ON THE RULES AND QUESTIONS REDUCES THE NUMBER OF POSSIBLE VARIABLES AND COMBINATIONS TO THE RELEVANT FEW.

When applied to the facts, the rules portion of the statement generally yields a number of conditions. And it is these conditions that are referred to by the questions. The rules limit the number of conditions you have to consider in selecting the best answer to a Relationships question.

THE QUESTION

The question brackets the answer selection to be made. As described previously, it also may add facts and rules to those that are common to the entire question set, further narrowing the relevant conditions with which you must deal. However, the question seldom reduces the relevant conditions to one.

Relationships questions are very straightforward. There are only three basic questions.

- Which of the following *must* satisfy the conditions/be true?
- Which of the following *could* satisfy the conditions/be true?
- Which of the following *cannot* satisfy the conditions/be true?

In most Relationships section-tests, you will find more *must* and *could* questions and fewer *cannot* questions. The test-maker is able to vary the presentation of these basic questions. The questions and their variations are illustrated in the diagram below.

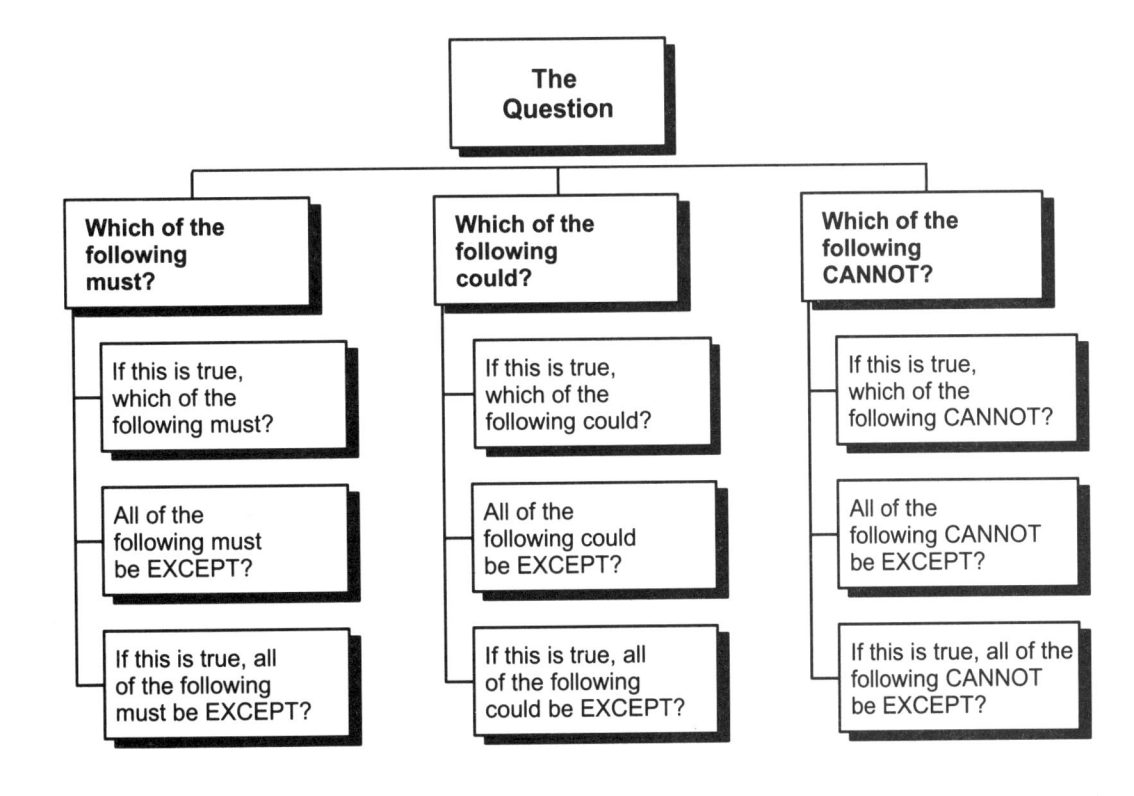

```
                          The
                        Question
        ┌─────────────────┼─────────────────┐
 Which of the        Which of the      Which of the
 following           following         following
 must?               could?            CANNOT?
   │                   │                   │
 If this is true,    If this is true,   If this is true,
 which of the       which of the       which of the
 following must?    following could?   following CANNOT?
   │                   │                   │
 All of the          All of the         All of the
 following must     following could    following CANNOT
 be EXCEPT?         be EXCEPT?         be EXCEPT?
   │                   │                   │
 If this is true, all  If this is true, all  If this is true, all of the
 of the following     of the following       following CANNOT
 must be EXCEPT?      could be EXCEPT?       be EXCEPT?
```

The first variation shows the supplemental statement format. The second is the converse of the basic question, requiring the selection of the answer option that is an exception to the conditions required by the question. The last variation combines the supplemental statement format with the converse of the basic question.

The test-maker also varies the appearance of questions by slipping synonyms in here and there. For instance, "might" may be substituted for "could," and "has to" or "is" may substitute for "must."

And that about says it all for Relationships questions. You have reviewed them all. There will be no surprises. *You now can predict every Relationships question that will appear on the LSAT.*

THE ANSWERS

The answer choices to Relationships questions are presented in both single- and multiple-option formats, with as many as 25 percent of them in a section-test using the multiple-option format. You will recall that, in the multiple-option format, one, two, or all three of the Roman numeral options could satisfy the question conditions. You should also remember that there are many possible answers that would satisfy the question conditions, but only one of those is included in the five options of an answer set.

The test-maker's selection of answer options gives you the wrong-answer advantage. Not only are there just five answers from which to select, but four of them do not satisfy one or more of the conditions required by the problem. It is difficult for the test-maker to produce attractive wrong answers, since every wrong answer fails to satisfy the conditions required by the combined statement and question. The test-maker attempts to disguise this failure, but, for most answer options, it is relatively easy to detect. In fact, for most questions using the single-option format, the failure is easy to detect in three of the five answer options.

✓ THE TEST–MAKER USUALLY OFFERS JUST ONE ATTRACTIVE WRONG ANSWER OPTION.

Wrong answers follow patterns that can assist in your detection of them. Recall that the best answer option is the only one that satisfies *all* of the relevant conditions. If the question is "Which of the answer options **must** be true?" options that *could* be true or *cannot* be true are wrong—they fail to satisfy all of the conditions.

If the question is "Which of the answer options **could** be true?" options that *cannot* be true are wrong. They, too, fail to satisfy all of the conditions. (Note that the test-maker accepts that an answer choice that **must** be true satisfies a question asking for the choices that *could* be true.)

If the question is "Which of the answer options **cannot** be true?" options that *must* be true and *could* be true are wrong, failing as they do to satisfy all of the conditions.

With Relationships questions, the test-maker usually uses the **too-little-too-much** technique (and a variation we will encounter a little later) to create wrong answer options. This simply means that the answer option overstates or understates conditions that would satisfy the question.

Notice that the following example of a Relationships problem employs a supplemental statement in the question. For the purposes of illustration, all of the answer options offered here are wrong. This would not be the case with an actual LSAT question. Remember also that the identifiers used here do not appear on the LSAT.

STATEMENT

Facts
The twelve-member board of directors of Acme International, Inc., is divided into four committees: the Audit Committee, the Finance Committee, the Planning Committee, and the Shareholder Relations Committee.
Rules
    At least one of the directors is a member of the Audit, Finance, and Planning committees.
    At least one of the directors is a member of the Audit, Finance, and Shareholder Relations committees.

QUESTION
1. If each committee has three members, and no two committees share more than two members, which of the following must be true?

ANSWER CHOICES
(A) All members of the Audit Committee are members of the Planning Committee.
(B) No member of the Audit Committee is a member of the Planning Committee.
(C) The Audit and Finance committees have at least two members in common.
(D) The Planning and Shareholder Relations committees have only one member in common.
(E) The Audit Committee has exactly twice as many members in common with the Finance Committee as does the Shareholder Relations Committee.

Since the question asks for that which **must** be true, wrong answers will be those that *could* or *cannot* be true.

Answer option A overstates what must be true. The supplemental statement requires that no more than two of the three members of a committee be shared with another committee. Thus, all three committee members *cannot* be shared by two committees.

Answer option B understates what must be true. The common statement requires that one director be a member of both the Audit and Planning committees. Thus, it *cannot* be that no committee members are shared by the two committees.

Answer option C overstates what must be true. The common statement requires that *one* member of the Audit and Finance committees be shared, not two. The supplemental statement requires that no more than two members of a committee be shared with another committee—it does not require that two members be shared. Thus, it *could* be that two committee members are shared by two committees, but it is not necessarily so.

Answer option D both understates and overstates what must be true. The common statement does not require that the member of the Audit, Finance, and Planning committees be the same person who is shared by the Audit, Finance, and Shareholder Relations committees. It is possible but not required. The supplemental statement requires that no more than two members of a committee be shared with another committee. It does not require that any members be shared. Thus, it *could* be that the Planning and Shareholder Relations committees have only one member in common, but it need not be so.

Answer option E illustrates a variation of the **too-little-too-much** technique sometimes used by the test-maker. It is wrong because it is far too precise to meet the stated conditions. This technique can be disconcerting and distracting to a test-taker who fails to recognize it and tries to develop some conclusive proof.

By identifying a condition implicit in the answer option that fails to satisfy the question, you can determine that an answer is wrong and dump it. The wrong-answer patterns and obfuscatory tactics are summarized below.

For **must** questions, wrong answer options are those that *could* or *cannot* satisfy required conditions, even though they use

- the **too-little-too-much** tactic
- the **overprecision** tactic

For **could** questions, wrong answer options are those that *cannot* satisfy required conditions, even though they use

- the **too-little-too-much** tactic
- the **overprecision** tactic

For **cannot** questions, wrong answer options are those that *must* or *could* satisfy required conditions, even though they use

- the **too-little-too-much** tactic
- the **overprecision** tactic

How does the test-maker create more difficult questions?

As you have seen, making more difficult questions is not a simple matter of asking tougher questions. Rather, the test-maker creates more difficult questions by creating better answers. The test-maker wants the substantial majority of questions on any section-test to be of medium difficulty, with some 40–60 percent of test-takers selecting the best answer. A smaller proportion of questions is to be relatively easy, with more than 60 percent of test-takers selecting the best answer. And an even smaller proportion is to be relatively tough, with fewer than 40 percent of test-takers selecting the best answer.

To adjust the difficulty level of a question or question set, the test-maker use two basic techniques. First, the complexity of the relationships can be varied. This is demonstrated in the preceding example by the inclusion of the supplemental statement, which defines the size of the committees and limits the nature of their composition.

✓ IN GENERAL, THE GREATER THE COMPLEXITY OF THE STATED RELATIONSHIPS, THE MORE DIFFICULT THE QUESTION.

The second technique used by the test-maker to create more difficult questions involves the answer options. Again, this is demonstrated in the preceding example. Answer options A and B are determined to be wrong by direct reference to a condition in the statement or the question. If all the wrong answer options could be similarly eliminated, the question would be relatively easy; it is made slightly more difficult by the inclusion of answer options C, D, and E, which require a more complicated review of conditions to determine that they are wrong.

With respect to your test plan, it makes sense to complete questions in the order of increasing difficulty. This strategy applies even more to question sets than to questions within sets. However, except for using the techniques described above, the test-maker provides no clues about the difficulty of questions.

✓ UNLIKE MANY OTHER STANDARDIZED TESTS, THERE IS NO ORDER OF DIFFICULTY AMONG LSAT QUESTIONS OR QUESTION SETS.

Later question sets are no more difficult than earlier ones, nor are later questions harder than earlier ones. Fatigue may sometimes make later question sets appear to be more difficult, but this is illusory.

How can you handle the complexity of Relationships questions?

Visualization is a critical efficiency device for working with the format of Relationships questions. How do you visualize? If you are told to put yourself in Mary's position and that John is standing to Mary's left and Betty to her right, what do you project onto the screen in your mind? If you "see" three people in a line, two women together and a man on one end or the other, your visualization technique is working well. If you "see" a woman, another woman, and a man standing in a line from left to right, your visualization is slightly more efficient, because you have defined the exact placement of the three on the basis of Mary's position. If you "see" something else or nothing at all, you will find the **node-and-line** visualization technique particularly helpful.

By using a single visualization as the basis for selecting answers to many questions, you maximize your use of test time and minimize the potential for confusion. The technique uses *nodes* to depict variables (usually things) and *lines* to depict connections (usually relationships) between them. On the following page is a visualization of the John-Mary-Betty statement in the previous paragraph.

```
  B ———— M ———— J
right              left
```

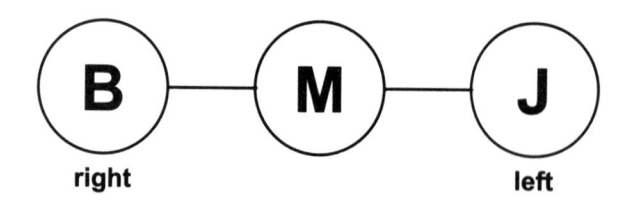

How do you apply the visualization technique?

First, you read the facts and rules. It is rare that these alone will provide sufficient information for you to develop an effective visualization, so you must next scan the questions. At this point, the core of information you will be working with becomes clear, and you can begin your visualization.

You usually will find some space to record your visualization on the pages of the question set, but occasionally you will encounter a full page with no white space. Scratch paper and shirt cuffs are forbidden. What to do? Just fold the preceding or succeeding page in half, and use the space thus exposed.

In the LSAT, relationships are defined in relative rather than specific terms. You will find such statements as "Mary is older than John and younger than Betty." You will not read that "Mary is 10, John is 8, and Betty is 12." The most efficient visualization must anticipate this lack of specificity and allow for the shifts that inevitably will be required by the questions. You must remember that the lines in your visualization do not depict exact relationships—they are more akin to rubber bands, capable of extending or contracting as circumstances require. In fact, a squiggly line can be used to remind you of this important point. (The varieties of visualization will be thoroughly illustrated in the next session.)

After you complete your visualization, consider the questions. As you work through them, you may have to adjust your visualization slightly to accommodate a supplemental statement or some other attribute of the question. Consider each answer option, seeking the condition that will make it wrong by failing to satisfy the requirements of the question and statement. Use comparison, identifying the conditions in the answer option and comparing them to those in your visualization. When you find the condition that fails to satisfy the requirements, dump that answer choice. One unsatisfactory condition is sufficient—compare no more.

Repeating the process, you select the best answer option and circle it in the test book. Once you have completed all six questions in the set, transfer all of your answers to the answer sheet *at the same time*. This provides a natural break before you move on to the next Relationships problem.

TRAINING SESSION

9

Relationships Problems in Depth

There is one Relationships section-test on each LSAT, which translates into some 25 percent of the questions. Relationships question sets appear in five forms: the line-up, family-tree, cluster, map, and schedule contexts.

Since there are four sets of Relationships questions on each 35-minute section-test, it is clear that all five contexts cannot be represented on each section-test. In fact, a section-test may include only two or three of them. The line-up, cluster, and schedule contexts appear with much greater frequency than do the family-tree and map contexts. In fact, the family-tree and map contexts have been almost completely phased out by the test-maker, and it is unlikely that you will encounter them. However, they will be covered just in case.

In what order should Relationships problems be considered?

While individual experiences differ, certain contexts are generally more difficult for test-takers than others. The line-up and family-tree contexts are generally the least difficult, the cluster and map contexts somewhat more difficult, and the schedule context usually the most difficult. Therefore, you should work on them in that order, from least to most difficult.

✓ WORK ON RELATIONSHIPS PROBLEMS IN THE ORDER OF DIFFICULTY OF THEIR CONTEXTS—FROM THE LINE–UP TO THE FAMILY–TREE, CLUSTER, MAP, AND SCHEDULE CONTEXTS.

In most instances, the question sets do not appear on the section-test in the order in which it is best to consider them. So your first assignment when beginning a Relationships section-test is to identify the context of each of the four question sets and number the sets in the order you will work on them.

What is the line-up context?

Most question sets include at least one question using the **line-up** context. You are already familiar with this context in its basic form. It involves simply putting items in order. A teacher arranges the students in a row, from shortest to tallest, from fastest to slowest, or from youngest to oldest—this is what is meant by the line-up context.

How do you work with the line-up context?

You begin by reading the statement, noting the facts and rules.

ARF dog food comes in six sizes—Small, Medium, Large, Jumbo, Giant, and Colossal.

Colossal weighs more than Large.
Large weighs more than Small.
Medium weighs less than Jumbo.
Large weighs more than Giant.
Giant weighs more than Jumbo.

The facts and rules announce the line-up context and suggest that the question set will focus on weight. A brief review of the questions confirms this suggestion. Now that the focus for the questions is clear, you can visualize.

The facts tell you that ARF comes in six sizes. These are the variables that will be nodes in your visualization. Abbreviate them as S, M, L, J, G, and C. (The test-maker generally uses names beginning with different letters to facilitate abbreviation.)

✓ RUN A CHECK TO BE CERTAIN THAT EACH VARIABLE IS INCLUDED.

The differences in weight are expressed in the relative terms "lighter" and "heavier." The lines in your visualization will depict these transitive relationships.

✓ AGAIN, RUN A CHECK TO BE CERTAIN THAT EACH RELATIONSHIP IS REPRESENTED.

Then combine these representations into a single visualization. After you complete the visualization, consider the questions. Do not return to the statement for any reason. This is a time-waster and is to be avoided.

FIRST STEP IN VISUALIZING THE VARIABLES

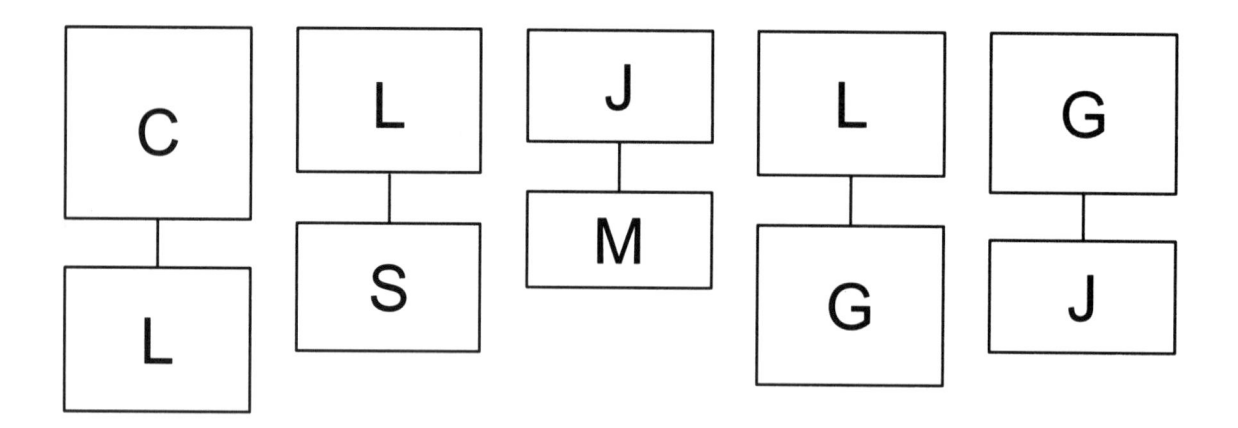

```
C        L        J        L        G
|        |        |        |        |
L        S        M        G        J
```

SECOND STEP IN VISUALIZING THE VARIABLES

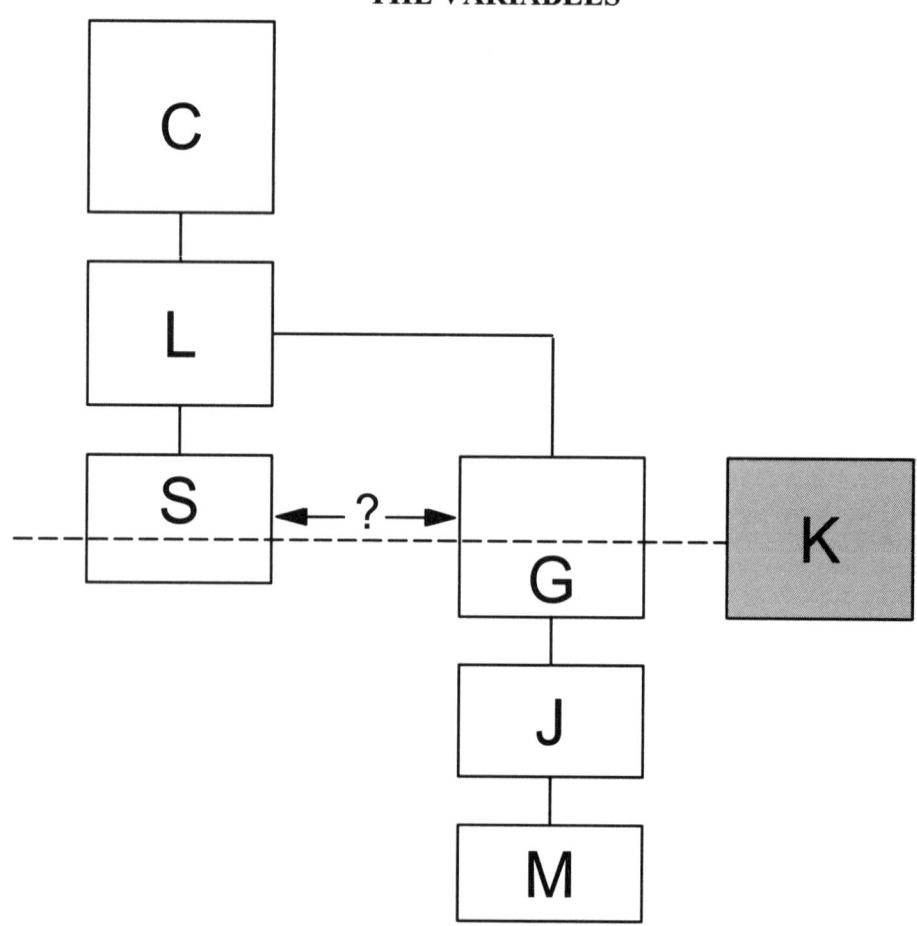

```
C
|
L ————————┐
|         |
S  ←?→    G ———— K
          |
          J
          |
          M
```

✓ AS YOU WORK THROUGH THE QUESTIONS, REFER TO THE VISUALIZATION ONLY.

1. Which of the following must be true?

   (A) Large is heavier than Jumbo.
   (B) Large is lighter than Jumbo.
   (C) Small is lighter than Medium.
   (D) Large is lighter than Giant.
   (E) Giant is heavier than Small.

This is a **must** question. Refer to the visualization, and start work with answer option A. You determine that Jumbo weighs less than Giant, which weighs less than Large. This means that Large is heavier than Jumbo, and option A is the best answer. Since you know there can be only one answer that satisfies all conditions, and you have determined that option A does this, there is no reason to go any further in considering options.

2. Which of the following CANNOT be true?

   (A) Jumbo is heavier than Large.
   (B) Jumbo is lighter than Large.
   (C) Small is lighter than Medium.
   (D) Large is heavier than Giant.
   (E) Giant is heavier than Small.

This is a **cannot** question. Again, refer to the visualization, and start work with answer option A. As you noted in the previous question, Jumbo weighs less than Giant, which weighs less than Large. This means that Jumbo cannot be heavier than Large. Option A is the best answer—it satisfies all conditions. There is no reason to go beyond A in considering options.

Notice that the best answers for questions 1 and 2 are opposites. The test-maker frequently uses such an approach. By being alert to take advantage of this circumstance, you can reduce the time required to respond to questions and become more efficient.

3. How many sizes must be lighter than Giant?

   (A) 0
   (B) 1
   (C) 2
   (D) 3
   (E) 4

This is a **must** question. The wrong answers are those that *could* or *cannot* be lighter than Giant. By referring to the visualization, you determine that Jumbo weighs less than Giant, and Medium weighs less than both. You also determine that, because both Large and Colossal weigh more than Giant, they *cannot* be lighter. Finally you determine that Small *could* be lighter than Giant. Thus, three sizes either *could* or *cannot* be lighter than Giant, leaving two that **must** be lighter. Therefore, option C is the best answer.

4. How many sizes must be heavier than Jumbo?

   (A) 1
   (B) 2
   (C) 3
   (D) 4
   (E) 5

This is a **must** question. The wrong answers are those that *could* or *cannot* be heavier than Jumbo. By referring to the visualization, you determine that Jumbo weighs more than Medium, which *cannot* then be heavier. You also determine that Jumbo could be lighter than Small, which means that Small *could* be heavier. Thus, two sizes either *could* or *cannot* be lighter than Giant, leaving three that **must** be heavier. Option C is the best answer.

5. If Kennel size is added to the ARF line, and it is lighter than three of the six original sizes, which of the following must be true?

   (A) Giant is heavier than Kennel.
   (B) Large is heavier than Kennel.
   (C) Jumbo is heavier than Kennel.
   (D) Small is lighter than Kennel.
   (E) Small is heavier than Kennel.

This is a **must** question that involves a **supplemental statement**. The wrong answers are those that *could* or *cannot* be true. First you must add the supplemental information to the visualization (K on page 50). By referring to the augmented visualization, you determine that Colossal and Large are the two heaviest sizes; what is uncertain is the third size that is heavier than Kennel. A review of the conditions discloses that you have no information through which certainty can be reached. Thus, it is likely that the best answer will not involve the uncertainty. Answer option A directly involves the uncertainty: since Giant *could* be heavier than Kennel, option A is wrong. Because Large weighs more than all sizes other than Colossal, it **must** be heavier than Kennel, making option B the best answer. Since you know that only one answer option satisfies all conditions, and you have determined that B satisfies all conditions, there is no reason to consider further options.

6. If Kennel size is added to the ARF line, and it is heavier than three of the six original sizes, which of the following CANNOT be true?

   (A) Kennel is heavier than Small.
   (B) Kennel is heavier than Jumbo.
   (C) Kennel is heavier than Giant.
   (D) Kennel is lighter than Large.
   (E) Kennel is lighter than Jumbo.

This is a **cannot** question that involves a **supplemental statement**. The wrong answers are those that *must* or *could* be true. First you must add the supplemental information to the visualization. The supplemental information, though conflicting with that in question 5, yields the same visualization. What is uncertain is the third size that is lighter than Kennel. Again, a review of the conditions discloses that you have no information through which certainty can be reached. Thus, once more it is likely that the best answer will not involve the uncertainty. Answer options A and C directly involve the uncertainty: since Kennel *could* be heavier than Small and Giant, A and C are wrong. Because Jumbo weighs less than all sizes other than Medium, it *must* be lighter than Kennel, and option B *must* be true, making it wrong when what is asked for is a **cannot** answer. And because Large weighs more than all sizes other than Colossal, it *must* be heavier than Kennel, and option D must be true, making it similarly wrong. Thus, the best answer is E.

What is the family-tree context?

You are probably familiar with the **family-tree** context, which focuses on the terminology of family relationships. One of the reasons that this context is being gradually eliminated from the LSAT has to do with the fact that this terminology is perhaps too familiar to many test-takers and too unfamiliar to others from different cultural backgrounds.

It is worth refreshing your memory about the designation of generations. "Grand" is used to indicate two generations removed: granddaughter, grandfather, grandaunt, etc. "Great-grand" is used to indicate three generations removed: great-granddaughter, great-grandfather, great-grandaunt, etc. A cousin, brother, and sister are in the same generation. A son, daughter, mother, father, niece, nephew, aunt, and uncle are one generation removed. "Blood" is used to speak of a biological family relationship, and "in-law" and "by marriage" are used to indicate a nonbiological family relationship.

How do you work with the family-tree context?

You begin working with the family-tree context by reading the statement.

The following is known about a particular family:
Doris is Eve's mother, and Fay is Eve's daughter.
Hanna is Ruth's mother, and Tess is Ruth's daughter.
Hanna and Lori are Fay's daughters.
Mary, Nancy, and Paula are Lori's only daughters.

The statement declares the family-tree context. After reading the statement and determining the probable focus of the questions, complete your visualization. The facts present ten family members who can be abbreviated D, E, F, H, R, T, L, M, N, and P. These are the variables that will be nodes in your visualization. The lines in your visualization will depict the family relationships. As before, check to see that each variable and relationship is visualized. A notation of the generations can be added to minimize the chance of confusing them with ages and other conditions.

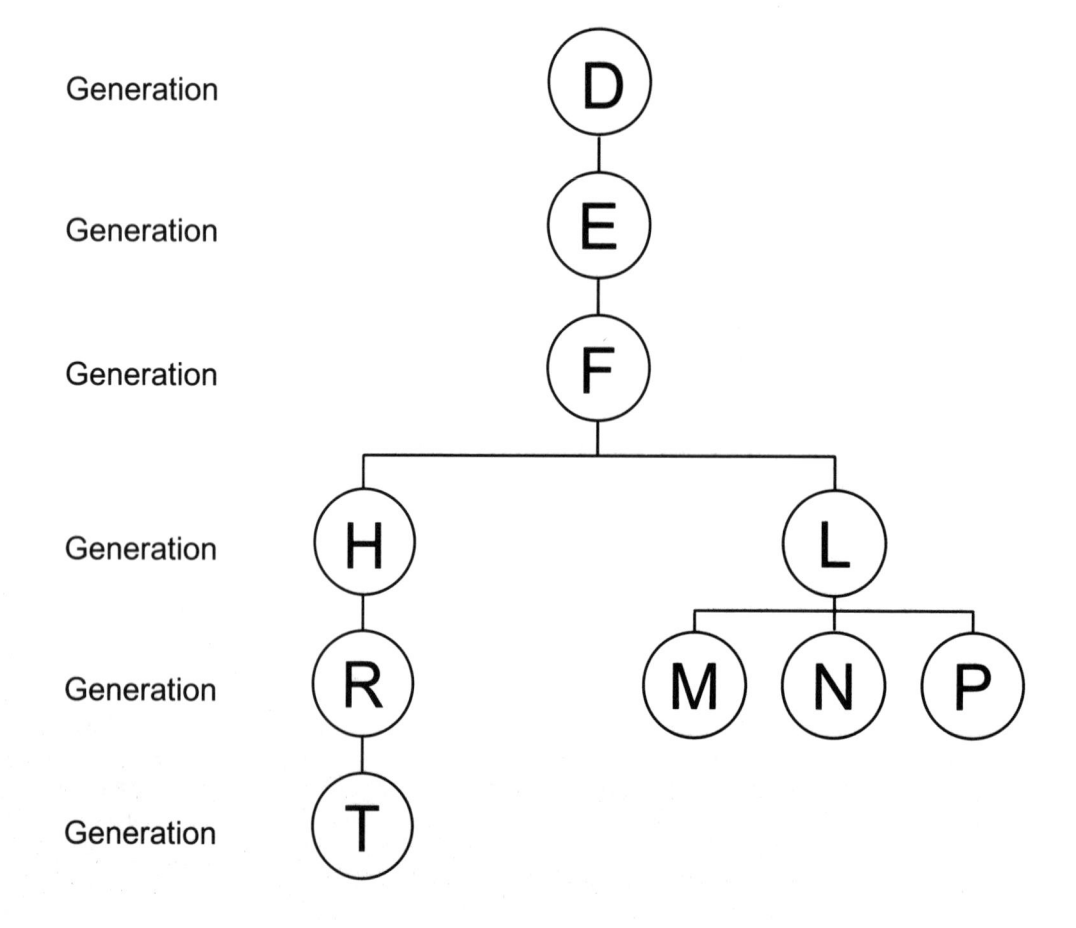

```
Generation         D
                   |
Generation         E
                   |
Generation         F
                  / \
Generation       H   L
                 |  /|\
Generation       R M N P
                 |
Generation       T
```

After you complete your visualization, consider the questions. Recall that you will be referring only to the visualization as you work through the questions. You will not return to the statement.

1. Hanna must be Eve's
   (A) niece
   (B) cousin
   (C) granddaughter
   (D) aunt
   (E) grandaunt

This is a **must** question. The wrong answers are those that *could* or *cannot* be true. The relationship being sought is determined by its distance from Eve. By referring to the visualization, you determine that Hanna is two generations from Eve. Answer options A and D are only one generation removed and are wrong because they *cannot* satisfy the conditions of the question. Option B is in the same generation, which also fails to satisfy the conditions. Option C is two generations removed in the direction of the subsequent generations and is the best answer option. While answer option E is also two generations removed, it is in the direction of the previous generations and *cannot* satisfy the conditions with respect to Eve.

2. If Lori is married, her husband is Ruth's
   (A) brother-in-law
   (B) father-in-law
   (C) uncle
   (D) cousin
   (E) granduncle

This is a **must** question that involves a **supplemental statement**. The wrong answers are those that *could* or *cannot* be true. First add the husband to the visualization, and then note Ruth as the point of reference. (Augment your visualization in a manner similar to the one used to add Kennel dog food to the diagram on page 50.) From the visualization, it is clear that Lori is in the generation immediately preceding Ruth's. Because brother and cousin are in the same generation, answer options A and D are wrong: they *cannot* satisfy the conditions. Options B and C are the two that are one generation removed. Since Ruth's marital status is not involved in this question, her father-in-law is obviously not relevant, and option B is wrong. Thus, option C is the best answer, because it is the only choice that is relevant and involves a relative one generation removed from Ruth.

3. If Ruth has a brother, he is Eve's
   (A) great-grandson
   (B) nephew
   (C) grandson
   (D) cousin
   (E) grandnephew

This is a **must** question that involves a **supplemental statement**. The wrong answers are those that *could* or *cannot* be true. First add the brother to the visualization, and then identify the point of reference by the possessive, which is "Eve's" in this case. From the visualization, it is clear that Ruth and her newly introduced brother are three generations removed in the direction of the subsequent generations. This means that the best answer option will have "great-grand" in it. Option A is the only answer that satisfies this condition. There is no reason to consider the other options.

4. Eve could have any of the following numbers of great-granddaughters EXCEPT
   (A) 3
   (B) 4
   (C) 5
   (D) 6
   (E) 7

This is a **could EXCEPT** question. The combination of "could" and "EXCEPT" is confusing—it is equivalent to a **cannot** question. Thus, the wrong answer options are those that *must* or *could* satisfy the conditions of the question. Eve's great-granddaughters are three generations removed in the direction of the subsequent generations. By reference to the visualization, you determine that Eve has at least four great-granddaughters—R, M, N, and P—and that answer option B *must* be true, making it a wrong answer. Since there is nothing in the statement to indicate that these four are Eve's only great-granddaughters, answers C, D, and E *could* satisfy the conditions of the question and are also wrong. Option A is the only one that **cannot** be true, and it is therefore the best answer choice. (Note that the test-maker interprets option A to mean *only* three great-granddaughters. We know that Eve has at least four.)

5. If Hanna is older than Lori, which of following must be true?
   I. Paula is older than Tess.
   II. Nancy is younger than Ruth.
   III. Lori is younger than Fay.
   (A) I only
   (B) II only
   (C) III only
   (D) I and III only
   (E) II and III only

This is a **must** question that involves a **supplemental statement** and the **multiple-option** format. Make a note on your visualization that Hanna is older than Lori. Then consider Roman numeral I. Even though you determine from the visualization that Paula and Tess are in different generations, this alone tells you nothing about their ages. It only means that Paula *could* be older than Tess. Since *could* is a wrong answer to a **must** question, mark Roman numeral I with an F for false. From this you know that answers A and D are wrong options, and you dump them. Next consider Roman numeral II. The fact that Ruth's mother, Hanna, is older than Nancy's mother, Lori, tells you nothing about Ruth's and Nancy's respective ages. It only means that Nancy *could* be younger than Ruth, and since *could* is a wrong answer to a **must** question, Roman numeral II is false also. From this, you determine that answers B and E are wrong options, and you also dump them. This means that answer C is the best option.

6. Ruth could have any of the following number of cousins, EXCEPT
   (A) 1
   (B) 3
   (C) 5
   (D) 7
   (E) 9

This is another **could EXCEPT** question—remember that this is equivalent to a **cannot** question. The wrong answer options are those that *must* or *could* satisfy the conditions of the question. Ruth's cousins are in the same generation. By reference to the visualization, you can see that Ruth has at least three cousins—M, N, and P—and that answer option B *must* be true, which is a wrong answer to a **cannot** question. Since there is nothing in the statement to indicate that these three are Ruth's only cousins, answers C, D, and E *could* satisfy the conditions and are also wrong. Option A is the only one that **cannot** be true, which makes it the best answer choice. (Note that the test-maker interprets option A to mean *only* one cousin. We know that Ruth has at least three.)

What is the cluster context?

You probably have some familiarity with the **cluster** context. On the LSAT, the cluster context usually appears in problems involving groups and individuals within those groups. It introduces the complications that arise when individuals have dual status or are affected by more than one set of conditions. Some conditions may apply to groups only, some to individuals within groups, some to individuals alone, and some to combinations of these. This complication tends to make the cluster context somewhat more difficult than the line-up and family-tree contexts.

How do you work with the cluster context?

As usual, you begin by reading the statement, with its facts and rules, to determine the context. You will recognize the following statement from the previous session.

> The twelve-member board of directors of Acme International, Inc., is divided into four committees: the Audit Committee, the Finance Committee, the Planning Committee, and the Shareholder Relations Committee.
>
> At least one of the directors is a member of the Audit, Finance, and Planning committees.
> At least one of the directors is a member of the Audit, Finance, and Shareholder Relations committees.

The facts present a board of twelve directors and four committees. These are the potential variables. By scanning the questions, you determine that their focus is committee membership, so the committees become the nodes in your visualization: A, F, P, and S. The relationships are depicted by the lines in your visualization. Always check to be certain that each variable and relationship is visualized.

In this instance, you will need to produce two visualizations, because the facts and rules leave an uncertainty. The director who is a member of the Audit, Finance, and Planning committees may or may not be the director who is a member of the Audit, Finance, and Shareholder Relations committees. The first visualization depicts the facts and rules if there are two directors (X and Y) satisfying the conditions; the second one depicts the facts and rules if there is just one director (Z) satisfying the conditions.

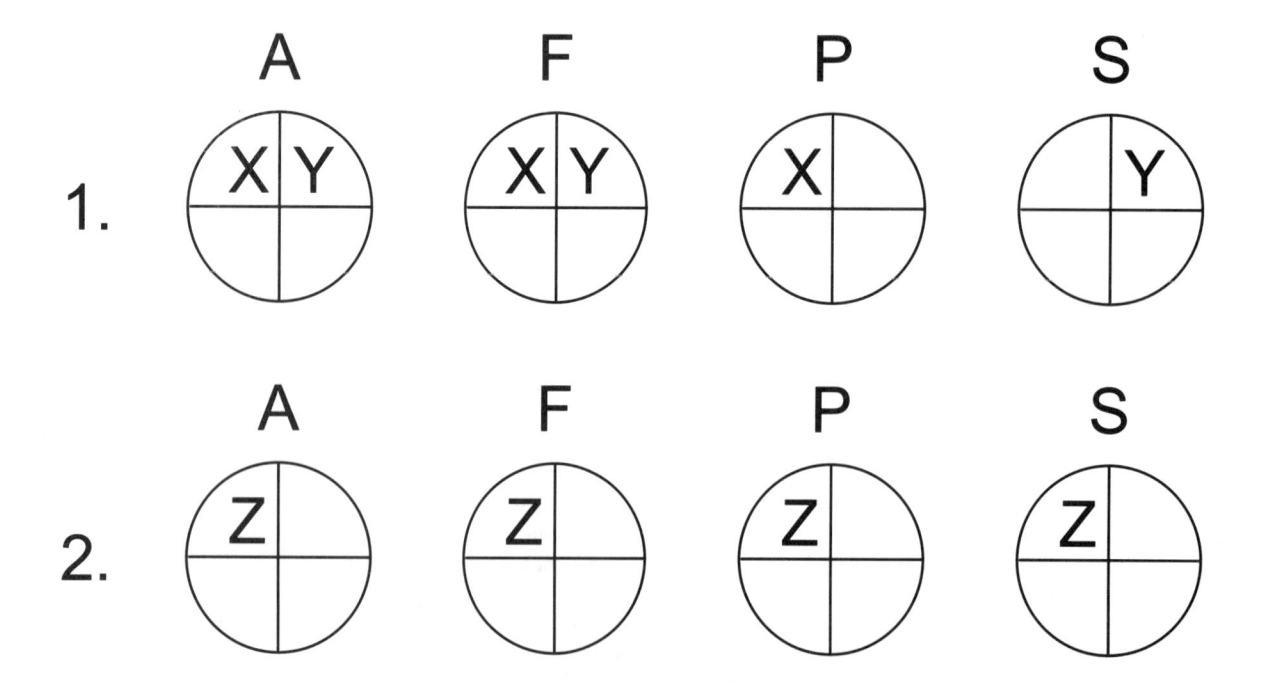

After completing the visualization, consider the questions, recalling that you will be referring only to the visualization as you work through the questions. For demonstration purposes, this question set emphasizes the multiple-option answer format, but there is no reason to expect that this format will be used more frequently in the cluster context than in any other.

1. Which of the following must be true?
   I. At least one member of the Finance Committee is a member of the Planning Committee.
   II. No member of the Planning Committee is a member of the Shareholder Relations Committee.
   III. The members of the Finance and Planning committees are the same people.
   (A) I only
   (B) II only
   (C) III only
   (D) II and III only
   (E) I, II, and III

This is a **must** question. Begin by considering Roman numeral I. Note from the visualizations that at least one member of the Finance Committee is a member of the Planning Committee. Since this option satisfies the conditions of the question, mark Roman numeral I with a T for true. Because they do not include Roman numeral I, you know that B, C, and D are wrong answer options. These three options are dumped. Next consider Roman numeral II. From the second visualization, you determine that at least one member of the Planning Committee *could* be a member of the Shareholder Relations Committee. Since *could* is a wrong answer to a **must** question, Roman numeral II is false and answer E is a wrong option. This means that A is the best answer option, and there is no reason to consider Roman numeral III.

2. Which of the following could be true?
   I. Some members of the Audit Committee are members of the Finance Committee.
   II. No member of the Audit Committee is a member of the Finance Committee.
   III. The members of the Audit and Finance committees are the same people.
   (A) I only
   (B) II only
   (C) III only
   (D) I and III only
   (E) I, II, and III

This is a **could** question. Considering Roman numeral I, you note from the visualizations that at least one member of the Audit Committee is a member of the Finance Committee. Since this option satisfies the conditions of the question, mark Roman numeral I with a T for true. B and C do not include Roman numeral I and are thus wrong answer options. Next you should consider Roman numeral III out of order, since, because it appears in D and E, it has the potential of identifying all of the remaining wrong answer options. From the visualizations, you determine that you have no information that would preclude the members of the Audit and Finance committees being the same people. Since this option satisfies the conditions of the question, Roman numeral III is marked with a T, but the advantage you hoped for is unrealized. You have to consider Roman numeral II after all. From the visualizations you determine that at least one member of the Audit Committee is a member of the Finance Committee, so Roman numeral II ca*nnot* be true, and you mark it with an F. From this, you determine that answer E is a wrong option, and D is the best option.

3. If Carter is a member of the Audit Committee, which of the following could be FALSE?
   I. Carter is a member of the Finance Committee.
   II. Carter is a member of the Planning Committee.
   III. Carter is a member of the Shareholder Relations Committee.
   (A) I only
   (B) II only
   (C) I and II only
   (D) I and III only
   (E) I, II, and III

This is a **could** question. Note that "could be false" also implies "could be true." First consider Roman numeral I. From the visualizations you determine that there is no information that requires Carter to be a member of the Finance Committee. This option satisfies the question conditions, and you mark Roman numeral I with a T. Also note that there is no information that requires Carter to be a member of the Planning and Shareholder Relations committees. Since these also satisfy the question conditions, Roman numerals II and III are also true. This means that options A, B, C, and D are wrong, and you dump them. Answer E is the best option.

4. If Gates is the only director that the Audit and Finance committees have in common, which of the following must be true?
   I. Gates is a member of the Planning Committee.
   II. Gates is a member of the Shareholder Relations Committee.
   III. The Planning and Shareholder Relations committees have at least one member in common.
   (A) I only
   (B) II only
   (C) I and II only
   (D) I and III only
   (E) I, II, and III

This is a **must** question with a **supplemental statement** that establishes the second visualization as the accurate representation of the question's conditions. Considering Roman numeral I, note on the visualization that Gates (Z) is a member of the Audit and Finance committees and a member of the Planning Committee. Since this option satisfies the conditions of the question, Roman numeral I is true. This makes B a wrong answer option, because it does not include Roman numeral I. Dump it. Next you consider Roman numeral II and determine from the visualization that Z is a member of the Audit, Finance, and Shareholder Relations committees. Since this option also satisfies the question conditions, Roman numeral II is also true. Because they do not include both I and II, A and D are wrong answer options. Coming to Roman numeral III, you determine from the visualization that Z is a member of the Planning and Shareholder Relations committees. This option also satisfies the conditions and is also true. This means that answer C is wrong, and E is the best option.

5. If Martin is the only director that the Finance and Planning committees have in common, which of the following could be true?
   I. Martin does not belong to both the Planning and Shareholder Relations committees.
   II. Martin does not belong to both the Audit and Planning committees.
   III. The Audit and Shareholder Relations committees have no members in common.

   (A) I only
   (B) II only
   (C) I and II only
   (D) I and III only
   (E) I, II, and III

This is a **could** question with a **supplemental statement** that establishes the first visualization as the accurate representation of the question conditions. Considering Roman numeral I, you note from the visualization that Martin (X) is the only member the Audit, Finance, and Planning committees have in common and that X could not also be a member of the Shareholder Relations Committee. Since this option satisfies the question conditions, you mark Roman numeral I with a T. Because it does not include Roman numeral I, B is a wrong answer option. Now consider Roman numeral II. From the visualization you determine that X m*ust* be a member of the Audit and Planning committees. Since this option *cannot* satisfy the question conditions, Roman numeral II is false, and C and E are wrong because they include it. In considering Roman numeral III, you determine from the visualization that Y is a member of the Audit and Shareholder Relations committees. Since this *cannot* satisfy the question conditions, Roman numeral III is false. Thus, E is wrong, and A is the best answer option.

6. If Titus and Varga are the only members of the Finance Committee, and neither is a member of all four committees, which of the following must be true?
   (A) Titus is a member of the Audit and Planning committees.
   (B) Titus and Varga are not both members of the Audit Committee.
   (C) Titus is a member of the Audit and Shareholder Relations committees.
   (D) Titus and Varga are not both members of the Planning Committee.
   (E) Varga is a member of the Planning and Shareholder Relations committees.

This is a **must** question with a **supplemental statement** that establishes the first visualization as the accurate one. By reference to that visualization, you can determine that Titus and Varga are X and Y, but you have no information to help you establish which is which. You consider the answer options in order. As to A, Titus *could* be a member of the Audit and Planning committees. Since *could* is a wrong answer to a **must** question, option A is dumped. As to B, the visualization establishes that Titus and Varga are both members of the Audit Committee, so it *cannot* be that they are not. This makes option B wrong, and you dump it. As to C, Titus *could* be a member of the Audit and Shareholder Relations committees. As with A, *could* is a wrong answer to a **must** question, so C is dumped. As to D, Titus and Varga *cannot* both be members of the Planning Committee. Option D satisfies the conditions and is the best choice. There is no need to consider option E.

What is the map context?

You are not likely to be familiar with the **map** context, which is a type of spatial exercise. It has many of the attributes of the line-up, although they are deployed in two-dimensional space instead of in a single line.

A few terms the test-maker uses are worthy of review. To indicate a precise direction, the test-maker uses such terms as "due," "directly," or "exactly." Therefore, "due north" means precisely north—0° and 360° on the compass. "North" means northerly; that is, anything in the northern direction bounded by the east/north/west hemisphere. "Northeast" means northeasterly; that is, anything in the direction of the quadrant bounded by north and east. These conventions apply to each of the compass directions—north, east, south, and west.

How do you work with the map context?

As with the other contexts, you begin by reading the statement, with its facts and rules.

> There are nine gasoline stations in the town of Mountain View: Amoco, Boron, Chevron, Exxon, Gulf, Hess, Mobil, Shell, and Texaco. The stations are located as follows:
> Amoco, Boron, Chevron, and Exxon are all west of Gulf, and all of the others are east of Gulf.
> Boron and Chevron are both due west of Gulf, and Amoco is due north of Boron.
> Exxon is due south of Chevron, and Mobil is due northeast of Gulf.
> Hess is due north of Mobil, and Shell and Texaco are both due south of Mobil.

The statement establishes the map context and suggests that direction and distance will be the focus of the question set. A brief look at the questions confirms this suggestion. Now you record your visualization.

The facts tell you that there are nine stations: A, B, C, E, G, H, M, S, and T. These variables will be the nodes in the visualization. The differences in direction are expressed in relative terms, and the lines in the visualization will depict these transitive relationships. As always, check to be certain that each relationship is visualized, and be especially careful not to confuse direction with relative distance.

Relationships Problems in Depth 57

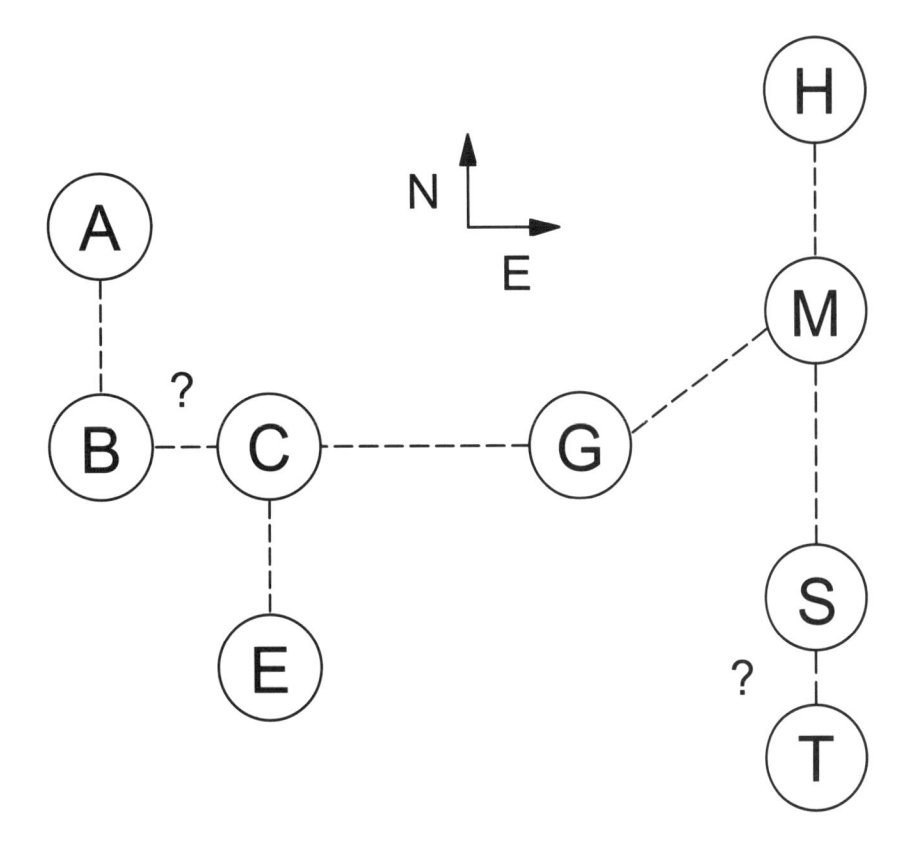

Complete your visualization, and consider the questions. Note that, because directions are relative, you should take care to consider the answer options from the position declared in the question. Remember to refer to the visualization only.

1. Hess lies in which direction from Chevron?
   (A) due east
   (B) southeast
   (C) due north
   (D) northeast
   (E) southwest

Even though it does not use the term, this is a **must** question. Locate C and H by referring to the visualization. H is east of C but also north. Thus, answer options A, B, and C *cannot* be true. They do not meet the conditions and are dumped. Option D, however, does meet the north and east conditions of the question and is the best answer option. There is no need to consider option E.

2. If a person were to travel directly west from Mobil, what is the maximum number of stations the person could encounter?
   (A) 0
   (B) 1
   (C) 2
   (D) 3
   (E) 4

This is a **could** question. From M's position on the visualization, you determine that B, C, E, G, S, and T are all south and *cannot* be due west of M. *Cannot* is the wrong answer to a **could** question. H is north of M and *cannot* be due west of it. Again, *cannot* is the wrong answer to a **could** question. Since A is due north of B, which is southwest of M, A **could** be directly west of M, depending on how far north A is from B. All nine variables are thus accounted for, and only A **could** be directly west of M. Answer options A, C, D, and E *cannot* be true; they do not satisfy the question conditions and are dumped. Option B satisfies the conditions and is the best answer.

3. Which of the following could be true?
   I. The Exxon, Shell, and Texaco stations are south of the Gulf station.
   II. The Boron, Chevron, and Exxon stations are north of the Gulf station.
   III. The Amoco, Shell, and Texaco stations are north of the Gulf station.
   (A) I only
   (B) II only
   (C) III only
   (D) I and III only
   (E) II and III only

This is a **could** question with a **multiple-option** format. Consider Roman numeral I first. From G's position on the visualization, you determine that E is south of C, and, because C is due west of G, E must also be south of G. Since *cannot* is the only wrong answer to a **could** question, so far you have found no reason why Roman numeral I is untrue. Even though M is north of G, there is no information about how far south S and T are from M. They **could** be so far south as to be south of G. Roman numeral I thus satisfies the conditions, so mark it with a T for true. Because Roman numeral I is not included in answer options B, C, and E, they are wrong and are dumped. Only A and D **could** satisfy the question conditions, so you skip to Roman numeral III because it is included in option D. From G's position on the visualization, you determine that A is north of B, and, because B is due west of G, A must also be north of G. This satisfies the conditions of the question. As noted previously, M is north of G, and there is no information about how far south S and T are from M. They could be such a short distance south of M as to be north of G. Roman numeral III thus satisfies the question conditions and is marked with a T. Option A does not satisfy the conditions and is wrong; D does satisfy the conditions and is the best answer.

4. How many stations must be south of the Boron station?
   (A) 1
   (B) 2
   (C) 3
   (D) 4
   (E) 5

This is a **must** question. Referring to the location of B on the visualization, you determine that A is north of B, and both B and C are due west of G. This means A, C, and G *cannot* be south of B. Because E is south of C, and both B and C are due west of G, E must also be south of B. Since *could* and *cannot* are the only wrong answers to a **must** question, A, C, and G do not satisfy the conditions of the question, and E does. Since B is due west of G, M is north of G, and H is north of M, H and M *cannot* be south of B and do not satisfy the conditions of the question. There is no information about how far south S and T are from M, so they *could* be so far south as to be south of B, but they might not be. S and T do not satisfy the conditions. Answer options B, C, D, and E *cannot* be true; none of them meet the question conditions. Answer option A does satisfy the conditions of the question, and it is the best answer option.

5. Which of the following could be true?
   I. The Amoco station is west of the Chevron station.
   II. The Exxon station is west of the Boron station.
   III. The Boron station is west of the Chevron station.

   (A) I only
   (B) I and II only
   (C) I and III only
   (D) II and III only
   (E) I, II, and III

This is a **could** question with a **multiple-option** format. First consider Roman numeral I. By referring to your visualization, you see that A's east-west position is determined by the position of B. Since B could be west of C or vice versa, A *could* be west of C. This option satisfies the question conditions, so you mark Roman numeral I with a T. This means that option D is wrong, and it is dumped. Next work with Roman numeral II. The visualization shows you that E's east-west position is determined by the position of C. Since C could be west of B or vice versa, E *could* be west of B. This option satisfies the question conditions, and you mark Roman numeral II with a T also. This means that options A and C are wrong. Next you consider Roman numeral III. Locating B on the visualization, you determine that B *could* be west of C (or vice versa). Since this option also satisfies the question conditions, Roman numeral III is marked with a T. Therefore, option D is wrong and is dumped. Option E satisfies the conditions and is the best choice.

6. What is the maximum number of stations that could be southeast of the Amoco station?
   (A) 4
   (B) 5
   (C) 6
   (D) 7
   (E) 8

This is a **could** question. Studying the visualization, you determine that A is due north of B and, consequently, that B *cannot* be southeast of A. Since *cannot* is the only wrong answer to a **could** question, B does not satisfy the conditions of the question. There is no information in the statement or question from which you can determine that B and A are not westernmost among the stations, nor can you determine how far north of B station A is located. So if A is located sufficiently far north, all stations other than B **could** be southeast of A. This means that seven stations **could** be southeast of A, and answer options A, B, C, and E *cannot* be true. They do not meet the conditions and are dumped. Option D does satisfy the conditions and is the best answer option.

What is the schedule context?

You may have some familiarity with the **schedule** (or "assignment") context. As used on the LSAT, it expands upon the complication of the cluster context, with some conditions applying to individuals, some to locations, some to times, and some to combinations of the three. This complication generally makes the schedule context the most difficult of the five Relationships contexts, which is why you should schedule schedule problems last when working on the Relationships section-test of the LSAT.

How do you work with the schedule context?

You begin, as always, by reading the statement to establish the facts and rules. The sample problem that follows is probably more difficult than any you will find on the LSAT. It is included to make the point that appearances can be deceiving. Despite its difficulty, the question set can be managed by following the Relationships protocol that is becoming familiar to you.

A circus presents a twelve-act show in three rings. Ring 1 is adjacent to ring 2, which is adjacent to ring 3. During a show, which is divided into four equal segments, each act is presented exactly once. Three acts are presented simultaneously in each segment. The acts are: acrobats, bears, clowns, dogs, elephants, horses, jugglers, lions, seals, trapeze artists, unicyclists, and wire-walkers.

  Only ring 2 has wire-walking, unicycling, and trapeze rigging.
  The lions and bears must perform in ring 3, the only ring with a cage.
  Because of the cage, the clowns, elephants, and horses cannot perform in ring 3.
  Two adjacent rings may not present an animal act at the same time.
  The acrobats, dogs, and lions perform at the same time.
  The trapeze artists and wire-walkers cannot follow immediately after each other, and the clowns must perform between the two to provide relief from the tension.

The many facts and rules tell you that this is the schedule context and suggest that order and location are the ideas on which the question set will focus. A brief survey of the questions confirms this suggestion. Now you are ready to visualize a schedule.

The facts tell you that there are twelve acts (individuals), four time slots, and three rings (locations). The individuals are A, B, C, D, E, H, J, L, S, T, U, and W. The intersection of time and location determines the nodes of your visualization, which results in a 3 x 4 matrix. Check to be certain that each variable is included, and apply the rules to the individuals, noting the results in the matrix as follows.

The first rule tells you that T, U, and W perform only in ring 2. The second rule tells you that L and B perform only in ring 3. Since rule three provides that animal acts cannot be presented in adjacent rings at the same time, rule four provides that dogs and lions (and acrobats) perform at the same time, and rule two provides that lions perform in ring 3, it follows that dogs must perform in ring 1 (not adjacent to another animal act) and acrobats in ring 2. *You have now determined all of the acts for ring 2: A, T, U, and W.*

Rule two provides that C, E, and H cannot perform in ring 3, and ring 2 is full, so C, E, and H must perform in ring 1 with D. *This determines all of the acts for ring 1: C, D, E, and H.*

The remaining acts must perform in ring 3. *Thus you have determined all of the acts for ring 3: B, J, L, and S.*

Take note that the clowns must perform between the trapeze artists and the wire-walkers.

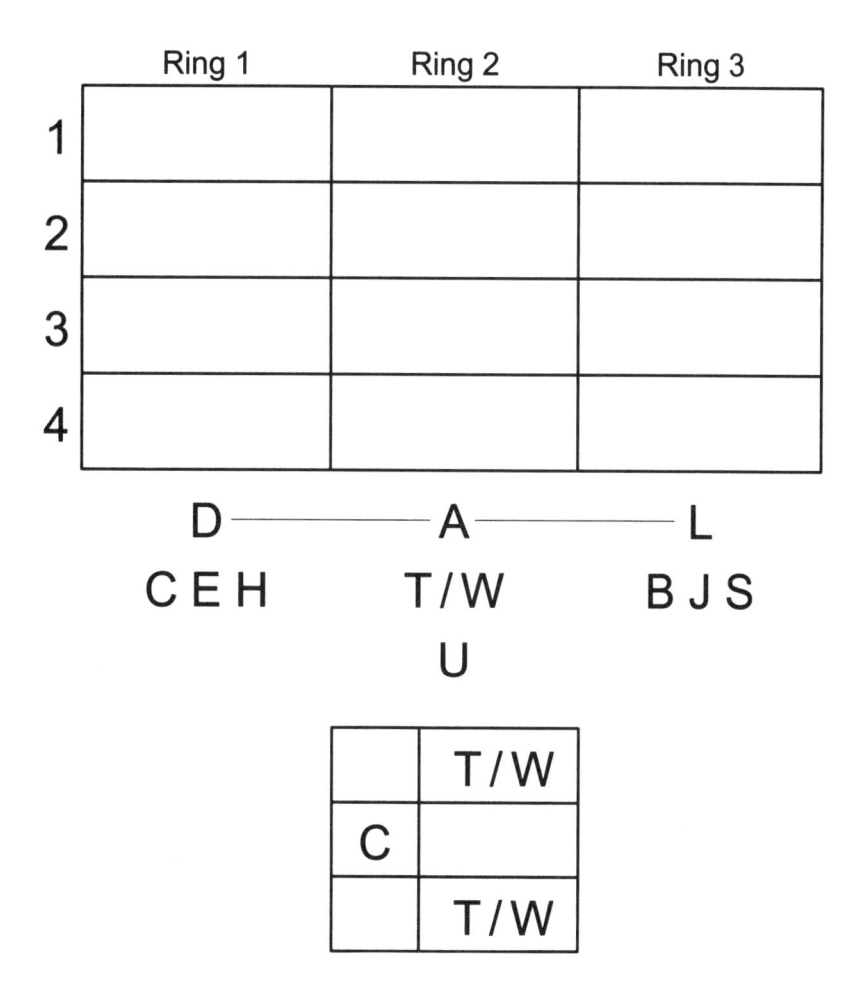

	Ring 1	Ring 2	Ring 3
1			
2			
3			
4			

D————A————L
C E H   T/W   B J S
         U

	T/W
C	
	T/W

60 Inside the LSAT

1. Which of the following must be true?

   (A) There are no animal acts in ring 1.
   (B) There are no animal acts in ring 2.
   (C) All acts presented in ring 3 are animal acts.
   (D) All acts presented in ring 2 are animal acts.
   (E) Animal acts perform in all three rings.

   This is a **must** question. Beginning with answer option A, you refer to your visualization and determine that dogs perform in ring 1. Option A *cannot* be true, as it does not satisfy the conditions of the question, and is dumped. Moving on to option B, you refer to the visualization and determine that A, T, U, and W perform there. None are animal acts, so option B is true, does satisfy the conditions of the question, and is the best answer. There is no reason to consider options C, D, and E.

2. Which three acts CANNOT start the show in rings 1, 2, and 3, respectively?

   (A) elephants, trapeze artists, bears
   (B) horses, unicyclists, seals
   (C) dogs, acrobats, lions
   (D) clowns, wire-walkers, jugglers
   (E) elephants, unicyclists, jugglers

   This is a **cannot** question. Beginning with answer option A, you refer to the visualization and determine that E performs in ring 1, T in ring 2, and B in ring 3. There is no other information to suggest that it **cannot** be true, so option A *could* be true, does not satisfy the conditions of the question, and is dumped. Working with option B, you refer to the visualization and determine that H performs in ring 1, U in ring 2, and S in ring 3. As with option A, option B *could* be true and is therefore dumped. Answer option C goes the same way, since D performs in ring 1, together with A in ring 2 and L in ring 3, and option C *could* be true. When you arrive at option D, you refer to the visualization and determine that C performs in ring 1, W in ring 2, and J in ring 3. However, C must perform between W and T; therefore, C and W **cannot** perform at the same time, and option D **cannot** be true, satisfies the conditions of the question, and is the best answer. There is no reason to consider option E.

3. If the lions are presented in the first segment, which of the following must be true?

   (A) The clowns are the third act presented.
   (B) The elephants are the second act presented.
   (C) The wire-walkers are the fourth act presented.
   (D) The horses are the first act presented.
   (E) The bears are the third act presented.

   This is a **must** question with a **supplemental statement**. The supplemental statement dictates that D (ring 1), A (ring 2), and L (ring 3) are the first acts presented. This means that either T or W must perform second in ring 2, since C must perform between them. This means that C **must** be among the third acts presented. Answer option A **must** be true, satisfies the conditions of the question, and is the best answer. There is no reason to consider options B, C, D, and E.

4. If the trapeze act is presented second, which of the following could be true?

   I. The elephant act is presented second.
   II. The lion act is presented third.
   III. The clown act is presented fourth.

   (A) I only
   (B) II only
   (C) III only
   (D) I and II only
   (E) II and III only

   This is a **could** question with a **supplemental statement** and the **multiple-option** answer format. From the supplemental statement that T is presented second and the requirement that an act be presented between it and W, it follows that W must be presented fourth. Since C must be presented between T and W, it must be third. We know that D, A, and L must be presented together, and the only time left for them to perform is first.
   Roman numeral I tells you that E performs second. Referring to the visualization, you determine that there is no reason this *cannot* be true. Since this option satisfies the question conditions, you mark Roman numeral I with a T for true. Because options B, C, and E do not include Roman numeral I, they are dumped. Move on to Roman numeral II. Since the supplemental statement dictates that L be presented first, it *cannot* be presented third. Since this option does not satisfy the question conditions, you mark Roman numeral II with an F for false. This means that option D must be wrong, and it is dumped. Answer option A satisfies the question conditions and is therefore the best answer.

5. If the acrobats are presented in the first segment, which of the following CANNOT be true?

   (A) The unicyclists are presented second.
   (B) The horses are presented second.
   (C) The seals are presented second.
   (D) The jugglers are presented second.
   (E) The elephants are presented second.

   This is a **cannot** question with a **supplemental statement**. The supplemental statement dictates that D, A, and L are the first acts presented. Either W or T must perform second in ring 2, since C must perform between them. This means that U *must* be among the third acts presented. Answer option A **cannot** be true, satisfies the conditions of the question, and is the best answer. There is no reason to consider options B, C, D, and E.

6. If the clowns and dogs are presented in the second and fourth segments, respectively, which of the following could be true?

   (A) The unicyclists are presented first.
   (B) The horses are presented third.
   (C) The wire-walkers are presented second.
   (D) The acrobats are presented first.
   (E) The elephants are presented fourth.

   This is a **could** question with a **supplemental statement**. The supplemental statement dictates that D, A, and L are the fourth acts presented. Either W or T must perform first in ring 2, since C must perform second between them. This means that U *cannot* be among the first acts presented. Answer option A *cannot* be true, does not satisfy the conditions of the question, and is dumped. As to answer option B, the supplemental statement says that C performs second and D fourth in ring 1. This means that E or H **could** perform third, since there is no information that dictates they cannot. Answer option B **could** be true, satisfies the conditions of the question, and is the best answer. There is no reason to consider answer options C, D, and E.

TRAINING SESSION 10

Relationships Pretests and the 9-12-18 System

How will the 9-12-18 system apply to your Relationships training?

In Session 6, you learned and applied the techniques of the 9-12-18 test planning system to a Relationships question set. You will recall that the system is based on two concepts. First, your performance is maximized by identifying and planning on achieving your optimal balance between speed and accuracy—this will probably mean that you achieve your goal of selecting fewer wrong answer options by planning to work on fewer question sets in the section-test. Second, you use a pretest process similar to the test-maker's to find your optimal speed and balance on each section-test.

✓ UTILIZING THE 9-12-18 PLANNING SYSTEM, YOU WILL DETERMINE WHETHER IT MAXIMIZES YOUR SECTION–TEST SCORE TO COMPLETE FOUR, THREE, OR TWO QUESTION SETS IN THE 35 MINUTES ALLOWED.

As you apply the techniques presented in the previous two sessions, they will become familiar and easy to use. As they do, you will probably experience a change in your balance between speed and accuracy, and the familiarity you gain will give you a greater sense of control and reduced anxiety. Familiarity will also improve your proficiency with the question sets. The combination of greater control and improved proficiency will result in more accurate answer selection. You will identify wrong answers and, consequently, best answers more efficiently. And with this increase in efficiency, you may have to adjust your test plan.

How do you develop your Relationships section-test plan?

Suppose that your initial Relationships pretest (in Session 6) indicated that you would achieve optimal performance by completing three of the four question sets in a section-test (and only guessing on the fourth). Working with the Relationships training techniques described in the previous two sessions, you will apply the 9-12-18 process to a pretest and update your performance record with the results. After working through these techniques a number of times, you may notice that your pretest results suggest making a change in your plan for balancing speed and accuracy. It now may be clear that completing all four sets of questions on the Relationships section-test would yield a better score than completing only three and guessing on one.

✓ CHANGE YOUR TEST PLAN ONLY WHEN THE RESULTS OF THE 9-12-18 PRETEST PROCESS INDICATE IT.

Your having arrived at this point does not mean that you should put your Relationships training aside and concentrate on other aspects of the test. You must maintain your level of familiarity and proficiency by working through the Relationships sessions regularly and monitoring your performance with 9-12-18 pretests.

How do you use Relationships pretests?

This session closes with six Relationships pretests. They are to be used one at a time. Each time you review Sessions 8 and 9, take one of the Relationships pretests to update your performance record. This means that you should work through the Relationships training techniques at least six times and complete at least six pretests.

Upon completion of the six training and update sessions, your performance record is likely to have stabilized, and your plan for the Relationships section-test will be "set." Your plan will indicate the number of question sets you should complete and the number you should guess on the Relationships section-test at any sitting of the LSAT.

How do you take Relationships pretests?

To reiterate the pretest process, first you read the statement and scan the questions until you are satisfied that you understand the general focus of the questions. Then you complete your visualization. For your visualization to be effective, it must represent all of the conditions set out in the facts and rules of the statement. It should be the sole reference you need for the efficient and accurate identification of the wrong and best answers to every question. Thus time spent on your visualization is time well spent. Depending upon your reading speed, you can comfortably allocate 3 to 5 of the first 9 minutes you spend on a question set reading the statement, scanning the questions, and preparing your visualization.

After completing the visualization, select answers to the number of questions you can comfortably handle in the remainder of the first 9 minutes allocated to the pretest set. It is important that you not push your pace beyond your comfort level.

At the end of the 9-minute period, you will have selected an answer for each of the six questions in the set through your own combination of considering and guessing. Place a circle around these answer choices, which constitute your 9-minute set.

Next, take an additional 3 minutes (for a total of 12) to reconsider questions and answer selections. You can be flexible, either focusing on questions you did not have time to consider in the first 9 minutes or reviewing questions about which you were uncertain. Without erasing or changing the circles you made during the first 9 minutes, place a box beside each of the answers you selected during this 3-minute period. If you did not change an answer, simply place a box beside the circled answer. If you did, place the box beside the new selection. The boxed answers are your 12-minute set.

In the final 6 minutes, go back and answer any questions you did not get to during the first 12 minutes, or review and change answers if you wish. Be flexible. Concentrate on questions about which you are uncertain, and take care not to rethink previously selected answers about which you are confident. Place an asterisk beside each of the answers you selected during this 6-minute period, without erasing or changing the circles and boxes you made during the first 12 minutes. If you did not change an answer, place an asterisk beside the boxed answer. If you did, place an asterisk beside the new selection. The answers identified with asterisks are your 12-minute set.

After you have completed the pretest, turn to the Pretest Answer Key for this session at the back of the book. For each pretest set, determine the number of best answers you selected during the 9-minute set (circled), 12-minute set (boxed), and 18-minute set (asterisked). Apply the numbers to the following formula, and complete the calculations indicated.

The largest total indicates the optimal number of question sets (two, three, or four) that you transfer to your Performance Tracking Worksheet (page 39). As you develop this record, it will clearly indicate the number of Relationships question sets you should plan to complete when taking the LSAT. Completing this number will yield the highest test score for you.

Relationships Set
Circles   _____ x 5 + 0 = _____
Boxes   _____ x 4 + 1 = _____
Asterisks   _____ x 3 + 2 = _____
Largest total _____

To repeat, every time you work quickly through Sessions 8 and 9, reviewing the main points, you complete one of the pretests. This process will take about 30 minutes. Don't be tempted to complete a pretest without working through the techniques; it is familiarity with and proficiency in the use of the techniques that will have the greatest impact on your performance. Conversely, working through a series of pretests or question sets without first working through the techniques is the least effective way of making an impact on your performance. You want high impact, not low impact or no impact.

✓ TRAINING WITH THE TECHNIQUES—
THEN UPDATING YOUR PERFORMANCE
RECORD WITH THE RESULTS OF A
PRETEST—IS THE KEY TO THE
DEVELOPMENT OF YOUR TEST PLAN.

As your performance improves, your test plan reflects the changes. Upon the completion of the seven pretests provided (one in Session 6 and six in this session), you will have a performance record that is stable. You will know whether your optimal performance will result from completing two, three, or four question sets. You will have a test plan for the Relationships section-test of the LSAT.

Only after your performance and test plan have stabilized will practicing question sets serve to maintain your achievements. Now your challenge becomes having the discipline to stick to your plan during the actual LSAT.

✓ ONLY BY FOLLOWING YOUR PLAN CAN
YOU MAXIMIZE YOUR TEST
PERFORMANCE AND SCORE.

Should you do more pretests?

Once you have completed six training workthroughs, you probably will have realized the high-impact gain that you were looking for before taking the LSAT. For most, further workthroughs and pretests will have much less impact, if any. But it is important to maintain familiarity and proficiency, and some people find they can also maintain control through regular practice. In any event, you may want to work with additional Relationships question sets.

There are three good sources of additional sets. The first is this guide—the simulated LSAT can be used as a source of additional question sets. Also Law School Admission Services sells disclosed tests. And finally, there are a number of preparation books that contain little more than simulated tests. (If you use these, take care that the questions use only the same specifications as the LSAT itself. It is not helpful to work with questions that employ different structures.)

You can use test materials that are not presented as question sets by converting them into sets. This is exactly what you do when taking the LSAT. You isolate a question set and think of it as "the test" until you have completed it. Then you move on to the next set. By breaking the test down into its components, you gain maximum control over it and are in the best position to execute your test plan.

What are the directions for completing the pretests?

Complete a pretest only after you have worked through the Relationships training techniques in Sessions 8 and 9. The directions are the same for each of the following Relationships question sets. Each set of questions is based on a number of conditions. A diagram is helpful in the answer selection process. Choose the best answer to each question from the five options presented, and mark your answers as described in the text.

RELATIONSHIPS PRETEST 10-1

Questions 1-6

Ten students, L, M, N, O, P, Q, R, S, T, and U, graduated from Naquapaug High School in the years 1971–1975, two students per year.

M graduated the year before Q.
P and R graduated together before 1975.
Q and N did not graduate in the same year.
S and T graduated together.

1. All of the following are possible orders of graduation, starting with the 1971 pair of graduates, EXCEPT
   (A) S, T; P, R; M, O; Q, N; L, U
   (B) S, T; P, R; M, N; Q, O; L, U
   (C) O, U; M, N; Q, L; P, R; S, T
   (D) P, R; M, U; Q, L; N, O; S, T
   (E) L, U; M, N; Q, O; P, R; S, T

2. Which of the following could be in the pairs that graduated in 1971, 1973, and 1975, respectively?
   (A) O, U, N
   (B) O, L, U
   (C) L, N, S
   (D) S, N, P
   (E) L, O, U

3. If Q, T, and U graduated in 1972, 1973, and 1975, respectively, and O and M graduated together, which of the following must be true?
   (A) L graduated in 1972.
   (B) N graduated in 1974.
   (C) P graduated two years before N.
   (D) R graduated before 1974.
   (E) S graduated the year before O.

4. If O and U graduated together, and Q graduated in 1974, which of the following must be true?
   I. N graduated in 1973.
   II. L graduated in 1974.
   III. S graduated in 1975.
   (A) I only
   (B) II only
   (C) III only
   (D) I and II only
   (E) II and III only

5. If P graduated in 1973, and L and O graduated together, which of the following are the only years in which N could have been one of the pair of graduates?
   (A) 1971 and 1972
   (B) 1971 and 1974
   (C) 1971 and 1975
   (D) 1972 and 1974
   (E) 1972 and 1975

6. If L, O, and U each graduated in an even-numbered year, which of the following must be true?
   (A) P graduated in 1971.
   (B) O graduated in 1972.
   (C) Q graduated in 1972.
   (D) N graduated in 1973.
   (E) S graduated in 1975.

RELATIONSHIPS PRETEST 10-2

Questions 1-6

On any day their schedules permit, Adam, Beth, Cary, Dana, and Edith each set up a sales table at a flea market.

Edith will set up only when Cary does not.
Dana will set up only when Adam does not.
Cary will set up only when Dana does.
Beth will set up only when Edith does.
Adam will always set up.

1. Which will set up on a day when the schedules of only Adam, Beth, and Cary permit them to sell?
   I. Adam
   II. Beth
   III. Cary
   (A) I only
   (B) II only
   (C) III only
   (D) I and II only
   (E) II and III only

2. How many will set up on a day when the schedules of only Adam, Beth, and Cary permit them to sell?
   (A) 1
   (B) 2
   (C) 3
   (D) 4
   (E) 5

3. Which of the following groups of people could set up on the same day?
   (A) Adam, Beth, and Cary
   (B) Adam, Cary, and Dana
   (C) Cary, Dana, and Edith
   (D) Beth, Dana, and Edith
   (E) Beth, Cary, and Edith

4. A buyer wants to be certain that both Beth and Cary are set up on the same day. Which of the following must also be set up?
   (A) Dana and Edith
   (B) Adam
   (C) Edith
   (D) Adam and Dana
   (E) Adam and Edith

5. Which of the following could set up on a day when the schedules on only Beth, Cary, and Edith permit them to sell?
   I. Beth
   II. Cary
   III. Edith
   (A) I only
   (B) II only
   (C) III only
   (D) II and III only
   (E) I and III only

6. How many will set up on a day when the schedules of only Beth, Cary, and Dana permit them to sell?
   (A) 0
   (B) 1
   (C) 2
   (D) 3
   (E) 4

RELATIONSHIPS PRETEST 10-3

Questions 1-6
A, B, and C are dentists, and S, T, U, and V are hygienists assigned to work for them.

  A and B each have exactly two hygienists assigned to them.
  C sometimes is assigned one hygienist and sometimes two.
  T is assigned to A and one other dentist.
  Each hygienist is assigned to at least one dentist.

1. If S and T are assigned to the same two dentists, V must work for
   (A) both A and B
   (B) both A and C
   (C) either A or B
   (D) either A or C
   (E) either B or C

2. If V is assigned to both B and C, which of the following must be true?
   (A) U is assigned to B.
   (B) S is assigned to A.
   (C) T and U are assigned to the same dentist.
   (D) S and T are assigned to the same dentist.
   (E) U is assigned to only one dentist.

3. If T and V both are assigned to the same two dentists, S must work for
   (A) both A and B
   (B) both A and C
   (C) either A or B
   (D) either A or C
   (E) either B or C

4. If U is assigned to B and C, and V is assigned to B, S must work for
   (A) A only
   (B) B only
   (C) C only
   (D) both A and B
   (E) both A and C

5. Whenever S is assigned to only one dentist and C is assigned only one hygienist, which of the following must be true?
   I. S is assigned to C.
   II. V is assigned to two dentists.
   III. U is assigned to only one dentist.
   (A) I only
   (B) II only
   (C) III only
   (D) I and II only
   (E) II and III only

6. If S is assigned to both B and C, which of the following must be true?
   (A) T and V are assigned to the same dentist.
   (B) V is assigned to A.
   (C) U and V are assigned to the same dentist.
   (D) U is assigned to B.
   (E) U is assigned to only one dentist.

RELATIONSHIPS PRETEST 10-4

Questions 1-6
The state presidents of the Half Century Club are comparing ages at the Club's annual meeting.

The Kansas president is older than the Wyoming president. The Ohio president is younger than the Maine president.

1. If the president from Ohio is younger than the president from Wyoming, which of the following CANNOT be true?
   (A) The Kansas president is younger than the Maine president.
   (B) The Maine president is younger than the Wyoming president.
   (C) The Ohio president is younger than the Kansas president.
   (D) The Wyoming president is younger than the Maine president.
   (E) The Kansas president is younger than the Ohio president.

2. If the president from Wyoming is older than the president from Ohio, which of the following must be true?
   (A) The Kansas president is older than the Maine president.
   (B) The Wyoming president is older than the Kansas president.
   (C) The Maine president is older than the Kansas president.
   (D) The Wyoming president is older than the Maine president.
   (E) The Kansas president is older than the Ohio president.

3. If the Texas president is older than the Maine president, which of the following must be true?
   (A) The Texas president is the oldest president.
   (B) The Texas president is older than the Kansas president.
   (C) The Wyoming president is older than the Texas president.
   (D) The Texas president is older than the Ohio president.
   (E) The Kansas president is older than the Texas president.

4. If the Vermont president is younger than the Maine president, the Wyoming president is older than the Maine president, and the Ohio president is the youngest, which of the following is the second-oldest president?
   (A) Vermont
   (B) Wyoming
   (C) Maine
   (D) Kansas
   (E) Ohio

5. If the Utah president is older than the Ohio president, the Florida president is younger than the Wyoming president, and the age of the Maine president is between the ages of the Utah and Florida presidents, which of the following CANNOT be true?
   (A) The Utah president is older than the Wyoming president.
   (B) The Florida president is older than the Ohio president.
   (C) The Florida president is older than the Kansas president.
   (D) The Maine president is older than the Ohio president.
   (E) The Wyoming president is older than the Florida president.

6. If the Alaska president is older than the Iowa, Maine, and Wyoming presidents, which of the following must be true?
   (A) The Iowa president is older than the Maine president.
   (B) The Iowa president is older than the Wyoming president.
   (C) The Iowa president is older than the Ohio president.
   (D) The Alaska president is older than the Ohio president.
   (E) The Kansas president is older than the Alaska president.

RELATIONSHIPS PRETEST 10-5

Questions 1-6

There are four parallel train tracks at a railroad station, numbered 1 through 4 from left to right. Tracks 1 and 2 are northbound, tracks 3 and 4 are southbound. A train coming from the north will arrive on a southbound track. A train coming from the south will arrive on a northbound track.

> A round-trip train must arrive on a track adjacent to a track going in the other direction.
> A local train can only arrive immediately after either an express or a metroliner.
> Two consecutive trains cannot use the same track.

1. If three trains, P, Q, and R, arrive at the station on tracks 2, 4, and 1, respectively, and in that order, what could be true about the trains?
   I. P is an express.
   II. P and R are metroliners.
   III. Q and R are locals.
   (A) I only
   (B) II only
   (C) III only
   (D) I and II only
   (E) I, II, and III

2. If two northbound locals, a southbound express, and a round-trip metroliner coming from the north are all approaching the station, what is the order in which the tracks can be used, from first to last?
   (A) 2, 3, 4, 1
   (B) 1, 2, 3, 4
   (C) 3, 2, 1, 4
   (D) 1, 3, 2, 4
   (E) 4, 1, 3, 2

3. If five trains arrive on tracks 1, 3, 1, 4, and 2, in that order, and the second train to arrive is not a local, what is the maximum number of trains that could be locals?
   (A) 1
   (B) 2
   (C) 3
   (D) 4
   (E) 5

4. Train Q, a northbound express; train R, a round-trip express coming from the south; train S, a northbound metroliner; and trains T and U, both southbound locals, are arriving at the station, though not necessarily in that order. In what order and on what track can each train arrive?
   (A) S on track 1, U on track 4, Q on track 2, T on track 4, R on track 3
   (B) R on track 2, T on track 3, S on track 1, Q on track 1, U on track 4
   (C) R on track 2, U on track 3, S on track 1, T on track 3, Q on track 2
   (D) Q on track 2, T on track 4, R on track 3, U on track 4, S on track 1
   (E) T on track 3, Q on track 2, S on track 1, U on track 4, R on track 2

5. If six trains arrive on tracks 1, 2, 1, 3, 4, 3, in that order, and there are two locals, what are the maximum and minimum numbers of trains that could be expresses, in that order?
   (A) 3, 0
   (B) 3, 2
   (C) 4, 2
   (D) 2, 1
   (E) 4, 0

6. If four trains arrive at the station, and none of them arrive on track 3, what must be true about the trains?
   (A) None are round-trip trains.
   (B) Two of the trains are not northbound locals.
   (C) The number of locals equals the number of southbound trains.
   (D) There are more northbound trains than there are southbound trains.
   (E) The greatest number of locals cannot exceed the greatest number of express trains.

RELATIONSHIPS PRETEST 10-6

Questions 1-6
Five friends—Carol, Ed, Jenny, Rick, and Walt—go to the beach. Each person either brings something (food, blankets, or umbrella) or does something for the trip (drives or pays the tolls along the route).

Two people are brother and sister. They are the only two in the group of friends who are related to each other.
One person meets the others on the beach when they arrive. This person brings the umbrella. The driver of the group that meets the person on the beach is male.
When Ed brings the food, Walt does not drive.
The brother pays the tolls.
When Carol or Jenny brings the blankets, Rick drives.

1. If Ed brings the food, which of the following must be true?
   (A) Carol brings the blankets.
   (B) Rick drives.
   (C) Jenny does not bring the blankets.
   (D) Carol does not bring the umbrella.
   (E) Jenny meets the others at the beach.

2. If Rick drives, what CANNOT be true?
   (A) Jenny brings the umbrella.
   (B) Ed pays the tolls.
   (C) Ed brings the food.
   (D) Walt is Jenny's brother.
   (E) Carol is Rick's sister.

3. If Walt brings the food, Rick CANNOT
   I. bring the blankets
   II. bring the umbrella
   III. pay the tolls
   (A) I only
   (B) II only
   (C) I and II only
   (D) I and III only
   (E) I, II, and III

4. If Carol brings the umbrella, which of the following CANNOT be true?
   (A) Carol is Rick's sister.
   (B) Ed pays no tolls.
   (C) Jenny brings neither blankets nor food.
   (D) Ed brings the food.
   (E) Jenny does not bring the blankets.

5. If Ed brings the food, Rick must
   (A) drive
   (B) pay tolls
   (C) bring the blankets
   (D) bring the umbrella
   (E) be someone's brother

6. If Jenny brings the blankets, which two people CANNOT be related?
   I. Carol and Ed
   II. Carol and Rick
   III. Jenny and Walt
   (A) I only
   (B) II only
   (C) III only
   (D) I and II only
   (E) II and III only

TRAINING SESSION 11

Arguments and Passages Problems

This session will look at Arguments and Passages, the other two question formats found on the LSAT. These formats appear to be more familiar than Relationships questions, but appearances can be deceiving. While the formats may be familiar, the material is not. In fact, the test-maker selects material that is extremely unlikely to be familiar in order to make sure that your reasoning skill is being measured, not your knowledge of the material. You should not treat Arguments and Passages as if they were academic material simply because there is a superficial resemblance in the formats.

While Arguments and Passages appear to be very different from each other, they share common characteristics that are more important to your test performance than their apparent differences. In this session we will examine their similarities, and in later sessions we will consider in depth their distinctive qualities.

What are the components of Arguments and Passages problems?

Like Relationships problems, both Arguments and Passages present the four-component LSAT problem profile: directions, a statement, questions, and answer options. The directions and statements of Arguments and Passages problems differ in notable respects, while the questions and answers are very similar. (Directions will be discussed in detail in Sessions 12 and 14.)

What are the statements like?

The most apparent difference between Arguments and Passages statements is their format. Passages statements are long and heavy on detail. They contrast with Arguments statements, which are short and offer little detail. These differences conceal their underlying similarity: each statement presents an argument.

Applied to the LSAT, the term "argument" means that the statement involves premises, propositions, and reasons that lead to, support, or imply a conclusion. The combination of different elements in the argument produces the conditions upon which Arguments and Passages questions and answer options are based.

The fact that Arguments and Passages statements involve arguments is comforting to most test-takers. The argument provides a context and a starting position for the consideration of question and answer options that seem to be similar to those encountered in an academic environment. This perceived similarity seems to be sufficient to make the average test-taker more comfortable with these question types than with Relationships. Whether for this reason or others, Arguments are the least difficult for test-takers, Passages more difficult, and, finally, Relationships the most difficult.

What are the questions like?

Arguments and Passages questions are very much alike. They are of two basic types: the **description** question and the **extension** question.

Description questions ask you to select the answer option that best embodies or *describes* the conditions set out in the statement. They look familiar because they refer to the statement or the conditions presented. Description questions often relate directly to key words or concepts found in the statement.

1. According to the passage, the Technocrats were

    (A) twentieth-century politicians
    (B) frustrated modern inventors
    (C) overpaid factory workers
    (D) precursors of today's scientists
    (E) nineteenth-century economists

The extension question asks you to select the answer option that best represents an *extension* of the conditions set out in or required by the statement. An example follows.

71

1. The passage suggests that which of the following might occur if governments increased control over the means of public communication?
   I. Newspapers would become more conservative.
   II. Free speech would be threatened.
   III. Individual rights to privacy would be better respected.
   (A) I only
   (B) II only
   (C) III only
   (D) II and III only
   (E) I, II, and III

The reasoning task involved in Arguments and Passages problems is the same as in all LSAT questions. Because the task is the same, the questions have the same basic format. As you learned in previous sessions, there are three basic question types that require you to determine which of the answer options **must, could,** or **cannot** satisfy the conditions. These questions are put directly in the Relationships section-test, but the test-maker is less direct in the Arguments and Passages section-tests. Seldom is a basic question asked directly, so each question type needs to be identified before you can proceed to the answer options.

✓ IN ARGUMENTS AND PASSAGES PROBLEMS, YOU NEED TO IDENTIFY THE QUESTION THAT IS BEING ASKED.

While this identification can be challenging, the wrong-answer advantage that results is worth the effort. The work of identification is assisted by the test-maker's dominant use of **could** questions in both the Arguments and Passages section-tests. (*Must* and *cannot* options do appear regularly, but they are far less frequent than **could** answer options.) As you recall, every wrong answer to a **could** question is an answer option that *cannot* satisfy the conditions. Most test-takers identify *cannot* wrong answer options more readily than either *must* or *could* options. Consequently, Arguments questions are, on average, the least difficult for test-takers.

Arguments and Passages questions share another common trait: neither one adds to or alters information contained in the statement.

✓ IN AN ARGUMENTS OR PASSAGES QUESTION, THERE IS NEVER A SUPPLEMENTAL STATEMENT TO CONFUSE OR OBFUSCATE.

How is the interaction between questions and answers structured?

The questions and answer options for Arguments and Passages are presented in three formats. The first is the familiar **question-and-answer** format. As the name implies, a question is posed to which the answer options are responses. The second format is the **question-question**, in which the question asks you to select the question that is answered by the information given or implied by the statement. The last format is **sentence completion**. The question is the first part of a sentence that the answer options complete in various ways. There is no question mark.

The variety of formats serves to obfuscate the question, and, just to make things more confusing, each of the three formats can be presented in either the **single-option** or **multiple-option** configuration. You will remember that the multiple-option configuration permits one, two, or all three of the Roman numeral options to satisfy the conditions of the question. The formats are summarized in the illustration on the facing page.

What are the answers like?

Answer options to Arguments and Passages questions are similar in structure.

Description questions are drawn directly from the statement, and the test-maker has little leeway in interpreting the information when constructing questions and answer options.

✓ ANSWERS TO DESCRIPTION QUESTIONS CONNECT DIRECTLY TO THE STATEMENT.

The direct connection between statement and question means that the focus of the question is immediately apparent. This often seems too easy to test-takers, so many of them seize the opportunity to convert a relatively straightforward question into one that is much more difficult by entertaining assumptions or interpretations that are unwarranted and uncalled-for.

When constructing extension questions, the test-maker interprets the information contained in the statement and thus obfuscates the focus of the question.

✓ ANSWERS TO EXTENSION QUESTIONS CONNECT TO INTERPRETATIONS OF THE STATEMENT.

More than in any other LSAT format, you need to rely on the answer options to cut through this obfuscation. The best answer option generally provides a focus for the question that the other options do not.

You will recall that the test-taker eliminates questions that do not work as predicted. A question-and-best-answer combination that does not attract a consensus of those it was designed to snag is discarded. This gives you a big advantage where Arguments and Passages questions are concerned, because the questions that pass all of the trials and are placed on the LSAT are not going to be followed by answer options that are too obscure to be identified. The best answer choice is right in front of you. Selecting it can be difficult, but the wrong-answer advantage assists your efforts with Arguments and Passages even more than it does with Relationships.

Question Formats

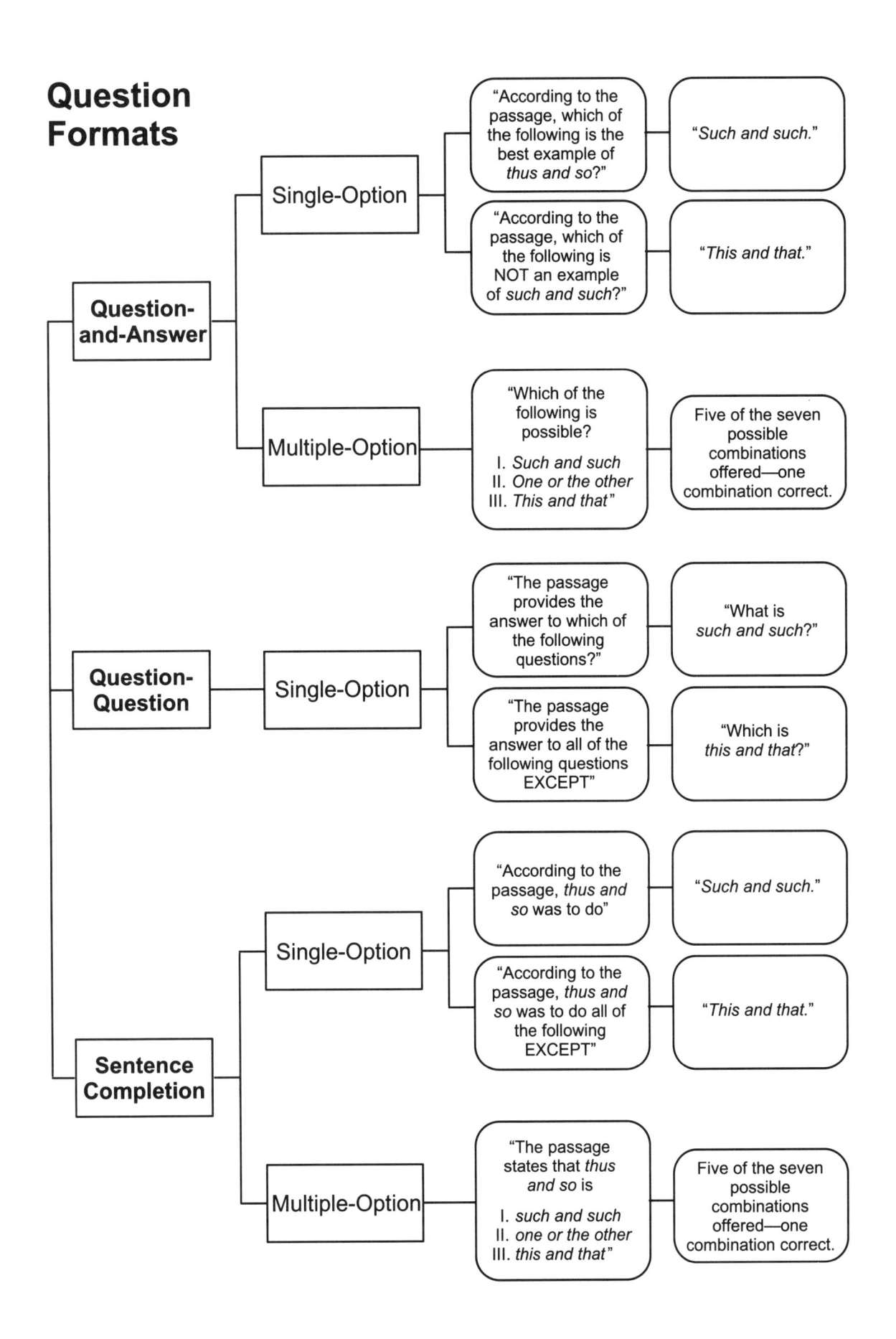

- **Question-and-Answer**
  - Single-Option
    - "According to the passage, which of the following is the best example of *thus and so*?" → "*Such and such.*"
    - "According to the passage, which of the following is NOT an example of *such and such*?" → "*This and that.*"
  - Multiple-Option
    - "Which of the following is possible?
      I. *Such and such*
      II. *One or the other*
      III. *This and that*" → Five of the seven possible combinations offered—one combination correct.

- **Question-Question**
  - Single-Option
    - "The passage provides the answer to which of the following questions?" → "What is *such and such*?"
    - "The passage provides the answer to all of the following questions EXCEPT" → "Which is *this and that*?"

- **Sentence Completion**
  - Single-Option
    - "According to the passage, *thus and so* was to do" → "*Such and such.*"
    - "According to the passage, *thus and so* was to do all of the following EXCEPT" → "*This and that.*"
  - Multiple-Option
    - "The passage states that *thus and so* is
      I. *such and such*
      II. *one or the other*
      III. *this and that*" → Five of the seven possible combinations offered—one combination correct.

What distinguishes the wrong answer options?

Every wrong answer on the LSAT fails to satisfy the conditions required by the combination of statement and question. It is worth repeating that, even though the test-maker attempts to disguise it, it is relatively easy to detect this failure in most answer options. You won't be surprised to hear that there are certain disguises that obfuscate more effectively than others, nor will you be shocked to find out that these are the very disguises the test-maker uses for the wrong answer options in the Arguments and Passages section-tests.

✓ BY TRAINING YOURSELF TO IDENTIFY WRONG–ANSWER DISGUISES, YOU ENHANCE YOUR WRONG–ANSWER ADVANTAGE.

When you combine the fact that the test-maker usually includes just one attractive wrong answer option among the four offered with your knowledge of the disguises and understanding of the wrong-answer patterns for the three basic question types, you will be positioned to take full advantage of the wrong answer options to every Arguments and Passages question.

Take a moment to recall that the best answer option is the only one that satisfies all of the relevant conditions set out in the statement and question. When you identify a question as a variation of "Which of the answer options *could* be true?" the options that *cannot* be true fail to satisfy all of the conditions and are wrong. With a variation of "Which of the answer options **cannot** be true?" the options that *must* and *could* be true fail to satisfy all of the conditions and are wrong. With a variation of "Which of the answer options **must** be true?" the options that *could* and *cannot* be true fail to satisfy all of the conditions and are wrong.

What are the wrong-answer disguises?

The test-maker uses four basic disguises for wrong answer options. Briefly stated, they are the **same-language** disguise, the **too-little-too-much** disguise, the **true but** disguise, and the **false-assertion** disguise.

It is not beneath the test-maker to cumulate disguises. That is, a particular wrong answer option may simultaneously wear a same-language and a false-assertion disguise.

The **same-language** disguise is simple. It consists of a repetition of the same language that was in the statement. This disguise attracts test-takers because it connects directly to the statement, and the language is usually so obscure as to create an impression of subtle significance.

The **too-little-too-much** disguise is used to overstate or understate something in the answer option so that it fails to satisfy the conditions required by the question.

The **true but** disguise means what it says. The answer option is true, but it does not satisfy the conditions required by the statement and the question. It attracts the test-taker because it is true and makes good sense. Its veracity obscures its irrelevance.

The **false-assertion** disguise is used to misstate information in the answer option. That is, the answer option misinterprets or wrongly characterizes a proposition or conclusion in the problem. It is often combined with the same-language disguise. It is attractive because it is obscure and authoritatively put.

How do Argument and Passages problems work?

Your knowledge of wrong-answer patterns and disguises will assist you in the identification of wrong answer options. By dumping wrong answer options, you can expeditiously locate the cream-of-the-crap answer option—the best answer option—the one that satisfies the conditions required by the statement and question. The way wrong-answer patterns and disguises are combined is illustrated in the following discussion.

STATEMENT
It is worth repeating that studies show that teenagers' exposure to the news is one measure of the extent of youthful political involvement in this society. In addition, the patterns of exposure to the news that develop during the teens continue throughout life. Even though we have confidence in these observations, the conclusions drawn from them by many media experts are simply not valid because so little is understood about the variables that are involved.

QUESTION
1. Which of the following best states the conclusion to which the author's statements lead?

ANSWER CHOICES
(A) It is worth studying teenagers' exposure to the news.
(B) Confidence in the observations of the variables that are involved in patterns of exposure to the news supports the conclusions drawn by many media experts.
(C) Understanding teenagers' exposure to the news is critical to understanding human behavior.
(D) The conclusions of many media experts about exposure to the news involve little-understood variables.
(E) Adult patterns of exposure to the news will ultimately reflect the fact that teenagers are more politically active.

This questions calls for selection of the answer option that **could** satisfy the conditions set out in the statement and question. Wrong answer options are those that *cannot* satisfy the conditions.

Answer option A is the best selection, though it is unlikely that you would select it as best after a quick reading. A careful reading will disclose that there is nothing in the answer option that conflicts with the conditions in the statement and question. It is an attractive cream-of-the-crap answer.

Answer option B is a **cannot** wrong answer option in a **same-language** disguise. Every word of this answer is taken from the statement, which connects it to the statement and makes it seem attractive. However, it cannot satisfy the statement conditions because, among other reasons, confidence cannot support the conclusions of media experts.

Option C is a **cannot** wrong answer option in **too-much** and **same-language** disguises. The answer option overstates by using much of the language of the statement to declare that what was "one measure" is actually "critical" and that it encompasses not just "youthful political involvement" but all "human behavior." By using what could be misperceived as paraphrase rather than overstatement, the answer might attract a few test-takers.

Option D is a **cannot** wrong answer option in a **true but** disguise. The answer option is a "true" statement, but it is irrelevant to the question posed. The author's conclusion, not the media experts', is what is sought.

Option E is a **cannot** wrong answer option in **false-assertion** and **same-language** disguises. It misstates the information given. Among many other things, there is no mention in the statement of the degree of teenage political activity involved, nor is it suggested that such activity is related causally to exposure to the news.

What variations on the wrong-answer disguises does the test-maker use?

The ways the test-maker varies the four basic disguises are often fuzzy, although they are predictable. Their outlines are always identifiable, and they frequently can assist your identification of the basic disguise and wrong-answer pattern. However, for this knowledge to work to your advantage, you have to have a certain tolerance for imprecision.

> ✓ IT IS IMPORTANT THAT YOU NOT GET CAUGHT UP IN TRYING TO IDENTIFY WRONG–ANSWER DISGUISES PRECISELY. YOUR SENSE THAT THEY ARE WRONG IS SUFFICIENT.

In the examples that follow, note that the number of answer options fluctuates atypically between four and five, depending on the number of variations being illustrated.

SAME–LANGUAGE VARIATIONS

There are four variations on the **same-language** wrong-answer disguise that the test-maker usually uses.

- The first reaches an incorrect conclusion, using the language of the statement.
- The second contradicts the statement, using the language of the statement.
- The third refers to a topic or point not in the statement, using the language of the statement.
- The fourth misinterprets points made in the statement, using the language of the statement.

STATEMENT
It is worth repeating that studies show that teenagers' exposure to the news is one measure of the extent of youthful political involvement in this society. In addition, the patterns of exposure to the news that develop during the teens continue throughout life. Even though we have confidence in these observations, the conclusions drawn from them by many media experts are simply not valid because so little is understood about the variables that are involved.

QUESTION
1. Which of the following can be inferred from the statement?

ANSWER CHOICES
(A) Youthful political involvement in this society is extensive.
(B) The variables that are involved in patterns of exposure to the news support the conclusions drawn by many media experts.
(C) Patterns of exposure to the news are measured by observation.
(D) The conclusions of many media experts about youthful political involvement are based on little-understood variables.

This question requires an answer option that **could** satisfy the conditions set out in the statement. Wrong answer options will be those that *cannot* satisfy the conditions.

Option A is a **cannot** wrong answer option in which the **same language** is used with a dash of **too much** to express an incorrect conclusion. There is nothing in the statement to suggest that youthful political involvement is extensive.

Option B is a **cannot** wrong answer option using the **same language** to contradict the statement. The statement says that the variables are the reason media experts' conclusions are invalid. This is the opposite of supporting the conclusions.

Option C is a **cannot** wrong answer option using the **same language** as the statement to refer to a different topic or point. There is nothing in the statement to suggest the method used to measure patterns of exposure to the news.

Option D is a **cannot** wrong answer option that misinterprets a point in the statement while using the **same language** as the statement. The statement does not indicate what the experts' conclusions are based on, although it is possible to interpret it as suggesting that observations were involved. To infer that the variables provide the base for their conclusions is a clear misinterpretation of the statement.

TOO–LITTLE–TOO–MUCH VARIATIONS

There are four primary variations on the **too-little-too-much** wrong-answer disguise used by the test-maker.

- One contradicts the statement, taking a part of the statement for the whole.
- Another agrees with the statement, taking a part of the statement for the whole.
- Another is too narrow, answering part of the question but not all of it.
- The last is too broad, answering all of the question and much more.

STATEMENT
It is worth repeating that studies show that teenagers' exposure to the news is one measure of the extent of youthful political involvement in this society. In addition, the patterns of exposure to the news that develop during the teens continue throughout life. Even though we have confidence in these observations, the conclusions drawn from them by many media experts are simply not valid because so little is understood about the variables that are involved.

QUESTION
1. Which of the following best describes the observations of exposure to the news made in the statement above?

ANSWER CHOICES
(A) It can be comprehensively measured by youthful political involvement.
(B) It can measure youthful political involvement in all societies.
(C) It can measure youthful political involvement.
(D) It measures political involvement in most societies, and its patterns explain both teenage and adult behavior.

This question calls for the selection of the answer option that **could** satisfy the conditions set out in the statement and question. The wrong answer options are those that *cannot* satisfy the conditions.

Option A is a **cannot** wrong answer option that contradicts the statement by declaring that exposure to the news is comprehensively (**too much**) measured by youthful political involvement. The statement indicates just the opposite—that youthful political involvement is measured by exposure to the news. It also ignores the second observation in the statement—patterns of exposure to the news that develop during the teens continue throughout life—thus taking a part of the statement for the whole.

Option B is a **cannot** wrong answer option that agrees generally with the statement but overstates it (referring to "all societies" instead of "this society"). It also ignores the observation that patterns of exposure to the news that develop during the teens continue throughout life, thus taking a single observation for the whole.

Option C is a **cannot** wrong answer option that takes the first observation in the statement into account but understates it (**too little**), in that it ignores the second observation entirely.

Option D is a **cannot** wrong answer option that goes too far, in that it answers the question and much more. It declares that exposure to the news measures all political involvement (not just among teenagers) in most societies (not just this society) and that its patterns explain all behavior (no behavior is involved in the statement).

TRUE BUT VARIATIONS

There are five primary variations on the **true but** wrong-answer disguise used by the test-maker. The wrong answer option is true, but

- it refers to a part of the statement not involved in the question.

- it does not match the information in the statement, although it is a logical response.
- it is not responsive to the question, although it is a logical response.
- it answers a different question.
- it implies a point or judgment not made in the statement.

STATEMENT
It is worth repeating that studies show that teenagers' exposure to the news is one measure of the extent of youthful political involvement in this society. In addition, the patterns of exposure to the news that develop during the teens continue throughout life. Even though we have confidence in these observations, the conclusions drawn from them by many media experts are simply not valid because so little is understood about the variables that are involved.

QUESTION
1. Which of the following best summarizes the observations about exposure to the news made in the above statement?

ANSWER CHOICES
(A) Accurate studies do not always reach accurate conclusions.
(B) Exposure to the news changes over a lifetime in response to changes in the way news is reported.
(C) Those reporting news should take teenagers' interests into account.
(D) Exposure to the news is a lifelong experience.
(E) Patterns of exposure to the news are important to media experts.

Again, the best answer option is one that **could** satisfy the conditions set out in the statement and the question. Wrong answer options are those that *cannot* satisfy the conditions.

Answer option A is a **cannot** wrong answer option that may be **true, but** it makes reference to parts of the statement (the studies and the invalidity of the experts' conclusions) that are not involved in the question.

Option B is a **cannot** wrong answer option that may be **true, but** it does not match the statement, which declares that patterns of exposure to the news continue rather than change over a lifetime.

Answer option C is a **cannot** wrong answer option that may be **true, but** it is not responsive to the question, which focuses on observations drawn from studies about exposure to the news.

Option D is a **cannot** wrong answer answer option that may be **true, but** it is answering a different question, not the one asked.

Option E is a **cannot** wrong answer answer option that may be **true, but** it implies a point or judgment that is not made in the statement—that patterns of exposure to the news are important to media experts.

FALSE–ASSERTION VARIATIONS

There are four variations on the false-assertion wrong-answer disguise.

- The first misinterprets or negates a statement premise.
- The second uses a false assertion to contradict the statement.
- The third uses a false assertion to agree with the statement.
- The fourth is a logical response but does not match the premises of the statement.

STATEMENT
It is worth repeating that studies show that teenagers' exposure to the news is one measure of the extent of youthful political involvement in this society. In addition, the patterns of exposure to the news that develop during the teens continue throughout life. Even though we have confidence in these observations, the conclusions drawn from them by many media experts are simply not valid because so little is understood about the variables that are involved.

QUESTION
1. Which of the following best describes the conclusions reached by the media experts referred to in the above statement?

ANSWER CHOICES
(A) Youthful political involvement is a measure of teenagers' exposure to the news.
(B) Youthful political activity is the result of increased exposure to the news.
(C) Youthful political involvement is measured by media experts.
(D) The conclusions are not valid because the observations upon which they are based are not complete.

This question again requires that you select the answer option that **could** satisfy the conditions set out in the statement. Wrong answer options are those that *cannot* satisfy the conditions.

Answer option A is a **cannot** wrong answer option that misinterprets or negates a premise of the statement (that exposure to the news measures political involvement) by making the **false assertion** that political involvement measures exposure to the news.

Option B is a **cannot** wrong answer option that uses a **false assertion** that contradicts the statement. It declares that there is a causal relationship between political activity and exposure to the news.

Option C is a **cannot** wrong answer option involving a **false assertion** that agrees with the statement to the extent that it notes that political involvement is being measured. It is false because it asserts that media experts do the measuring, a fact neither included not implied in the statement.

Answer option D is a **cannot** wrong answer option that is a logical response to the question but makes the **false assertion** that observations are not complete. This assertion does not match the premise in the statement that experts' conclusions are not valid because little is understood about the variables involved.

How difficult are Arguments and Passages questions?

As noted earlier, the test-maker wants the substantial majority of questions on each section-test to be of medium difficulty, with some 40 to 60 percent of test-takers selecting the best answer. A smaller proportion of the questions are to be relatively easy, with more than 60 percent of test-takers selecting the best answer. And a smaller proportion are to be relatively tough, with fewer than 40 percent of test-takers selecting the best answer.

In Arguments and Passages section-tests, there is no order of difficulty among sets. Question sets appearing later in a section-test are not necessarily more difficult, nor are questions appearing later in a question set harder, than those that come first. Later questions sometimes appear to be more difficult, but this is usually due to the cumulative effect of having reviewed many questions and answer options. Fatigue may make later question sets appear more difficult, but, while the fatigue may be real, the apparent difference in difficulty is not.

TRAINING SESSION 12

Arguments Problems in Depth

In this session you will work with Arguments questions on their own. There are two Arguments section-tests in every LSAT. This means that Arguments comprise about half of all of the questions on the test. Quantitatively, Arguments are twice as important as other question types.

What is the fundamental approach to Arguments problems?

An Arguments section-test contains between 3,000 and 4,500 words, with 4,000 the average. If you use all of the time allotted to read the section-test material, you must read at the rate of about 115 words per minute. While not too fast for careful reading, this is not a slow pace. Taking into account the time you need to make decisions about answer options, you may find that such a reading pace is demanding and difficult to maintain. Your pace when reading carefully will influence your optimal balance between speed and accuracy. You should also be mindful of the fact that answer options, not statements, provide much of the reading burden in an Arguments section-test. In order to keep your test-taking mechanics consistent throughout, there is a small task you should complete before you begin an Arguments section-test. Only one or two Arguments questions are based on a common statement, so the questions are not presented in sets.

✓ YOU, RATHER THAN THE TEST–MAKER, PACKAGE THE QUESTIONS INTO SETS.

You will package the questions into sets of six. Sets are easily built by combining questions 1 through 6, 7 through 12, etc., as summarized below. In this way, you create four sets of Arguments questions in each 35-minute section-test.

- Question set 1: questions 1–6
- Question set 2: questions 7–12
- Question set 3: questions 13–18
- Question set 4: questions 19–24+

In what order should Arguments question sets be considered?

Previously it was stated that you should work on the least difficult question set first and the most difficult last. However, when this principle is applied to Arguments questions, a problem arises. In general, the effort it takes to identify the questions in terms of their difficulty outweighs any advantage you might realize from the effort. So, simply work through Arguments questions in the order in which they appear.

Instead of reordering question sets according to their difficulty, you will approach the questions according to your test plan. If your plan is to complete all four questions sets in the section-test, you will work through the questions in sets of six.

If your plan is to complete three question sets, you have a choice of two strategies. The more straightforward one is to work through the first three sets of questions and guess the answers to the fourth set. A more sophisticated strategy is to omit six questions as you work through the four question sets. Pass over six long question-and-answer combinations or confusing questions, since you have the poorest prospects of selecting the best answer options to these questions. (Of course, you will select answers to the omitted questions by guessing.) Either question-selection strategy will meet the objectives of your test plan and maximize your wrong-answer advantage.

If your plan is to complete two question sets in a section-test, you apply the strategy described above, in this instance either working through the first two sets of questions and guessing your answers on the last two sets or omitting twelve questions as you work through the four question sets, passing over twelve long question-and-answer combinations or confusing questions.

How are Arguments problems constructed?

Arguments are generally drawn from informal sources. Letters to the editor are good sources, because they are often implausible and unpersuasive while appearing to be logical. Advertisements are also used for source material, because they often encourage unjustified assumptions. Books, periodicals, editorials, speeches, and reported conversations provide Arguments statements, too. Whatever the source, the statement has usually been heavily edited to ensure that it is compatible with the LSAT format.

Each argument is selected for its possession of three major characteristics. Evidence, or a premise, is always involved. And a point or purpose—the conclusion—is also involved. A structured process connects the evidence and conclusion. This is sometimes called reasoning, and it accounts for the Arguments sections being called tests of "logical reasoning" by many people. This designation is misleading, however, since no formal logic is required, even when the form and content of the argument are unfamiliar.

✓ NO KNOWLEDGE OF FORMAL LOGIC IS REQUIRED FOR YOU TO HANDLE ARGUMENTS PROBLEMS EFFECTIVELY.

To summarize, every argument is selected because it involves evidence that is used to support or reach a conclusion through a structured process. But the customary order of a series of pieces of evidence leading to a conclusion is not always followed by the test-maker. The order of presentation is varied. Sometimes the conclusion is placed in the statement. It may come first, last, or between pieces of evidence. It also may be placed in the answer options. And evidence may be placed in the statement or in the answer options. Possible arrangements look like this:

Evidence ⟶ Conclusion
Conclusion ⟵ Evidence
Evidence ⟶ Conclusion ⟵ Evidence

How do Arguments questions work?

As you know, the profile of an Arguments problem is the same as for other LSAT problems. There are directions, a statement, questions, and answer options.

THE DIRECTIONS

In the directions the test-maker tells you to evaluate the reasoning contained in brief statements and that the best answer is a "conceivable solution to the particular problem posed" by the question. The test-maker also says that the best answer is the one that does not require you to make what are by common-sense standards implausible, superfluous, or incompatible assumptions.

For many test-takers, these directions obfuscate rather than clarify what is expected of them. It is difficult to extract the practical meaning of the directions from the language used by the test-maker. However, the directions can be translated into more familiar terms, especially when it comes to wrong answer options. And you know how important it is to your performance to be able to identify wrong answer options to LSAT questions. Identifying and dumping wrong answer options is the most efficient way of selecting the best answer options—the cream of the crap.

To reiterate, a wrong answer option is one that does not satisfy the conditions of the statement and question. Thus, if the question seeks an answer that **must** satisfy the conditions, answer options that *could* or *cannot* satisfy the conditions are wrong. If the question seeks an answer that **could** satisfy the conditions, options that *cannot* satisfy the conditions are wrong. And last, if the question seeks an answer that **cannot** satisfy the conditions, answers that *must* or *could* satisfy the conditions are wrong.

There are two basic reasons why an answer option can fail to satisfy required conditions: one is that it conflicts directly with the statement, and the other is that is makes unjustified assumptions. The wrong answer looks like it satisfies the required conditions only by your making a related but unjustified assumption. So all you have to do is avoid making unjustified assumptions when working through Arguments questions—this seems to pose no great challenge.

And it is not much of a challenge if you heed the directions we looked at earlier. Translated, the test-maker's directions tell you that unjustified assumptions are those that exceed the terms of the statement, are inconsistent with the terms of the statement, or are unfounded given the terms of the statement. Avoid these things, and you will identify wrong answer options readily and efficiently select best answers, right?

Unfortunately, experience shows that this is easier said than done. Assumptions are the stock-in-trade of the able student, for whom the ability to justify assumptions and positions persuasively is a necessary skill rewarded in examination papers, essays, debates, and other such exercises. The temptation to apply this ability in the context of the LSAT can be almost irresistible. When a test-taker gives in to this temptation, the result is the erroneous selection of a wrong answer option as the best answer to an Arguments question, so fight it with everything you've got. Your section-test performance will benefit.

✓ AVOID EVERY ASSUMPTION THAT IS NOT CLEARLY SUPPORTED BY THE ARGUMENTS STATEMENT.

THE STATEMENT

Arguments statements are generally short. Their brevity can make them seem deceptively simple. The brevity is often the result of the test-maker's strategy of obfuscation by omission. Many Arguments questions seek omitted evidence or a conclusion—in other words, the information required to complete the argument.

Arguments statements always involve a position or point of view. Although the position or point of view may not be clearly articulated, the statement is never neutral. A statement consists of 75 to 125 words. It defines the context for either one or two question-and-answer sets. Usually a statement supporting two questions has a slightly smaller reading burden than a statement supporting only one.

THE QUESTION

Arguments questions are straightforward. They directly present the decision that must be made. They do not contain supplemental statements, which means that questions never modify or add to the argument. In most section-tests, there are more instances of the statement supporting one question than two. When two questions are supported by a single statement, each question is independent of the other.

As was discussed in the preceding session, there are two basic Arguments question types: **description** questions and **extension** questions. There are two variations on the description question:

- One requires you to recognize the point, purpose, premise, or reasoning of a statement.
- The other requires you to recognize a stated presumption.

There are four variations on the extension question:

- The first requires you to identify a pattern.
- The second requires you to identify inferences and conclusions.
- The third requires you to identify assumptions.
- The fourth requires you to assess evidence.

These six cover all of the questions that will appear in an Arguments section-test.

✓ YOU NOW CAN PREDICT EVERY ARGUMENTS QUESTION THAT WILL APPEAR ON THE LSAT.

THE ANSWERS

The answer options complete the Arguments question; without them the question has little practical meaning. Take a typical Arguments question: "Which of the following is the underlying point of the above?" You are being asked, "What's the point?" As you know, this is not an invitation to extemporize or demonstrate your ability to synthesize. Your activity should be confined to the selection of the answer option that best satisfies the conditions of the question and statement. You achieve this by viewing each answer option in relation to the question. Only then can you select answers in the way the LSAT requires.

✓ THE ANSWER OPTIONS PRESENT YOU WITH A FIELD OF CHOICES FROM WHICH YOU MUST DECIDE. YOU SELECT ONLY FROM THE FIVE OPTIONS PRESENTED.

Your objective with Arguments questions is to identify wrong answer options quickly so that you can locate the best answer to the question posed.

In addition to obfuscating by omission, the test-maker will attempt to disguise both the question and the wrong answer options. Often the test-maker does not present the question explicitly. This means that you must first determine whether you are being asked to select the answer option that **must, could,** or **cannot** satisfy the conditions of the question and statement. And, until you work through the answer options, it is very difficult to tell which statement conditions are relevant and which are not. In order to make the best use of the time available, you need to minimize the number of times you deal with an answer option. The decision technique you will use to work through answer options involves comparison and contrast.

Comparing an answer option against the statement only once meets the objective of efficiency. The answer options are compared against the conditions required by the statement and question. When the comparison makes it clear that an answer option fails to satisfy the conditions, you know that it is a wrong answer option and chuck it.

If comparison fails to produce all four wrong answers, contrast the remaining options (usually two). Using this technique often makes it possible to identify differences that highlight the failure of one or both answer choices to satisfy the conditions required by the statement and question.

✓ COMPARISON AND CONTRAST FACILITATE YOUR IDENTIFICATION OF WRONG ANSWERS AND YOUR DECISION MAKING ABOUT ANSWER OPTIONS.

To review the patterns of wrong answer options, think of them in terms of an *if-then* format. *If* you determine that the question seeks an answer option that **could** satisfy required conditions, *then* options that *cannot* satisfy all of the conditions are wrong. These **could** questions are the most frequently asked in the Arguments section-test. *If* you determine that the question seeks an answer option that **must** satisfy required conditions, *then* options that *could* or *cannot* satisfy all of the conditions are wrong. And *if* you determine that a question seeks an answer option that **cannot** satisfy required conditions, *then* options that *must* or *could* satisfy all of the conditions are wrong.

To make wrong answer options attractive, the test-maker disguises them by using the **same-language, too-little-too-much, true but,** and **false-assertion** disguises we have met before. The patterns and disguises are combined in the following summary of wrong answer options.

For **could** questions, wrong answer options are those that *cannot* satisfy required conditions, even though they use

- the **same-language** disguise
- the **too-little-too-much** disguise
- the **true but** disguise
- the **false-assertion** disguise

For **must** questions, wrong answer options are those that *could* or *cannot* satisfy required conditions, even though they use

- the **same-language** disguise
- the **too-little-too-much** disguise
- the **true but** disguise
- the **false-assertion** disguise

For **cannot** questions, wrong answer options are those that *must* or *could* satisfy required conditions, even though they use

- the **same-language** disguise
- the **too-little-too-much** disguise
- the **true but** disguise
- the **false-assertion** disguise

Knowing wrong-answer patterns and disguises is advantageous to you, as is knowing that the test-maker usually includes just one very attractive wrong answer option among the four offered. When you combine this knowledge with the ability to predict the six basic questions that appear on the Arguments section-test, you will be ready for anything.

What is the best response technique for Arguments questions?

Even though the question appears after the statement, the first thing you do is *read the question*. You need to determine whether it is a **could, must,** or **cannot** question. Note your decision next to the question. You want to be able to tell as quickly as possible which information in the statement is relevant to the question and which is superfluous. Reading the question first gives you clues about what will be relevant.

Now *read the statement*. As you do so, highlight or underline key words, assertions, and the conclusion, if there is one. If there is no conclusion in the statement, it is likely that the question will ask for a conclusion in some form.

Next, *work through each answer option*. Arguments answer options are presented in both the single- and multiple-option formats. You will remember that the multiple-option format permits one, two, or all three of the Roman numeral choices to satisfy the conditions required by the statement and question. In most Arguments section-tests, a very small percentage of the answers may be presented in the multiple-option format.

As you work through the answer options, you will use comparison and contrast to identify the options that fit a wrong-answer pattern, keeping alert for disguises. When you find a condition in an answer option that fails to satisfy the requirements of the question or statement, you chuck it. Repeating this process as necessary, you *select the best answer option* and *circle it in the test book*.

Once you have completed all of the questions in the set of six, you *transfer all your answers to the answer sheet* at the same time. This gives you a natural break before you move on to the next Arguments question set.

What are the six basic questions, and how do you work with them?

The test-maker uses six basic question types in the Arguments section-test. The techniques used to work through them are detailed in the following sections. These techniques are applicable to any version of the six questions. It might also help you familiarize yourself with the thinking required if, after this discussion, you review each question and answer option, specifically identifying the disguises used by the test-maker. (For example, option C in question 4 uses the **same language** as the statement to disguise the wrong answer. Option A in question 2 uses the **too-much** disguise. Option B in question 3 takes advantage of the **true but** disguise, and option B in question 1 applies the **false-assertion** disguise to a wrong answer choice.)

DESCRIPTION QUESTIONS

Description questions make direct reference to the argument. There is no need to go beyond the argument to identify the answer option that satisfies the conditions of the question and statement. Description questions take two forms. The first asks you to identify a point, purpose, premise, or form of reasoning used in the argument. The second asks you to identify a stated presumption.

A *what's-the-point?* question uses a direct format that takes the form "Which of the following best describes (or is) the point, purpose, premise, or form of reasoning used in the argument?" An example follows. Remember to read the question first.

1. Too little staging rather than too much is the failure of producers of wild animal movies. The indifferences recently displayed by an "Animals in the Wild" film crew is hard to excuse as it zealously filmed a newly born killer whale agonizingly drowning in an overwhelming flood tide.

    Which of the following is the underlying point of the above?
    (A) Producers should not stage animal action shots.
    (B) Producers should document the inhumanity of whalers, because their cruelty can be stopped only by exposure.
    (C) Producers should not continue as observers when doing so is incompatible with humane behavior.
    (D) Producing real-life films is a brutal business, because it requires people to sacrifice their feelings in order to record events.
    (E) Producers should commit themselves to reducing suffering and promoting humane behavior.

The question in this example asks you to select the answer option that **could** express the point of the statement. The first sentence of the statement clearly accepts staging, whereas answer choice A rejects it. Thus, A *cannot* satisfy statement conditions and is wrong. Answer option B *cannot* satisfy required conditions because it refers to matters not involved in the statement, such as the inhumanity of whalers and the prevention of cruelty. Options D and E are wrong for the same reason as B. They refer to matters not involved in the statement, such as people's feelings and their obligations. Thus, answer option C is the best selection, since it does not require anything inconsistent with the statement.

The second form of description question asks you to identify a *stated presumption*. The format for this question type is usually direct, although the test-maker varies the question structure. The following example uses a conversation structure. Read the question first.

2. *Mark*:
   Everyone who was a fighter pilot during the Korean War suffered battle fatigue.
   Harry:
   That is untrue. Many veterans of the Korean War who were in the infantry had an acute psychological reaction to their wartime experience.

   Harry's response indicates that he interpreted Mark's remark to mean that
   (A) fighter pilots are more likely to have suffered battle fatigue than any others
   (B) only those who were fighter pilots suffered from battle fatigue
   (C) battle fatigue is a mental rather than physical reaction to stress
   (D) flying fighter planes was more stressful than being a foot soldier
   (E) some who were not fighter pilots suffered battle fatigue

The question in this example requires careful reading. It asks you what Harry presumes Mark meant. Answer options A and D *cannot* satisfy the required conditions because they compare such items as the likelihood of battle fatigue and differences in job stress. Nothing in the statement suggests such comparisons. Option C *cannot* satisfy the required conditions because there is nothing in the statement to suggest a disagreement about the nature of battle fatigue. Option E *cannot* satisfy the required conditions because it is Harry's position, not Harry's interpretation of Mark's position. Option B is the best selection because it does not conflict with the conditions of the statement in any way.

EXTENSION QUESTIONS

Extension questions require you to go beyond the argument to identify the answer option that satisfies the question and statement conditions. You will have to draw inferences or define assumptions or reach conclusions. The answer options do not connect to the statement directly.

Extension questions take four forms, in which you are asked to identify a matching pattern, determine inferences and conclusions, recognize assumptions required for a conclusion, or assess evidence.

Pattern questions ask you directly to select the answer option that has a structure or principle in common with or analogous to that of the statement. Rarely, you might be asked to identify a logical flaw in a statement. It takes the form "The above is most like which of the following?"

3. The automation of industry throws people out of work; therefore, machines are harmful.

   The argument above is most like which of the following?
   (A) Hitler was a fascist; therefore, he was evil.
   (B) Fatty foods are harmful; therefore, eating butter is dangerous.
   (C) The senator steals public funds; therefore, he is dishonest.
   (D) Alcoholic beverages are high in calories; therefore, beer is fattening.
   (E) Pigeons spread disease; therefore, birds are nuisances.

This pattern-recognition question asks you to select the answer option that **could** satisfy the requirements of the statement and question. Many people approach such a question by trying to find a rational explanation for a similarity in subject matter between the statement and the answer option. This technique is not productive. Rather, you should compare the statement and answer option to determine a difference between them. Option A is wrong for a number of reasons. It *cannot* satisfy the question conditions because of the verb in the first phrase of the statement: "throws" is active, while "was" in the answer is not. Also, the subject of the first and second phrases in the answer option is the same ("Hitler" and "he"), while in the statement it is different ("automation" and "machines"). Option B also exhibits the first-phrase verb difference ("throws" versus "are"). For the same reason, answer option D is wrong. There are other differences, if you want to seek them out, but you should avoid such unnecessary hunts when taking the test. Option C is also a wrong answer. The verb pattern in the statement and answer is the same, but the subject pattern is not: in the statement the subjects of the two phrases are different ("automation" and "machines"), but they are the same in the answer option ("senator" and "he"). So the best answer option is E, which shares both the verb and subject patterns of the statement.

While the pattern is not always based on sentence structure, very often an analysis at the sentence level will quickly produce the best answer.

Inference and conclusion questions ask you to select the answer option that expresses an inference or conclusion drawn from the statement. The format is very direct, asking, "Which of the following conclusions can be logically inferred?"

4. Children perceive the world spontaneously and unself-consciously. But as they grow into adulthood, learning more facts about reality, they lose their capacity for direct perception and immediate response.

   If the statements above are true, which of the following conclusions can be logically inferred?
   (A) Children's perceptions are better than those of adults.
   (B) Facts are unimportant in the process of perceiving.
   (C) Children and adults do not perceive the world in the same way.
   (D) It is impossible for adults to recapture spontaneous perception.
   (E) Children do not distinguish clearly between fact and fantasy.

This conclusion question asks you to select the answer option that **could** satisfy the requirements of the statement and question. Answer option A does not satisfy the conditions because it introduces a value term, "better," as a conclusion. There is nothing in the statement or question to suggest values. Option B is wrong for the same reason—the value term here is "unimportant." Option D is wrong because it declares that something cannot be recaptured, when the statement gives no indication that what is lost—spontaneous perception—cannot be regained. Option E introduces two concepts, fantasy and distinguishing, that are not suggested in any way by the statement. This leaves option C as the best answer, since if offers nothing contrary to the conditions of the statement and question.

Assumption questions ask you to select the answer option that provides the evidence necessary to permit the conclusion in the statement to be reached. The question format is usually direct. It asks, "The above requires (or is based on) which of the following assumptions?"

5. Since Byron's fingers are so short and stubby, he will never be an outstanding pianist.

    The statement above is based on which of the following assumptions?

    I. The size and shape of fingers are important attributes for a professional musical career.
    II. Piano playing requires long, thin fingers.
    III. Physical characteristics can affect how well one plays the piano.

    (A) III only
    (B) I and II only
    (C) I and III only
    (D) II and III only
    (E) I, II, and III

This question asks you to select the answer option or options that express the assumptions that **could** be made in order to satisfy the requirements of the statement and question. Recall that you must always try to identify the conclusion when you read an Arguments statement. In this statement, the conclusion is "he will never be an outstanding pianist." Roman numeral I is a wrong answer to a **could** question. The conclusion in the statement involves only the type of pianist ("outstanding"), not whether the pianist is an amateur or professional or has a musical career or not. The references made in Roman numeral I *cannot* account for the conclusion. Since Roman numeral I is a wrong answer, it eliminates the options in which it appears—B, C, and E. Because Roman numeral II is involved in both of the remaining answer options, you work through it next. The statement clearly implies that Byron plays the piano, even though he does not have long, thin fingers. Thus, Roman numeral II contradicts the statement and *cannot* satisfy its conditions. This makes option D wrong and leaves A as the best answer option.

While you must avoid going any further with your analysis when taking the actual LSAT, we can work through option A at our leisure here. "Short" and "stubby" are physical characteristics. If physical characteristics can affect the way a person plays the piano, as Roman numeral III states, the length and shape of Byron's fingers could account for the conclusion that he will never be an outstanding pianist.

Evidence-assessment questions appear in a number of forms in the Arguments section-test. They ask you to select the answer option that strengthens or weakens an argument, criticizes an argument, or distinguishes between fact and opinion in an argument. The format for the evidence-assessment question varies, but it is usually direct.

6. The British economy is stagnant, which can only be the result of its overgenerous governmental programs of social aid.

    Which of the following, if true, most seriously weakens the view expressed above?

    (A) Britain spends a lower percentage of its national income on medical care than does prosperous Germany.
    (B) Several countries in the world have found that certain governmental social-aid programs have absorbed an unexpectedly high percentage of government revenues.
    (C) The governmental social-aid programs of Britain meet many of the needs of its citizens and residents and yet cost less than similar programs elsewhere.
    (D) The Scandinavian nations, with more comprehensive governmental social-aid programs than Britain's, have similar economies that are thriving.
    (E) Italy, which has few governmental social-aid programs, has for many years been in economic difficulty to a degree that equals or exceeds that of Britain.

This evidence-assessment question asks you to select the answer option that **could** weaken the statement. The fact that the word "most" is used to modify "weaken" is of no importance; this degree of refinement is virtually never involved on the LSAT. You will need to identify the conclusion in the statement—"The British economy is stagnant."

Answer option A does not satisfy the requirements of the question and statement. It is wrong because nothing in the option suggests the proportion of income the Germans spend on social-aid programs. Also, it involves only medical care, which is just one social-aid program; therefore, it *cannot* be related to the statement. Options B and C *cannot* satisfy the statement conditions and are wrong because, among other things, they fail to indicate the condition ("stagnant"?) of the economies to which Britain's economy is being compared. Option E is wrong because it fails to indicate whether the amount Italy spends on its few social-aid programs is more, less, or the same as that spent by Britain. It *cannot* be related to the statement. This leaves D as the answer option that weakens the argument, because nothing in it conflicts in any way with the statement, and it affirms that countries with more comprehensive social-aid programs and economies similar to Britain's are not stagnant ("thriving").

Are there any cue clues?

Arguments statements and answer options are replete with cue words. These words indicate the nature of the information that follows them. For example, the appearance of the word "therefore" cues you that the conclusion is coming up. There are a bundle of similar cue words. They are not worth committing to memory, but a read-through may prove beneficial to your test performance. Some conclusion cues follow.

- so
- therefore
- hence
- thus
- accordingly
- can be inferred
- results
- follows

- indicates
- suggests
- proves
- means
- shows
- nevertheless
- however

There are also a number of cue words whose presence generally indicates that the information that follows is evidence. The evidence that it cues may or may not be relevant. Representative words are listed below.

- given
- since
- because
- assume
- suppose
- if
- insofar

- inasmuch
- as
- but
- except
- despite
- notwithstanding
- although

TRAINING SESSION 13

Arguments Pretests and the 9-12-18 System

How do you apply the 9-12-18 system to Arguments pretests?

You first completed an Arguments question set in Session 6, where you learned the techniques of the 9-12-18 test planning system. The system uses pretests to help you identify your optimal balance between speed and accuracy on each section-test. With this information you can plan your total test performance.

The LSAT rewards working smart rather than working hard. You maximize your performance by selecting best answers, not by rushing through questions and answers. In the Arguments section-test, most people select fewer wrong answers as best when they plan on working with less than all the available question sets.

✓ YOU DECIDE TO MAXIMIZE YOUR
SECTION–TEST SCORE BY COMPLETING
FOUR, THREE, OR TWO QUESTION
SETS IN THE 35 MINUTES ALLOTTED.

The techniques presented in the previous two sessions will become familiar and easy to apply to Arguments problems as you work with them. As you apply them, you may find that your optimal balance between speed and accuracy changes. The familiarity you have developed will give you a sense of control and reduce your anxiety. Familiarity will also improve your proficiency with the question sets. The combination of greater control and improved proficiency will result in more accurate answer selection. You will identify wrong answers more efficiently and, consequently, select more of the best answers. This increase in efficiency may lead to a change in your test plan.

How do you develop your Arguments section-test plan?

You are probably becoming very familiar with the process of using ongoing pretest information to revise your test plan. It has been explained previously, so feel free to skim the next few paragraphs if you are already comfortable with the pretest process.

Suppose your initial Arguments pretest (in Session 6) indicated that you would achieve your optimal performance by completing three of the four question sets in a section-test (and guessing on the fourth set). Working with the training techniques explained in the previous two sessions, you will use the 9-12-18 process to update your performance record with the results. After you have worked through a number of pretests, your performance record may dictate making a change in your plan for optimal performance. For instance, the results may now make it clear that you will achieve a better score by completing all four sets of questions on the Arguments section-test than you would by completing only three question sets and guessing on one.

✓ YOU WILL CHANGE YOUR TEST PLAN
ONLY WHEN THE RESULTS OF THE
9-12-18 PRETEST PROCESS INDICATE IT.

Even after you have arrived at a stable balance between speed and accuracy, working through Arguments question sets will maintain and enhance your level of familiarity and proficiency. Always work through the technique sessions first, and then monitor your performance with 9-12-18 pretests.

How do you use Arguments pretests?

This session ends with six Arguments pretests. Use them one at a time. Each time you work through all of the techniques in Sessions 11 and 12, complete one of the pretests. Use the results to update your performance record. This means you should review the Arguments training techniques at least six times and complete at least six pretests.

✓ UPON COMPLETION OF THE SIX
TRAINING AND UPDATE SEQUENCES,
YOU SET YOUR PLAN FOR THE
ARGUMENTS SECTION–TESTS.

After six times through the sequence, your performance record should have stabilized, and your plan can be set. It will indicate the number of question sets you should complete and the number you should guess on the Arguments section-test of the LSAT.

How do you take Arguments pretests?

On pretests you should follow the procedure of reading the question first and then the statement, looking for and noting key words, concepts, and the conclusion, if any. Next select your answer options. Repeat this procedure for the number of questions you can comfortably cover in the first 9 minutes allocated to the pretest set. It is important that your pace not exceed your comfort level. At the end of the 9-minute period, you will have selected an answer for each of the six questions in the Arguments set. Depending upon your pace, some of your answers may have been selected by guessing. *Circle* your answer choices. These constitute your 9-minute set.

Next use an additional 3 minutes to reconsider the questions and the answers you selected in the 9-minute period. Your use of the additional time will vary depending on the work you completed during the first 9 minutes: you can work through questions you did not have time to consider in the first 9 minutes or review questions about which you are uncertain. Place a *box* beside each of the answers you select during this 3-minute period. If you did not change an answer, place a box beside the circled answer. If you changed and answer, place a box beside the new selection. The boxed answers are your 12-minute set. Do not erase or change the circles you placed on the question sheet during the first 9 minutes of the pretest.

The next step is to use an additional 6 minutes. Go back to the set and answer questions you did not get to during the first 12 minutes, or review and change answers as necessary. Be flexible in using this period. Concentrate on questions about which you are uncertain, but avoid reworking previously selected answers about which you are confident. Place an *asterisk* beside each of the answers you select during this 6-minute period. If you did not change an answer, place an asterisk beside the boxed answer; if you did, place the asterisk beside your new selection. The answers identified with asterisks are your 18-minute set. Again, be sure not to erase or change the circles or boxes you placed on the question sheet during the first 12 minutes of the pretest.

After the pretest is completed, refer to the Arguments Pretest Answer Key at the back of the book. Determine the number of best answers you selected during the 9-minute (circled), 12-minute (boxed), and 18-minute (asterisked) question sets. Complete the calculations called for below. The results of these calculations are transferred to your Pretest Performance Tracking Worksheet (page 39). Enter the number of question sets that represent your optimal balance between speed and accuracy. As you work through the pretests and develop your performance record, the pattern of your greatest efficiency will emerge. This pattern will indicate the number of Arguments question sets you should plan to complete on the actual LSAT—the number that will yield the highest test score for you.

Circles _____ x 5 + 0 = _____
Boxes _____ x 4 + 1 = _____
Asterisks _____ x 3 + 2 = _____

Largest total _____ indicates the optimal number (2, 3, or 4) of question sets you will enter on your Performance Tracking Worksheet.

For the pretest process to work most effectively, you should complete a pretest only after you have reviewed the Arguments test-training techniques in Sessions 11 and 12. Do this before each pretest. It will take about 30 minutes. The familiarity and proficiency you gain with the techniques through this procedure will have the greatest impact on your performance and your test score. Going through a series of pretests or question sets without first working through the training techniques is the least effective way of having an impact on your performance. And your objective is high impact, not low or no impact.

✓ ONCE YOUR PERFORMANCE ON ARGUMENTS QUESTION SETS IS STABILIZED, SO IS YOUR TEST PLAN.

After the seven pretests have been completed (one in Session 6 and six in this session), your performance record should be sufficiently comprehensive to provide you with stable information. You will develop your test plan for the Arguments section-tests on the basis of this performance record. You will plan to complete two, three, or four question sets, depending on the optimal balance you have discovered between your speed and accuracy. Then your challenge is having the self-discipline to stick to your plan during the actual LSAT.

✓ FOLLOW YOUR PLAN TO MAXIMIZE YOUR TEST PERFORMANCE AND SCORE.

Should you do more pretests?

Once the high-impact gain you wanted before taking the LSAT is realized, further workthroughs and pretests will have much less, if any, impact on your score. But it is important to maintain familiarity and proficiency with Arguments, and practice with pretests provides a positive maintenance regimen for many prospective test-takers. For others, regular workthroughs of the techniques in Sessions 11 and 12 will maintain readiness.

If you want to practice with additional Arguments problems, there are three good sources of additional sets. There is the simulated test in this guide. Law School Admission Services sells disclosed tests. And there are a number of preparation books containing little more than simulated tests. (If you use such books, make certain that the problems are constructed to the same specifications as the real LSAT questions.)

When practicing with test materials, first convert them into question sets. This is exactly the same process you will use when taking the LSAT. You identify a question set, view that set as the test until you have completed it, then move on to the next set or test. By segmenting the section-test into its four component sets, you gain maximum control over the test, which puts you in the best position to execute your test plan.

What are the directions for completing the pretests?

In each of the following Arguments question sets, evaluate the reasoning contained in the brief statements, and select the best answer. The best answer is a "conceivable solution to the particular problem posed" by the question and does not require you to make what are, by common-sense standards, implausible, superfluous, or incompatible assumptions. Complete each pretest only after you have worked through the Arguments training techniques in Sessions 11 and 12.

ARGUMENTS PRETEST 13-1

1. Hitler was born in <u>1889</u> and became chancellor of Germany in <u>1933</u>. On December 7, 1941, he was <u>52</u> years old and had been in power for <u>8</u> years. Hirohito was born in <u>1901</u> and became emperor of Japan in <u>1926</u>. On December 7, 1941, he was <u>40</u> years old and had been in power for <u>15</u> years. The four underlined figures for each man total 3,882.
   Which of the following most accurately describes the total 3,882?
   (A) It is significant, but its meaning is not clear.
   (B) It is insignificant and coincidental.
   (C) Important leaders share significant events and figures.
   (D) It is politically significant only.
   (E) There is more significance in figures than is usually acknowledged.

2. It is acceptable to support one corrupt faction in a war against another in Nicaragua. And it is acceptable to send troops to Grenada to oust a Communist leader. But it is unacceptable to use force to get food to thousands of isolated and starving people in Sudan because it would interfere with that nation's internal affairs.
   The author makes a point by
   (A) identifying incongruities in the use of force
   (B) analyzing evidence of the use of force
   (C) attacking proprieties in the use of force
   (D) complaining about irrationality in the use of force
   (E) arguing for a more pervasive use of force

3. "Return my pocket watch!"
   "How did you get it?"
   "My father gave it to me."
   "How did your father get it?"
   "His father gave it to him."
   "How did your grandfather get it?"
   "He won it in a poker game."
   "Good, we will play poker for it."
   Which of the following is best inferred from the statement "Good, we will play poker for it"?
   (A) Gambling achieves objectives effectively.
   (B) Past practice validates future action.
   (C) Meaningful customs transcend generations.
   (D) Possession is a privilege, not a right.
   (E) Wanting another's possessions is instinctive.

4. Kaminski's disparaging reviews of the book call her abilities as a critic into question, since the book became an immediate bestseller.
   Which of the following, if true, would most weaken the author's questioning of Kaminski's critical ability?
   (A) Immediate success of books is quickly forgotten.
   (B) Book critics often disagree with one another.
   (C) Sales of a book are not always indicative of its value.
   (D) The significance of a book is not known for years.
   (E) Critics often change their views about books.

Questions 5-6
If writers are truly emotional, their writing will comprise their deepest feeling about the world; and one would expect such feelings to appear in their work, if not to dominate it. Many societies and people are very emotional, and their writing has as its principal function the expression and integration of deep feeling. This suggests that writing must be either emotional or trivial, that only emotional people can be great writers, and that writing cannot flourish in a technical society.

5. The fact that emotional writing integrates feelings does NOT prove that
   I. feelings are not integrated in other ways
   II. only emotional writing can be great
   III. one type of writing is better than another
   (A) I only
   (B) I and II only
   (C) I, II, and III
   (D) I and III only
   (E) II and III only

6. On which of the following assumptions is the author's position based?
   (A) Great writers must be emotional.
   (B) Societies must be emotional or technical.
   (C) Feelings dominate an emotional writer's work.
   (D) Writing is emotional or trivial.
   (E) A writer's purpose is to express emotion.

ARGUMENTS PRETEST 13-2

Questions 1-2

It is almost as safe to assume that artists of any dignity are against their country, i.e., against the environment in which chance placed them, as it is to assume that their country is against the artists. They differ from the rest of us mainly because they react sharply and in an uncommon manner to phenomena that leave the rest of us unmoved, or, at most, merely annoy us vaguely. Therefore, they pursue artistic endeavors, which are at once criticisms of life and attempts to escape from life.

The more the facts are studied, the more they bear out these generalizations. In those fields of art, at all events, that concern themselves with ideas as well as with sensations, it is almost impossible to find any trace of artists who were not actively hostile to their environment, and thus indifferent patriots.

1. Which of the following, if true, would most strongly refute the author's argument?

    (A) Artists are generally honored by their countries.
    (B) Artists best recognize life's difficulties.
    (C) Artists usually escape from their countries.
    (D) Artists generally venerate their countries.
    (E) Artists are best known in their own countries.

2. The author's argument depends most upon which of the following assumptions?

    (A) Most people are annoyed by phenomena that make an artist hostile.
    (B) Art defines in the abstract events and sensations that are uncommon.
    (C) The purpose of art is both to find fault with and to escape from life.
    (D) In order to be an artist of dignity, a person must be an indifferent patriot.
    (E) Life is actively hostile to the artistic endeavors of most artists.

3. In a recent survey, the majority of respondents answered "no" to the question "Should free hypodermic needles be provided by the government to drug addicts on welfare?"

    The survey results can best be criticized because the question structure

    (A) presented more than one issue to respondents
    (B) presented a choice that suggested a negative reply
    (C) presented respondents with an impossible value judgment
    (D) presented an issue to largely unaffected respondents
    (E) presented a controversial issue out of context

4. When it rains, the crops grow; but it hasn't rained recently, so the crops must not be growing.

    Which of the following arguments is logically most similar to the one above?

    (A) When people are old, they complain about their health; but our town has no health problems, so it must have no old people.
    (B) When a town has health problems, it must also have many old people.
    (C) When people are old, they complain about their health; but no people can complain about their health and yet not be old.
    (D) When people complain about their health, they get old; but no people are complaining about their health, so we must have no people getting old.
    (E) When a town has people complaining about their health, it must also have old people; our town has many people complaining about their health, so it must have many old people.

Questions 5-6

The proposal to divert one third of the flow of the Delaware River to supply New York City with water ought to be a matter of great concern to the people who live in the Delaware Valley. The interests of the people of the Delaware Valley are being put aside so that growth can continue in an already overdeveloped area. Fresh water is a natural resource in the same sense that oil and coal are natural resources. Do Texas and Alaska give away their oil? Does West Virginia give away its coal? Why should Pennsylvania and New Jersey supply New York or any other place with fresh water? If the growth of New York is capped by limited fresh water, so much the better.

5. The author assumes which of the following to be fact rather than opinion?

    I. Diverting the Delaware River is a matter of great concern to people in the Delaware Valley.
    II. The purpose of diverting the Delaware River is to allow New York City to continue to grow.
    III. Oil, coal, and fresh water are natural resources.

    (A) II only
    (B) III only
    (C) I and II only
    (D) II and III only
    (E) I, II, and III

6. Which of the following, if true, would most weaken the author's argument?

    (A) New York City is permanently committed to zero growth.
    (B) The diversion will not reduce water availability to people in the Delaware Valley.
    (C) New York City will pay Pennsylvania and New Jersey for each gallon of water diverted.
    (D) The diversion will reduce the risk of flooding in the Delaware Valley.
    (E) New York City will get water from Vermont if the Delaware River is not diverted.

ARGUMENTS PRETEST 13-3

1. If the present moment contains no living and creative choice, and is totally and mechanically the product of the matter and the moment before, then so was that moment the mechanical effect of the moment that preceded it, and so on, until we arrive at a single cause of every later event, of every act and suffering of man.

   Which of the following would NOT be supported by the above argument?

   I. A theory postulating a mechanistic origin of the universe.
   II. A theory postulating suffering as a requisite for creativity.
   III. A theory postulating a deterministic explanation of history.

   (A) II only
   (B) III only
   (C) I and II only
   (D) I and III only
   (E) II and III only

2. Baxter defends paternal authority and the preservation of the family in her most recent work. But other aspects of her thinking more convincingly demonstrate that she cannot be considered a feminist. For example, she fails to appreciate that the full realization of a woman's capacities depends on her securing the same political, economic, and civil rights as those afforded me.

   Which of the following inferences is NOT supported by the above argument?

   (A) Paternal authority is not generally supported by feminists.
   (B) The family is not generally supported by feminists.
   (C) Baxter feels that women do not need rights equal to mens'.
   (D) Women's capacities have not been fully realized.
   (E) Baxter feels that women and men have unequal capacities.

3. Many children in urban schools are forced to learn in dilapidated classrooms with few modern teaching aids. Compared to children in suburban schools, with their computers, labs, and the latest advances in educational resources, the urban student is truly deprived.

   The point of the author's argument is best stated by which of the following?

   (A) Modern educational aids should be provided for urban children.
   (B) Urban and suburban children should be educated in the same schools.
   (C) Urban school children should not be required to compete with suburban school children.
   (D) Unequal resources for urban and suburban children should be investigated.
   (E) Suburban school resources should be combined with those of urban schools if an ideal education is to be achieved.

4. A philosopher makes arguments that frequently are not logical in order to demonstrate that rationality is not as valuable as irrationality to us humans. Consequently, the philosopher should not be expected to use the same arguments as do those whose positions are rationally based.

   The argument above is most similar to which of the following?

   (A) A philosopher's arguments focus on the flaws in logical reasoning of those who oppose her.
   (B) A writer often uses great restraint when describing mayhem.
   (C) A female author was not taken seriously, so she used a male pseudonym when establishing her reputation.
   (D) A novel is judged to be boring because it describes a boring situation.
   (E) A philosopher's reasoning is complicated because he was trained in a tradition that often uses complicated reasoning.

Questions 5-6

United States treaty negotiations with Japan about trade involve the basic question "Can the Japanese be trusted?" But treaties are based on self-interest rather than on trust. There would be no need to have treaties if countries trusted one another. A treaty is an alternative to trust; one that formally recognizes that each country finds an advantage in the agreement.

5. Which of the following is an argument made above?

   (A) If the Japanese can be trusted, the United States should negotiate treaties with Japan.
   (B) If the Japanese cannot be trusted, the United States should not negotiate treaties with Japan.
   (C) If Japan and the United States have common trade interests, a treaty between the countries should be negotiated.
   (D) If Japan and the United States sign a treaty, interests of each will be served by the agreement.
   (E) If Japanese and United States interests are different, a treaty dealing with those interests will not be signed.

6. Which of the following is NOT supported by the author's argument above?

   I. Treaties are made only between countries that do not trust one another.
   II. Treaties do not serve mutual interests of countries.
   III. Treaties formally recognize an advantage one country has over another.

   (A) I only
   (B) II only
   (C) III only
   (D) I and II only
   (E) I and III only

ARGUMENTS PRETEST 13-4

1. Tests done on the employees of a chemical plant showed that 28 percent had abnormal chromosome patterns. Chemical fumes, radiation, and airborne particulates are among the causes of abnormal chromosome patterns.
   Which of the following would most support the conclusion that chemical fumes were responsible for abnormal chromosome patterns in the plant's employees?
   (A) Abnormal chromosome patterns can be altered.
   (B) Nonemployees in the area also develop abnormal chromosome patterns.
   (C) Employees of other chemical plants do not develop abnormal chromosome patterns.
   (D) Abnormal chromosome patterns are not necessarily harmful.
   (E) Employees of most chemical plants develop abnormal chromosome patterns.

2. "None of the legislators we polled are in favor of this bill."
   "That cannot be true. There are six legislators who introduced the bill and support it."
   Which of the following can be inferred from the above exchange?
   (A) Legislators who do not favor the bill may support it.
   (B) The only legislators who favor the bill are those who introduced it.
   (C) Only legislators who do not favor the bill were polled.
   (D) Some legislators refused to participate in the poll.
   (E) Legislators might indicate that they favor a bill when they do not.

3. The Audubon Society Falcon Watch reports that there were 2,487 more falcon sightings in 1988 than there were in 1987. This proves that an increase in the falcon population has finally been realized.
   Which of the following, if true, most weakens the above argument?
   (A) Falcons regularly move from area to area in search of food.
   (B) Falcons have been introduced into urban environments.
   (C) Development in falcon nesting areas is being restricted.
   (D) The Society intensified its falcon sighting program in 1988.
   (E) The Society database about falcons improved in 1988.

4. The following notice was received by Mary Castle, a scientist:
   "We regret that your article cannot be accepted. Page limitations in the Journal force the editor to return many worthy and well-written articles."
   All of the following may be inferred from the above EXCEPT
   (A) only well-written articles are accepted for publication
   (B) Castle's article was considered to be well written
   (C) Castle's article was found to be too long for the Journal
   (D) Castle's article was found to be worthy of publication
   (E) quality of writing was not the only factor in deciding which articles to publish

Questions 5-6

The drug Thalidomide caused unforeseen birth defects in thousand of babies; therefore, thorough testing of the effects of all new drugs should be required before their release to the public.

5. Which of the following is an assumption made in the argument above?
   (A) Birth defects caused by Thalidomide could have been prevented by testing.
   (B) Thalidomide produced more harmful birth defects than any drug before it.
   (C) The benefits of Thalidomide are not outweighed by its harmful side effects.
   (D) Thalidomide producers acted irresponsibly in putting such a dangerous drug on the market.
   (E) Less harmful drugs were available to treat the problems treated by Thalidomide.

6. The argument above is most similar to which of the following?
   (A) Exposure to loud music has been shown to be harmful to teenage hearing; therefore, teens should not be permitted to listen to loud music.
   (B) The value of research is hard to determine; therefore, amounts spent for research should be reduced.
   (C) The Ford Pinto has been found to have a design defect; therefore, it should be replaced by the manufacturer.
   (D) Teenage drivers have caused some of the worst auto accidents; therefore, driving tests for teenagers should be more rigorous than for others.
   (E) Generic drugs are less expensive than brand-name drugs; therefore, doctors should prescribe only generic drugs.

ARGUMENTS PRETEST 13-5

1. Six Hi-Fiber tablets a day reduce weight fast! Pounds disappear! (Warning: Hi-Fiber tablet dieters may eat only three balanced meals a day.)

   Which of the following most effectively argues against the claim that Hi-Fiber tablets will cause weight loss?

   (A) Weight loss is not the natural result of the consumption of food.
   (B) If the diet is followed and weight loss occurs, limiting food to three balanced meals a day is the cause.
   (C) Any weight loss that occurs after taking six tablets a day is the result of the diet.
   (D) Even though the advertisement says, "Pounds disappear!" it makes no claim as to when weight loss will occur.
   (E) Weight loss on any diet depends largely on the extent to which the dieter is overweight.

2. Rites of adulthood are more frequently found in societies where the differences between adults and children are not clear. The purpose of such rites is to formally impose adult responsibilities on participants.

   The above argument would be most strengthened if it were found that

   (A) children do not generally behave as adults prior to the rites
   (B) children generally accept the rites without question
   (C) adults generally approve of the rites
   (D) formal rites are prevalent in such societies
   (E) children do not generally accept adult responsibilities prior to the rites

3. Attempts to make public transportation facilities accessible to physically challenged people are misguided. Only the most athletic of the physically challenged are able to get to the stops and stations where it is possible for them to take advantage of special devices installed on buses and trains.

   Which of the following most strengthens the argument above?

   (A) It is extremely expensive to install special devices on buses and trains to accommodate the physically challenged.
   (B) More physically challenged people have access to motorized wheelchairs than ever before.
   (C) Very few physically challenged people use facilities in the places where they have been installed.
   (D) Special access facilities to public buildings have increased their use by physically challenged people.
   (E) Physically challenged people on buses and trains are at greater safety risk than others.

4. All quiet people are harmless.
   No harmless people are easily identified.

   The premises above lead to which of the following conclusions?

   I. Quiet people are not easily identified.
   II. Most people who are easily identified are harmless.
   III. No harmless people are quiet.

   (A) I only
   (B) III only
   (C) I and II only
   (D) II and III only
   (E) I, II, and III

Questions 5-6

Every time a business grants financial credit to an individual, the business assumes the risk of the individual not being able to make all the payments agreed upon. Credit bureaus assist businesses in their efforts to evaluate the risks involved with the extension of credit to individual purchasers. The financial history of individuals is maintained and reported on by credit bureaus. Credit bureaus assist debtors as well as creditors by preventing them from assuming greater debt than they can afford. Finally, the reduction of bad debts resulting from the work of credit bureaus holds losses and prices down and thus benefits consumers generally. The few concerns for individual privacy that have been raised about credit bureaus hardly offset their financial value to business and consumer alike.

5. Which of the following is assumed by the above argument?

   (A) Business would have no way to make credit decisions without credit bureaus.
   (B) Risk of nonpayment is difficult for most businesses to assess.
   (C) Purchasers attempt to secure more credit than they can afford.
   (D) Credit bureaus seldom make errors in their reports about individuals' financial histories.
   (E) Financial histories are complex and difficult to develop and maintain.

6. According to the above argument, any harm that results from the use of credit bureaus by businesses is

   (A) offset by the need for individual financial histories
   (B) minimal, because so few errors are made in their reports
   (C) acceptable, because business requires financial histories
   (D) justified by the economic value to business and society
   (E) essential to the effective extension of credit to individuals

ARGUMENTS PRETEST 13-6

1. The average salary of a college graduate is only 22 percent greater than that of a high school graduate. In 1969, the difference was 55 percent. In addition, college graduates' salaries have not kept up with inflation. For most, the rewards of a college education will not justify the cost of tuition and lost income while getting a degree.

   Which of the following, if true, most weakens the above argument?
   - (A) Since 1969, the incomes of few groups have kept pace with inflation.
   - (B) Since 1969, college education costs have outpaced inflation by nearly 100 percent.
   - (C) Since 1969, more high school graduates have decided to seek a college degree.
   - (D) Since 1969, the unemployment rate for college graduates is lower than that for high school graduates.
   - (E) Since 1969, there has been a steady decline in the number of high school graduates in the job market.

2. Genetic engineering places the nature and nurture argument in stark relief. Not only will physical qualities (nature) of individuals be altered by manufacturing processes, but intellectual, emotional, and spiritual qualities will be modified as well. Those who argue that the altering of human qualities violates the laws of nature ignore the reality that people are already the result of engineering in the form of their manufactured education, socialization, and environment (nurture).

   Which of the following, if true, supports the above argument?
   - I. Engineering of genes and environment are virtually the same.
   - II. Manufacturing of education and intellect are virtually the same.
   - III. Qualities of individuals and societies are virtually the same.
   - (A) I only
   - (B) II only
   - (C) III only
   - (D) I and II only
   - (E) II and III only

Questions 3-4

There is an inherent fallacy in the reasoning of Shea, who suggests that all of his readers ought to attend the retrospective of Beatles music offered by the Springfield Pops because "the Beatles have had as great an influence on the musical development of our day as Beethoven had on his." Stalin had great influence on the political development of his time, but no one suggests that people should rush to Moscow to pay homage at his tomb.

3. The point of the above argument is that
   - (A) Shea confuses influence with merit
   - (B) Shea confuses politics with music
   - (C) Shea confuses the Beatles with Beethoven
   - (D) Shea confuses honor with attendance
   - (E) Shea confuses popularity with importance

4. Which of the following is analogous to Stalin's tomb in the argument above?
   - (A) the Springfield Pops
   - (B) musical influence
   - (C) Beethoven
   - (D) attendance at the Beatles retrospective
   - (E) Shea's readers

5. Dictatorships or centralized governments result from the political indifference of a country's people. If people were not politically indifferent, all governments would be democratic or decentralized.

   Which of the following could NOT be inferred from the above argument?
   - (A) Democratic governments result from politically active people.
   - (B) Dictatorships exist only in countries whose people are politically indifferent.
   - (C) Politically active people are responsible for decentralized governments.
   - (D) A country with a democratic government must have a politically active people.
   - (E) Centralized governments are the responsibility of the politically indifferent.

6. Testing the reasoning abilities of illiterate people has proven to be particularly challenging to psychologists. When illiterate people are given tasks that are designed to require them to reason to a conclusion, they are relatively successful when the mechanical devices used in the test are familiar ones. But if the devices used in the test are unfamiliar, they are relatively unsuccessful at performing analogous tasks.

   Which of the following conclusions can be drawn reasonably from the information above?
   - I. Reasoning abilities of illiterate people should not be tested using tasks that do not involve familiar devices.
   - II. Literacy is required in order for the reasoning abilities of people to be tested through the use of mechanical devices.
   - III. Illiterate people can be tested for reasoning abilities.
   - (A) I only
   - (B) II only
   - (C) I and II only
   - (D) I and III only
   - (E) II and III only

TRAINING SESSION 14

Passages Problems in Depth

What are the fundamentals of Passages problems?

There is one Passages section-test on each LSAT, with four Passages problems in the section-test. Each Passages problem fits the LSAT profile: directions, a statement, a question, and answer options. Each statement supports a set of questions and answer options. There are seven questions per set, making the total number of questions in a section-test twenty-eight.

How are Passages problems constructed?

Passages are taken from law reviews and similar journals. This is not to suggest that some knowledge of law is required or even beneficial in working through Passages problems. In fact, the statements are chosen and edited to avoid jargon and legalese. They involve diverse topics—from technical subjects to topics drawn from the social sciences, the humanities, and other fields.

> ✓ PASSAGES STATEMENTS ARE CHOSEN FOR THEIR COMMON CHARACTERISTICS, NOT FOR THEIR SUBJECT MATTER.

From the test-maker's perspective, the topic of the statement is irrelevant. What is critical to the test-maker is that the Passages statement have six major characteristics:

- point or purpose
- key words or concepts
- authorities
- enumerations
- unusual words or phrases
- competing perspectives

This requires an adjustment in the way you read. You have probably been conditioned to read material of the type presented in Passages statements for information and understanding. However, successful performance on the LSAT Passages section-test depends upon your avoiding this conditioning.

> ✓ WITH PASSAGES STATEMENTS, YOU READ FOR THE CHARACTERISTICS OF THE STATEMENT, NOT FOR INFORMATION OR UNDERSTANDING OF THE TOPIC.

How do you handle all of that reading?

As you can see, Passages problems impose a substantial reading burden on test-takers—nearly twice that of the other LSAT section-tests. The Passages reading burden is a major factor in your performance on the Passages section-test, much more so than with Relationships and Arguments problems. There are between 4,000 and 7,500 words in a section-test. This means that, to complete all of the reading in a long section-test, a pace above 200 words per minute must be maintained. The required pace can go even higher when the time needed to select the best answer options is taken into account, since, for Passages problems, the questions and answer options require as much reading as the statements. It is difficult to read carefully at this pace.

> ✓ YOUR READING PACE CLEARLY INFLUENCES YOUR BALANCE BETWEEN SPEED AND ACCURACY.

By testing your pace, you can estimate the time you will need to complete the reading in the Passages section-test. Read the following example carefully. Keep a record of the time it takes you to complete the reading. Then divide the number of words in the statement (some 550) by the number of minutes you took to read the statement. This tells you your speed at reading a Passages statement. Suppose you took 5 minutes to read the statement carefully: this means that you read the statement at a pace of 110 words per minute.

Blackmail may be defined as the sale of information to an individual who would be incriminated by its publication, and at first glance it appears to be an efficient method of private enforcement of the law (the
(5) moral as well as the positive law). The value of the information to the blackmailed individual is equal to the cost of the punishment that the individual will incur if the information is communicated to the authorities and he is punished as a result, and so he will be willing to
(10) pay up to that amount to the blackmailer for the information. The individual is thereby punished, and the punishment is the same as if he had been apprehended and convicted for the crime that the blackmailer has discovered, but the fine is paid to the blackmailer rather
(15) than to the state.

Why then is blackmail a crime? One scholar's answer is that it results in underdeterrence of crimes punished by nonpecuniary sanctions because the criminals lack the resources to pay an optimal fine. The
(20) blackmailer will sell his information to the criminal for a price lower than the cost of punishment if the criminal cannot pay a higher price. A more persuasive explanation of why blackmail is a crime is that the decision to discourage blackmail follows directly from
(25) the decision to rely on a public monopoly of law enforcement in some areas of enforcement, notably criminal law. Were blackmail, a form of private enforcement, lawful, the public monopoly of enforcement would be undermined. Overenforcement of
(30) the law would result if the blackmailer were able to extract the full fine from the offender. Alternatively, the blackmailer might sell his incriminating information to the offender for a price lower than the statutory cost of punishment to the criminal, which would reduce the
(35) effective cost of punishment to the criminal below the level set by the legislature. This problem, however, could be solved by a system of public bounties equal to the cost of punishment (or lower, to induce the enforcement industry to contract to optimal size). Then
(40) the blackmailer could always claim a bounty from the state if the criminal was unable to pay a price equal to the optimal fine.

Consistent with this analysis, Axel's studies show that practices indistinguishable from blackmail, though
(45) not called by that name, are permitted in areas where the law is enforced privately rather than publicly because the overenforcement problem is not serious. No one seems to object to a person's collecting information about his or her spouse's adulterous activities, and
(50) threatening to disclose that information in a divorce proceeding or other forum, in order to extract maximum compensation for the offending spouse's breach of the marital obligations.

Blackmail and bribery appear to be virtually
(55) identical practices from the standpoint of the analysis of private enforcement. The blackmailer and the bribed official both receive payment in exchange for not enforcing the law. We therefore predict that in areas where there is a public monopoly of enforcement,
(60) bribery, like blackmail, will be prohibited, while in areas where there is no public monopoly, it will be permitted. And so we observe. The settlement out of court of negligence claims is a form of perfectly lawful bribery, although the term is not used in these situations
(65) because of its pejorative connotation.

If you read at a pace of 110 words per minute and assume a Passages section-test of about 5,000 words, you will be able to read 75 percent of the full burden or three of the four Passages problems. The reading burden puts a premium on the techniques you use to work through each Passages problem. You especially want to avoid rereading or other repetitive activities.

In what order do you consider Passages problems?

You should work on the least difficult Passages problem first and the most difficult last. There are two major factors determining Passages difficulty. The first and dominant one is the reading burden of the problem. (As elsewhere, "problem" refers to the combined statement, questions, and answer options.)

✓ THE GREATER THE READING BURDEN, THE MORE DIFFICULT THE PROBLEM.

The other factor is the subject matter of the statement. While we have said that the statement subject matter is less significant than it appears to be, many test-takers are significantly less proficient at reading a statement about a subject they dislike or find difficult.

✓ REORDER PASSAGES PROBLEMS ACCORDING TO THEIR DIFFICULTY.

You will proceed by working on the problems according to their degree of difficulty, from least to most. This means that you must first rank the problems by length. (The greatest variation in length occurs within the combination of seven questions and answer options that follows each statement.) You then consider the subject matter of the statements—if a statement involves subject matter that is problematic for you, rank that statement last. Otherwise, work through Passages problems in the order of their length, with the shortest first and the longest last.

Of course, the *number* of problems you will work through depends on your test plan. If your plan is to complete all four Passages problems in the section-test, you will work through all the questions in sets of seven. If your plan is to complete three problems, you will work through your selected three sets of questions and guess your answer selections on the fourth set. If your plan is to complete two problems, you will work through the first two question sets and guess your answer selections on the last two sets.

How do Passages questions work?

THE DIRECTIONS

In the directions to Passages questions, the test-maker tells you to select the best answer to the question based upon what is stated and implied in the statement. Beyond acknowledging the presence of the two basic question types—the description and extension types—these directions do not give you any information.

THE STATEMENT

Passages statements obfuscate. They are relatively long, generally between 500 and 550 words, and much of the material in them is not relevant to the questions. But the length of the statement presents most readers with fewer difficulties than do its other attributes. The absence of familiar structure can be disconcerting, and there are no titles to go by. Each statement has been heavily edited beforehand, with the result that the purpose of the statement is unclear, especially since it appears outside of its original context. The statement is compressed into three to five paragraphs, and the paragraphs often do not reflect different topics or points. The grammar is generally awkward, and the writing is in a technical rather than journalistic style.

The line numbers placed beside each statement are used to mark five-line increments, which facilitates the making of references to statement material in the questions. When a question refers to a specific word in the statement, the line number is used to indicate the location of that word.

Opinion is involved in virtually every Passages statement, although the point of view, purpose, or position is often veiled. The form and substance these opinions take are likely to be unfamiliar to you, and they can be confusing if you let yourself become involved with them.

✓ OVERLOOKING FORM AND CONTENT PERMITS YOU TO AVOID CONFUSION AND FOCUS ON THE ELEMENTS OF THE STATEMENT THAT ARE REALLY INVOLVED IN THE QUESTIONS.

You will recall that the pertinent elements of the statement are its point or purpose, key words or concepts, authorities, enumerations, unusual words or phrases, and competing perspectives. Most statements present competing perspectives, although the presentation may at first appear to be balanced by viewing the topic "on the one hand" and "on the other hand." Even if it is camouflaged, one of the views is preferred by the author. Key words and concepts usually can be identified by their being repeated or elaborated upon. References to authorities include such statements as "The Task Force study shows. . .". Enumerations are usually found in the statement and take the form "Examples of these are dogs, cats, canaries, tropical fish, and horses." Unusual words or phrases also appear regularly. Some examples are "syntactics," "on-all-fours," "credence goods," " post-Pigovian," "prose models," and "gentry controversy."

In other words, the statement presents elements upon which the set of questions and answer options is based. It supports all of the questions in the set.

THE QUESTION

Passages questions are limited in their coverage and structure. They directly state the decision to be made by test-takers. They do not contain supplemental statements. Passages questions do not modify or add to the statement, and each question is independent of every other one.

When a question refers to a line number, that reference ought to be taken in context. This means that you should consider the material before and after the specific reference at the same time that you look at the referenced material.

As you recall, there are two basic Passages questions types: description questions and extension questions. The variations on these questions are similar to those used in Arguments questions, but they are not exactly the same. The three variations on the description question require you to select an answer option that presents

- the summary, principal point, or purpose of the statement
- some specific detail
- some meaning in context

The summary, point, or purpose question almost always appears in Passages question sets. The four variations of the extension question require you

- to identify a perspective
- to identify a context
- to identify a pattern
- to assess evidence

These seven points cover all the types of questions that appear on a Passages section-test.

✓ YOU NOW CAN PREDICT EVERY PASSAGES QUESTION THAT WILL APPEAR ON THE LSAT.

THE ANSWERS

The answer options complete the question, which, by itself, means very little. The typical Passages question asks, "Which of the following best summarizes the point?" It does no more than tell you that the selection of an answer option will be necessary. Only when it is connected to the answer options does the question become sufficiently specific to permit answer selection.

✓ THE ANSWER OPTIONS PRESENT THE REAL DECISION TO YOU.

As with Arguments, you will use comparison and contrast to work through the answer options. These techniques assist you in detecting wrong answer disguises and identifying differences between options.

With most Passages problems, it is not clear whether the question requires the selection of an answer option that must, could, or cannot satisfy the question and statement conditions. This means that, before you work through the answer options, you must first determine the nature and, to the degree possible, the focus of the question. Is it must, could, or cannot? Does it focus on an enumeration, authority, unusual word, or some other statement characteristic? By doing this, you can take best advantage of the time available, minimizing the number of times you deal with the statement and answer options.

✓ REPEATED REVIEWS OF THE SAME MATERIAL ARE EFFICIENCY–BUSTERS OF THE WORST KIND.

Your efficiency objective is to compare an answer option against the statement conditions just once. When the comparison shows that an answer option fails to satisfy the conditions, you chuck it. In the contrast technique, one answer option is contrasted with another. This is useful when the comparison of an answer option against the required conditions has yielded more than one possible best answer. Contrasting answer options often identifies differences in them that make it clear that one or both fail to satisfy the required conditions.

✓ COMPARE AND CONTRAST FOR EFFICIENT WRONG–ANSWER IDENTIFICATION.

Take a moment to recall the other aids we have employed to identify wrong answer options efficiently: the wrong-answer patterns and disguises. For a question seeking an answer that **could** satisfy required conditions, the pattern predicts that options that *cannot* are wrong. These **could** questions are the ones most often asked on the Passages section-test. Questions asking for an answer that **must** satisfy required conditions are not completed by options that *could* or *cannot* satisfy all of the conditions. And questions asking for the answer that **cannot** satisfy required conditions are not completed by options that *must* or *could* satisfy the conditions.

As to disguises, the test-maker uses the **same-language**, **too-little-too-much**, **true but**, and **false-assertion** strategies to create answer options that are attractive but do not satisfy the conditions of the question and statement.

These patterns are combined in the following summary of wrong answer options.

For **could** questions, wrong answer options are those that *cannot* satisfy required conditions, even though they use

- the **same-language** disguise
- the **too-little-too-much** disguise
- the **true but** disguise
- the **false-assertion** disguise

For **must** questions, wrong answer options are those that *could* or *cannot* satisfy required conditions, even though they use

- the **same-language** disguise
- the **too-little-too-much** disguise
- the **true but** disguise
- the **false-assertion** disguise

For **cannot** questions, wrong answer options are those that *must* or *could* satisfy required conditions, even though they use

- the **same-language** disguise
- the **too-little-too-much** disguise
- the **true but** disguise
- the **false-assertion** disguise

Another strategy used by the test-maker to disguise the best answer option is **paraphrasing**. This disguise obfuscates the best answer and adds to the attractiveness of answer options that use the same language as the statement. Recognizing that an answer option paraphrases the statement can keep you from discarding it too quickly. Carefully check answer options that are clear paraphrases—they often satisfy all the required conditions.

What is the best response technique for Passages questions?

Efficient use of time is important to your performance on all LSAT section-tests. Passages provide you with many opportunities for efficiency. Your challenge is to take advantage of the opportunities.

The first order of business is to determine and mark the order in which you will work through the four Passages statements and question sets. Using the techniques described earlier in this session, you rank the Passages problems according to their difficulty, numbering them in the order in which you will work through them.

Next you begin to work on the statement you designated as first. Orient yourself to it briefly by taking 10 to 20 seconds to read the first sentence of each paragraph. This gives you a sense of the statement's orientation before you scan the questions. Both this and the question scan are important preparation for the one careful reading of the statement that follows.

Scan the questions. As you know, they are short and serve primarily as cues, but they often provide a good idea of the characteristic in the statement that is their focus. A clear example is the question that refers you to a specific line in the statement. Mark that line during your scan so that you can concentrate when it comes to the careful readthrough.

During the scan, designate the questions as **description** (D) or **extension** (E) types. This is so you can work through description questions first. Working through the questions that make direct reference to the statement first will improve your familiarity with the statement before you reach the extension questions that require you to go beyond the statement.

Next read through the statement carefully, focusing on the six characteristics and discarding the residual. There are two alternative techniques that facilitate this objective. The first is unfamiliar—as you read, use a marking pen to cross out extraneous material, leaving only the common characteristics for later reference. Not only does this make reference to the characteristics easy, but it eliminates the potential distraction of superfluous portions of the statement. The procedure creates insecurity in many test-takers, because the blackened text is gone, and there is no turning back. However, that text is unnecessary and a distraction.

> Blackmail ~~may be defined as the sale of information to an individual who would be incriminated by its publication, and at first glance~~ it appears to be an efficient method of private enforcement of the law ~~(the moral as well as the positive law). The value of the~~
> (5) ~~information to the blackmailed individual is equal to the~~ cost of the punishment ~~that the individual will incur if the information is communicated to the authorities and he is punished as a result, and so he will be willing to~~
> (10) ~~pay up to that amount to the blackmailer for the information. The individual is thereby punished, and the punishment~~ is the same as if he had been apprehended and convicted for the crime ~~that the blackmailer has discovered, but the fine is paid to the blackmailer rather~~
> (15) ~~than to the state.~~

The second technique is more familiar. It involves underlining or highlighting the common characteristics for later reference. (For an example, see the facing page.)

In doing either of these, you are connecting the statement to the predetermined analysis of the statement. You know that the **point or purpose, key words or concepts, authorities, enumerations, unusual words or phrases,** and **competing perspectives** in the statement will be the focus of the questions. No other material will be involved in the questions.

✓ DO NOT WASTE TIME WITH EXTRANEOUS MATERIAL.

Return to the statement earlier in this session. Using whichever technique you prefer, read the statement carefully and note the point or purpose, key words or concepts, authorities, enumerations, unusual words or phrases, and competing perspectives. After you have completed your reading, review the samples here and compare your results. Beside the underlined sample on the facing page are extracts of the noted material organized under headings reflecting the six characteristics used by the test-maker to select Passages statements.

Now you are ready to work through the description questions and then the extension questions. Determine whether the question seeks a must, could, or cannot answer option. Examine the answer options in order, using the techniques of comparison and contrast to identify the options that match a wrong-answer pattern. Be alert for the test-maker's disguises. When you find an answer option that fails to satisfy the requirements of the question and statement, you chuck it. *Repeat the process until you have selected the best answer option. Circle it in the test book.*

Once you have completed all of the questions in a set, *transfer all of your answers to the answer sheet* at the same time. This provides you with a natural break before moving on to the next Passages statement and question set.

Passages answers may be presented in both the single- and multiple-option formats. Recall that the multiple-option format permits one, two, or all three of the Roman numeral choices to satisfy the conditions required by the statement and question. In most Passages section-tests, the multiple-option format is used very sparingly.

How do you work with the seven basic questions?

DESCRIPTION QUESTIONS

Description questions always refer directly to the statement. Refer to the statement if necessary to make a decision about the conditions, but make only one such reference back.

Description questions take three forms. They ask you to recognize the principal point or purpose of the statement, identify a specific detail in the statement, or determine the meaning of a term or concept in context. (All of the examples of questions and answer options that follow are based on the previous passage about blackmail and bribery.)

Principal point or purpose questions employ a direct approach of the form "Which of the following best describes (or is) the principal point or purpose of the passage?"

1. Which of the following best summarizes the main point of the passage?
   (A) Blackmail and bribery are valuable forms of law enforcement.
   (B) Private law enforcement is more efficient than public law enforcement.
   (C) Punishment under private and public law enforcement is the same.
   (D) The law enforcement industry should contract to optimal size.
   (E) When public law enforcement is not threatened, blackmail and bribery are permitted.

Although not directly, the question asks for the answer option that **could** satisfy the required conditions. Answer option A makes a value judgment not made in the statement. The statement indicates that blackmail is an *efficient* method of private law enforcement but nowhere says that it is a *valuable* form of law enforcement or even a *valuable* form of *private* law enforcement. Option A does not satisfy the conditions of the statement and is wrong. (Be particularly alert to answer options that make value statements, which often employ the **too-little-too-much** disguise.) Answer option B *cannot* satisfy the required conditions because it compares the efficiency of public and private law enforcement. No such comparison is made in the statement. Option C is wrong because it involves a peripheral point, not the *main* point of the statement. It is an example of the **true but** wrong answer option, as is option D. Option D reflects the point made on line 39 of the statement but has nothing to do with the question, which seeks the *main* point of the statement. Option E is the best answer.

Blackmail may be defined as the sale of information to an individual who would be incriminated by its publication, and at first glance it appears to be an efficient method of private enforcement of the law (the
(5) moral as well as the positive law). The value of the information to the blackmailed individual is equal to the cost of the punishment that the individual will incur if the information is communicated to the authorities and he is punished as a result, and so he will be willing to
(10) pay up to that amount to the blackmailer for the information. The individual is thereby punished, and the punishment is the same as if he had been apprehended and convicted for the crime that the blackmailer has discovered, but the fine is paid to the blackmailer rather
(15) than to the state.

Why then is blackmail a crime? One scholar's answer is that it results in underdeterrence of crimes punished by nonpecuniary sanctions because the criminals lack the resources to pay an optimal fine. The
(20) blackmailer will sell his information to the criminal for a price lower than the cost of punishment if the criminal cannot pay a higher price. A more persuasive explanation of why blackmail is a crime is that the decision to discourage blackmail follows directly from
(25) the decision to rely on a public monopoly of law enforcement in some areas of enforcement, notably criminal law. Were blackmail, a form of private enforcement, lawful, the public monopoly of enforcement would be undermined. Overenforcement of
(30) the law would result if the blackmailer were able to extract the full fine from the offender. Alternatively, the blackmailer might sell his incriminating information to the offender for a price lower than the statutory cost of punishment to the criminal, which would reduce the
(35) effective cost of punishment to the criminal below the level set by the legislature. This problem, however, could be solved by a system of public bounties equal to the cost of punishment (or lower, to induce the enforcement industry to contract to optimal size). Then
(40) the blackmailer could always claim a bounty from the state if the criminal was unable to pay a price equal to the optimal fine.

Consistent with this analysis, Axel's studies show that practices indistinguishable from blackmail, though
(45) not called by that name, are permitted in areas where the law is enforced privately rather than publicly because the overenforcement problem is not serious. No one seems to object to a person's collecting information about his or her spouse's adulterous activities, and
(50) threatening to disclose that information in a divorce proceeding or other forum, in order to extract maximum compensation for the offending spouse's breach of the marital obligations.

Blackmail and bribery appear to be virtually
(55) identical practices from the standpoint of the analysis of private enforcement. The blackmailer and the bribed official both receive payment in exchange for not enforcing the law. We therefore predict that in areas where there is a public monopoly of enforcement,
(60) bribery, like blackmail, will be prohibited, while in areas where there is no public monopoly, it will be permitted. And so we observe. The settlement out of court of negligence claims is a form of perfectly lawful bribery, although the term is not used in these situations
(65) because of its pejorative connotation.

Point and Purpose

Blackmail . . . appears to be an efficient method of private enforcement of the law. . . .

Were blackmail, a form of private enforcement, lawful, the public monopoly of enforcement would be undermined.

blackmail . . . permitted in areas where the law is enforced privately. . . .

where there is no public monopoly, it will be permitted.

Key Words and Concepts

Blackmail

cost of the punishment . . . is the same as if he had been apprehended and convicted for the crime

cost of punishment . . . set by the legislature.

Blackmail and bribery appear to be virtually identical practices . . . payment in exchange for not enforcing the law.

Authorities

One scholar's answer. . . .

Axel's studies show. . . .

Enumerations

collecting information about his or her spouse's adulterous activities, and threatening to disclose that information . . . to extract maximum compensation for the offending spouse's breach of the marital obligations.

The settlement out of court of negligence claims is a form of perfectly lawful bribery. . . .

Unusual Words and Phrases

public monopoly of law enforcement

optimal fine

a system of public bounties equal to the cost of punishment

Competing Perspectives

Why then is blackmail a crime? . . . it results in underdeterrence of crimes. . . .

A more persuasive explanation . . . is that the decision to discourage blackmail follows directly from the decision to rely on a public monopoly of law enforcement in some areas. . . .

Specific detail questions also have a direct format. They focus on enumerations, a key word or concept, or an unusual word or phrase. Specific detail questions usually require a **must** or **cannot** answer option.

2. According to the passage, which of the following sets the cost of punishment?
   (A) the blackmailer
   (B) the offenders
   (C) the legislature
   (D) the criminal
   (E) the bribed official

This a **must** question. The blackmailer may set the *tribute* to be paid, but the tribute is not the cost of punishment. Answer option A does not satisfy the statement conditions and is wrong. Nothing in the statement suggests that the offenders, criminals, or bribed officials set the cost of punishment. Besides, they are practically the same in the context of this question. For both reasons, answers B, D, and E are wrong. Option C is best, and the statement makes the point clearly in lines 35 and 36.

Meaning-in-context questions use a straightforward format. They require direct reference to the statement, but the reference is to the context and not to the specific words involved. The meaning is drawn from the context, not from the dictionary.

3. In line 37, "public bounties" refers to
   (A) a claim made to establish optimal fines for blackmailers
   (B) a way to ensure that blackmailers receive the statutory cost of punishment
   (C) a way to ensure the optimal size of the law enforcement industry
   (D) a claim paid by the state to blackmailers to induce enforcement
   (E) a way to ensure that optimal punishment is enforced by blackmailers

This a **could** question. Answer option A fails to satisfy the conditions and is wrong. It declares that optimal fines are established by claims, a concept suggested nowhere in the statement. The statement does declare that blackmailers could make claims (line 40) but also suggests that such claims would be made to collect an amount equal to the optimal fine, not to establish the fine. Option C is drawn from a parenthetical aside (lines 38 and 39) on the meaning of public bounties and is thus a wrong answer option. Option D states the purpose of public bounties to be the inducement of enforcement, a concept that is outside the scope of the statement and therefore wrong. Answer option E fails similarly. Nowhere does the statement deal with the concept of optimal punishment. This leaves B as the best answer selection.

EXTENSION QUESTIONS

Extension questions always require that you go beyond the statement to arrive at the answer. You are required to make inferences and assumptions and draw conclusions from material you find in the statement. Reference to the statement may be helpful.

Extension questions take four forms. You are asked to determine a perspective, select the context from which the statement came, identify a pattern, or assess evidence.

Perspective questions ask you directly to select the answer option that reflects the view, attitude, or purpose of the statement's author or some other person involved with the statement. They may seek either general or specific perspectives. While they may go beyond the statement, they also may connect directly to material in the statement, often bridging the area between description and extension questions.

4. Which of the following best describes the author's attitude toward bribery?
   (A) It will be permitted in divorce proceedings.
   (B) It will be encouraged when overenforcement is not a serious problem.
   (C) It will be used in order to extract maximum compensation.
   (D) It will be permitted where there is no public law enforcement monopoly.
   (E) It will be permitted where private law enforcement is not a serious problem.

This is a **could** question. Answer options A and C fail to satisfy the statement conditions, since all the references to divorce proceedings in the statement involve something akin to blackmail, not bribery, which is the focus of the question. There is nothing in the statement to suggest that the overenforcement mentioned in option B is encouraged or should be. B is a wrong answer option. Option E also fails to satisfy the statement conditions, since there is no reference in the statement to private law enforcement being a serious problem, let alone its connection to bribery being permitted. Answer D is the best option and connects to the point made in lines 61–62.

Context questions are easily understood but not so easily dealt with. They ask you to determine the source of the statement or the text that either precedes or succeeds the statement. It is very difficult to determine context from a few paragraphs, but comparing and contrasting are often helpful techniques.

5. Which of the following law review articles is the most likely source of this passage?
   (A) The Private Enforcement of Law
   (B) Public Monopoly of Law Enforcement
   (C) Comparing Bribery and Blackmail
   (D) A Critique of Out-of-Court Settlements
   (E) Bounties as a Means of Law Enforcement

This is another **could** question. Answer options C, D, and E are not likely candidates when contrasted with A and B. They deal narrowly with specific matters considered in the statement. The statement provides the context for these answer options, not vice versa as the question requires. By comparing answer options A and B to the statement, it becomes clear that the focus of the statement is on private law enforcement, of which blackmail and bribery are examples and to which the public law enforcement monopoly is antagonistic. Because the passage concentrates on private enforcement, option B does not satisfy the statement conditions and is a wrong answer. Answer A is the best option.

Pattern questions ask you to identify answer options that are structurally or logically analogous to a point or concept expressed in the statement. These questions are sometimes obscure. Use the answer options to bring clarity to the question.

6. Which of the following most closely parallels the author's example of perfectly lawful bribery in the passage (lines 63–64)?
   (A) a plea bargain made by a public prosecutor with an indicted defendant
   (B) a pardon given by a governor to a convicted felon
   (C) a fine paid by a traffic violator to a magistrate
   (D) a holiday turkey given by a vendor to a city purchasing agent
   (E) a donation given by a landowner to a senator running for reelection

This a **could** question. The perfectly lawful bribery referred to in lines 63–64 is a variation of the process described in lines 57–58: "payment in exchange for not enforcing the law." The payment described in answer option C is made as a result of the enforcement of the law, the opposite of bribery. Thus, this answer is wrong. The payments described in options B, D, and E are not made in exchange for nonenforcement of the law. They too are wrong. Answer option A is the best answer. By accepting a plea bargain ("payment in exchange") for not pursuing the indictment ("not enforcing the law"), the public prosecutor's action parallels that of accepting a settlement for not pursuing a negligence claim in court.

Evidence-assessment questions take various forms in the Passages section-test. All ask you to select the answer option that strengthens, weakens, criticizes, or distinguishes between fact and opinion in the statement. The format for evidence-assessment questions varies slightly, but it is direct.

7. Which of the following, if true, most strengthens the author's position on the legality of blackmail?
   (A) Blackmail is not a crime in all countries where law enforcement is a public monopoly.
   (B) Bribery flourishes in countries where public law enforcement is weak or nonexistent.
   (C) Blackmail of such private dispute–resolution professionals as labor arbitrators is very rare.
   (D) Bribery of such public dispute–resolution professionals as judges is very rare.
   (E) Blackmail is a crime in all countries where people can choose between private and public law enforcement.

Once again, this is a **could** question. If answer choice A were true, it would weaken the author's position, not strengthen it. It *cannot* satisfy the question and statement conditions and is wrong. Answer options C, D, and E do not satisfy the required conditions, since they refer to matters not included in the statement. Use of the contrast technique makes it clear that there is no practical difference between answer options C and D, and, consequently, each is wrong. This leaves answer option B as the best answer.

The techniques used to work through the seven examples of Passages questions are applicable to all versions of those questions. If you found yourself attracted to a wrong answer option as you worked through the questions, you might benefit from returning to that option and identifying the disguise that made it attractive. By becoming familiar with the disguises that attract you, you can avoid being misled by them in the future.

TRAINING SESSION

15

Passages Pretests and the 9-12-18 System

How do you apply the 9-12-18 system to your Passages training?

In Session 6 you learned the 9-12-18 test planning system, including its application to a Passages problem. The system uses pretests to help you identify your optimal balance between speed and accuracy. This information is then used to develop your plan for the Passages section-test. Remember that working through fewer question sets than are available on a Passages section-test usually produces more best answers than rushing through all of the questions.

✓ PRETESTS HELP YOU DETERMINE WHETHER YOU WILL MAXIMIZE YOUR SECTION–TEST SCORE BY COMPLETING FOUR, THREE, OR TWO QUESTION SETS IN THE 35 MINUTES ALLOTTED.

Passages test-taking techniques will become familiar and easy to apply as you work with them. Familiarity will give you a sense of control and reduce your anxiety about the questions. It will also improve your proficiency with the question sets. The combination of greater control and improved proficiency will result in more accurate answer selection. You will be able to identify wrong answers more efficiently and, consequently, select more of the best answers. As this happens, your balance between speed and accuracy may change, and your test plan will change accordingly.

How do you develop your Passages section-test plan?

Once again, we will go through the process of using pretest information to revise the test plan. It is the same process that has been explained previously, so, if you are comfortable with the pretest process, skim the next paragraphs.

Suppose your initial Passages pretest (in Session 6) indicated that your optimal performance would result from completing three of the four question sets on a section-test (and guessing on the fourth set). Working with the Passages training techniques you have learned, you will use the 9-12-18 process to update your performance record with the results. After you have worked through a number of pretests, your performance record may suggest making a change in your plan for optimal performance. For instance, your efficiency may have improved so that your performance record shows you will achieve a better score by completing all four sets of questions on the Passages section-test rather than by completing only three question sets and guessing on one. This calls for a change in your test plan for the section-test.

✓ CHANGE YOUR TEST PLAN ONLY WHEN INFORMATION FROM THE 9-12-18 PRETEST PROCESS INDICATES THAT A CHANGE IS DUE.

Avoid the temptation to stop working through the Passages techniques and pretests at the point where your Passages performance record indicates that completing all four question sets will yield your best score. The workthroughs maintain and enhance your familiarity and proficiency.

How do you use Passages pretests?

There are six Passages pretests at the end of this session. After you have completed working through all of the Passages techniques in Sessions 11 and 14, complete one of the pretests. Then use the results to update your performance record. Work through the Passages test-training techniques at least six times and complete at least six pretests.

After you have been through the sequence six times, your performance record should have stabilized. Your performance record can then be translated into a plan for the number of question sets you will complete and the number you will guess on the Passages section-test of the LSAT.

How do you take Passages pretests?

On Passages pretests you should begin by reading the first sentence of each paragraph in the statement. Then scan the questions, noting the types of question, key words and concepts, and any references to line numbers in the statement. Next read the statement carefully, looking for elements of the six-part pattern. Underline or highlight the point or purpose, key words or concepts, unusual words or phrases, authorities, enumerations, and competing perspectives. All other information in the statement is extraneous.

Now you are ready to work through the questions and answer options. Complete the number of questions you can comfortably address in the first 9 minutes allocated to the pretest set. Maintain your pace at the comfort level. At the end of the 9-minute period, you will have selected an answer for each of the six questions in the Passages set. Depending upon your pace, some of your answers may have been selected by guessing. *Circle* your 9-minute answer choices—this is your 9-minute set.

Next take an additional 3 minutes to reconsider the questions and the answers you selected in the 9-minute period. Vary your use of the additional time according to the work you completed during the first 9 minutes. First work through questions you did not have time to consider in the first 9 minutes. Then review questions about which you were uncertain. Place a *box* beside each of the answers you selected during this 3-minute period. If you did not change an answer, place a box beside the circled answer. If you did, place the box beside the new selection. The boxed answers are your 12-minute set. Do not erase or change the circles you placed on the question sheet during the first 9 minutes of the pretest.

The next step is to use an additional 6 minutes. Return to the set and answer questions you did not get to during the first 12 minutes, or review questions and answers, making changes as necessary. Concentrate on questions about which you are still uncertain, but avoid reworking previously selected answers about which you are confident.

Place an *asterisk* beside each of the answers you selected during this 6-minute period. If you did not change an answer, place an asterisk beside the boxed answer. If you did, place the asterisk beside your new selection. The answers identified with asterisks are your 18-minute set. Again, do not erase or change the circles or boxes you placed on the question sheet during the first 12 minutes of the pretest.

After the pretest is completed, refer to the Passages Pretest Answer Key at the back of the book. Determine the number of best answers you selected during the 9-minute (circled), 12-minute (boxed), and 18-minute (asterisked) question sets. Complete the calculations called for, and then transfer the results of these calculations onto your Pretest Performance Tracking Worksheet (page 39). Enter the number of question sets that represents your optimal balance between speed and accuracy. As you work through the pretests and develop your performance record, the pattern of your greatest efficiency will emerge. This pattern will indicate the number of Passages question sets you plan to complete—the number that will yield the highest score for you.

Circles	_____ x 5 + 0 =	_____
Boxes	_____ x 4 + 1 =	_____
Asterisks	_____ x 3 + 2 =	_____

Largest total _____ indicates the optimal number (2, 3, or 4) of question sets you will enter on your Performance Tracking Worksheet.

For the pretest process to work effectively, you should complete a pretest only after you have reviewed the Passages test-training techniques in Sessions 11 and 14. Do this before each pretest. This should take you about 30 minutes. The familiarity and proficiency you will gain through this process will produce the greatest impact on your performance and your test score. Going through a series of pretests or question sets without first working through the training techniques will have little, if any, impact on your performance. And your objective, as you know, is high impact.

After the seven pretests have been completed (one in Session 6 and six in this session), your performance record should be sufficiently comprehensive to provide you with stable information. You will develop your test plan for the Passages section-test on the basis of this performance record. You will plan to complete two, three, or four question sets, depending on the optimal balance between your speed and accuracy. Then your challenge is having the self-discipline to stick to your plan during the actual LSAT.

✓ FOLLOW YOUR PLAN TO MAXIMIZE YOUR TEST PERFORMANCE AND SCORE.

How many pretests should you complete?

Once the high-impact gain you wanted before taking the LSAT is realized, further workthroughs and pretests will have much less, if any, impact on your score. But it is important to maintain familiarity and proficiency with Passages, and practice with pretests meets this objective for many prospective test-takers. Others maintain their efficiency by regular workthroughs of Sessions 11 and 14.

If you want to work with additional Passages question sets, there are three good sources. The first is this guide—if you choose, you can use the simulated test included here as a source of four additional question sets. Law School Admission Services sells disclosed tests, and there are a number of preparation books containing little more than simulated tests. (If you use these, be sure the problems are constructed to the same specifications as the real LSAT questions.)

When practicing with test materials, first convert them into question sets. This is exactly the same process you will use when taking the LSAT. You identify a question set, viewing it as *the test* until you have completed it, and then move on to the next set or test. By dividing the section-test into its four component sets, you gain maximum control, which puts you in the best position to execute your test plan.

What are the directions for completing the pretests?

For each of the following Passages question sets, select the best answer option to the question on the basis of what is stated or implied in the statement.

PASSAGES PRETEST 15-1

Without doubt, the role of firearms in American violence is much greater today than a decade ago. Rates of gun violence and the proportion of violent acts that are committed with guns have increased substantially even
(5) after the Gun Control Act went into effect. Behind these increases lies the probability that handgun ownership has become at least a subcultural institution in the big cities which are the main arena of American violence. During this period, regional differences in gun ownership and use
(10) have been moderated as the large northeastern cities that were traditionally areas of low ownership and use have experienced large increases in handgun use.

The special role of the handgun in urban violence is one of the more obvious lessons of the data that are
(15) reported. Over the past ten years, rates of handgun homicide have increased more than three times as much as homicides by all other means. The data reported suggest, but do not compel, other conclusions about patterns of handgun ownership and violence in the United
(20) States. First, the sharp rise in the proportion of violence attributable to handguns in northeastern cities may lead to modification of the hypothesis that general patterns of handgun ownership determine the extent to which handguns are used in violent episodes. While it is still
(25) true that those regions with the highest general levels of gun ownership have the highest proportion of gun use in violence, the past decade has produced an increase in handgun use in the Northeast that leaves cities in that region closer to but still below the average handgun share
(30) of violence. This could be due to a substantial rise in handgun ownership in the general population in these cities, but that would mean that a vast northeastern urban handgun arsenal has been accumulating during the past ten years. It is more likely that handgun ownership
(35) increased substantially among subcultural groups disproportionately associated with violence without necessarily affecting other parts of the population.

If one adopts a "subcultural" explanation of the relationship between gun ownership and violence,
(40) hypotheses about the effect of increases or decreases in handgun ownership on handgun violence should take a slightly more complicated form. One would predict that high levels of handgun ownership produce high levels of handgun violence for two reasons: more handguns are
(45) available at a moment of perceived need, and high ownership rates necessarily suggest high levels of handgun availability to all potential consumers. Low general levels of handgun ownership, on the other hand, become the necessary but not sufficient condition of low
(50) levels of handgun violence. If the lower-than-average general ownership levels are still high enough to create relatively easy handgun availability, and if both handgun ownership and propensity for violence are concentrated in discrete subpopulations, lower-than-average general
(55) ownership is an inadequate insurance policy against increases in handgun violence. It is only when ownership levels are low enough to have an impact on handgun availability that low aggregate ownership will depress handgun involvement in rates of subcultural violence.
(60) Efforts to limit handgun supply on a national basis, by limiting legitimate production, or imports, or both, will not require a large federal street police force. At the point when market controls make illicit gun production profitable, some police work will obviously be needed,
(65) along the lines of controls on illicit liquor production

1. The primary purpose of the passage is to
   (A) criticize the Gun Control Act
   (B) describe the role of the handgun in urban violence
   (C) advocate limiting handgun availability
   (D) explain the growth of handgun violence
   (E) point out the increase in the urban handgun arsenal

2. If true, the "subcultural" explanation of gun ownership and violence means that
   (A) all parts of the population own more guns
   (B) general patterns of gun ownership determine their use in violent episodes
   (C) higher levels of gun ownership produce higher levels of violence
   (D) gun ownership by people associated with violence has greatly increased
   (E) guns are now primarily owned by the violent elements of urban society

3. The author refers to the Gun Control Act to
   (A) dramatize the increase in gun-related violence
   (B) criticize the government for gun-related violence
   (C) point out the statute's total ineffectiveness
   (D) minimize the importance of gun control legislation
   (E) argue for more enforcement of the statute

4. Which of the following, if true, would most weaken the author's argument concerning handgun ownership in northeastern cities?
   (A) Handgun ownership among Boston drug dealers has increased 300 percent in the last ten years.
   (B) Handgun ownership among organized crime figures in New Jersey has increased dramatically in the last ten years.
   (C) Handgun ownership among convicted criminals has increased in the last ten years.
   (D) Handgun ownership among middle-class New Yorkers has increased fourfold in the last ten years.
   (E) Handgun ownership among middle-class Philadelphians has increased slightly in the last ten years.

5. Which of the following may be inferred from the passage?
   (A) The rate of growth in gun ownership in the Northeast is greater than that of other regions.
   (B) Gun ownership is greater in the Northeast than in other regions.
   (C) There is little data available concerning the growth of gun ownership in urban areas.
   (D) High levels of handgun ownership do not necessarily result in increased violence.
   (E) High levels of handgun ownership in urban areas do not necessarily result in increased violence.

6. The passage suggests which of the following?
   (A) High levels of handgun ownership are not related to perceived needs among consumers.
   (B) More violent acts are committed by means other than handguns.
   (C) Urban violence is due to subcultural differences among residents.
   (D) The number of homicides not involving handguns has increased in the past ten years.
   (E) Lower-than-average handgun ownership will result in lower violence.

7. The author would be likely to agree that which of the following would reduce handgun violence?
   I. regulating import of handguns
   II. regulating production of handguns
   III. regulating possession of handguns
   (A) I only
   (B) II only
   (C) I and II only
   (D) I and III only
   (E) I, II, and III

PASSAGES PRETEST 15-2

Software is like hardware in that it causes machines to perform tasks. Software is merely a replacement for hardware components that could otherwise perform the same function. Software is often embedded in hardware
(5) and part of an overall hardware system. Like hardware, software can often serve as a tool for creating other items. Like hardware, software needs maintenance work from time to time to operate properly.

Software is unlike hardware, however, in a great many
(10) ways. Software, is, for example, easy and cheap to replicate as compared with hardware. Once the first copy has been produced, software can be almost endlessly replicated at almost no cost, regardless of how complex it is. One of the consequences of this characteristic is that
(15) the government tends to think that additional copies of software ought to be deliverable at a very low cost, whereas industry, which is concerned about recouping its research and development costs, and which tends to regard the sale of software as the sale of a production
(20) facility (as if one bought a General Motors factory when one bought a truck produced by GM), thinks that sales at higher price levels are necessary to make the software business viable. A second consequence of low-cost replicability is that the software industry, for the most
(25) part, tends to make its products available only on a highly restrictive licensing basis rather than selling copies outright.

Another important difference between software and hardware is that software may be wholly subject to a very
(30) lengthy lawful monopoly (i.e., a copyright) as well as being held as a trade secret, whereas hardware may be subject to a much shorter monopoly (i.e., a patent) and most often cannot be held as a trade secret. Moreover, quite often hardware is either not patented at all or only
(35) subject to partial patent protection. A high standard of inventiveness is required for patent, while copyright requires only the most minimal originality. Hardware, unlike software, cannot be copyrighted at all. As a result, it tends to be much harder to get competition for software
(40) procurements and maintenance than for hardware, which means that it is even easier for the government to find itself in a sole source position as to software rather than hardware. Moreover, because software engineering is still in the early stages of development, it is generally more
(45) difficult to specify how software, as opposed to hardware, should be developed for particular functions and to estimate the cost and development schedule for it.

Software, which consists of a stream of electrical impulses, is also virtually "invisible" as compared with
(50) hardware, which means that it is more difficult to detect if someone delivers very similar or nearly identical software on a second development contract. Again, because software engineering is a developing art, software is likely to contain many undetected defects that will need to be
(55) corrected while in the user's possession.

Unlike hardware, software is readily changeable; that is, new capabilities can be added to software without additional plant or material costs. Often, all that is required is some intellectual labor. All of these factors
(60) tend to make software maintenance and enhancement a much bigger part of computer system life-cycle planning than is the case with hardware.

1. The passage is primarily concerned with
   (A) correcting misimpressions about hardware and software
   (B) explaining the nature of software
   (C) Minimizing apparent difficulties with software
   (D) comparing hardware and software
   (E) describing computer system life-cycle planning

2. According to the passage, which of the following is true?
   I. Hardware and software can perform the same functions.
   II. Software can be located within hardware.
   III. Software can make hardware cheaper.

   (A) I only
   (B) II only
   (C) I and II only
   (D) I and III only
   (E) II and III only

3. According to the passage, all of the following are true EXCEPT
   (A) the cost of duplicating software is low
   (B) very little software is sold outright
   (C) hardware is often not patented
   (D) software requires minimum originality
   (E) hardware is readily changeable

4. According to the passage, which of the following characteristics does NOT apply to both hardware and software?
   (A) It can be held as a trade secret.
   (B) It can be copyrighted.
   (C) It can create other items.
   (D) It can be subject to a monopoly.
   (E) It can be maintained.

5. Which of the following can be inferred from the passage?
   (A) Hardware is more expensive than software.
   (B) It is more profitable to sell copies of software than hardware.
   (C) Software maintenance is a relatively competitive business.
   (D) Procurement of hardware is not a competitive business.
   (E) Software is licensed because it is too expensive to buy.

6. Which of the following can be inferred from the passage?
   (A) Ownership rights in software can be better protected than those in hardware.
   (B) Copyrighted software requires greater inventiveness than does hardware.
   (C) Ownership rights in hardware can be better protected those those in software.
   (D) Patented hardware requires greater inventiveness than does software.
   (E) Patented hardware is difficult to specify for particular functions.

7. The argument that one purchases the factory when one purchases a truck made at the factory (line 20) is most like which of the following?
   (A) One purchases the typewriter on which the manuscript was prepared when one purchases the book.
   (B) One purchases the cruise when one purchases the cruise ship.
   (C) One purchases the restaurant when one purchases the dinner prepared there.
   (D) One purchases the office building when one leases the office located in the building.
   (E) One purchases the health club when one purchases membership to use the club facilities.

PASSAGES PRETEST 15-3

We customarily identify the concept of status with its conventional indices, such as wealth, title, and occupation. But there is nothing sacred about these indices; they are merely the most convenient and concrete
(5) manifestations in everyday life of different social positions. If all members of society routinely tested their strength in court several times each year, instead of once or twice in a lifetime, we would immediately recognize court performance as a direct measure of social position,
(10) perhaps even more revealing of the pecking order than conventional indices.

Of course in no society, not even a litigious one like premodern New Haven, does the court play so vital a role as this in the life of the community. Nevertheless, if other
(15) societies show the same positive correlation between status and court performance found in New Haven, we will be compelled to admit that individual court appearances—infrequent though they are—are revelatory of group status when treated collectively. Of course one
(20) cannot assume on the basis of this one study of a single society that court performance is always and everywhere a reliable index of status. Only a considerable accumulation of confirmatory studies of other communities and courts could justify the use of the voluntary appearance ratio as
(25) an independent measure of status. But if, as in the case of New Haven, it can be shown for a given community that court performance is strongly correlated with the more conventional indices of status over a long period of time, then it seems reasonable to treat court performance itself
(30) as an index of status in that community. Doing so may be extremely advantageous because, unlike most indices of status, court performance can be reconstructed on a year-to-year basis.

If court performance can be shown to reflect the
(35) static distribution of power and advantage in the community—as has been done for New Haven—then by tracing court performance through time, on a year-to-year basis, it should be possible to reveal shifts of power and advantage as they take place. Court records exploited in
(40) this manner might serve as a weather vane of social change. The gentry controversy in English history stands as the classic illustration of the difficulty of reconstructing an account through time of the relative position of two classes, using only economic and demographic data. Of
(45) all the kinds of data relating to group status, none is more likely to be recorded and be preserved in as complete a form as court records. A continuous year-by-year account of group status would be virtually impossible to reconstruct from surviving economic data, but such an
(50) account may be feasible for societies with complete court records. Such a methodological tool should be useful to any historian who wants to test hypotheses postulating the rise or fall of a class or other large group.

1. The author views court records primarily as
    (A) surviving other available records about society
    (B) a source of more reliable data about society
    (C) reflecting distribution of power in society
    (D) a means of tracing changes in group status in society
    (E) reporting on tests of strength within a society

2. The term "positive correlation" in line 15 refers to which of the following?
    (A) the relationship between individual and group status
    (B) the relationship between group status and frequency of court appearance
    (C) the relationship between individual court appearance and social position
    (D) the relationship between the pecking order and group status in the community
    (E) the relationship between power shifts and frequency of court appearance

3. The passage suggests that which of the following is an indication of individual social status?
    I. wealth
    II. court performance
    III. occupation
    (A) I only
    (B) II only
    (C) I and II only
    (D) I and III only
    (E) I, II, and III

4. Which of the following, if true, would most weaken the author's thesis?
    (A) There is an inverse relationship between wealth and court appearances.
    (B) There is a negative relationship between age and court appearances.
    (C) There is a random relationship between occupation and court appearances.
    (D) There is a positive relationship between title and court appearances.
    (E) There is a direct relationship between land ownership and court appearances.

5. If true, which of the following would best support the author's thesis?
    (A) There is little correlation between the New Haven findings and those of other towns.
    (B) There is a positive correlation between the New Haven findings and those of other towns.
    (C) There is a positive correlation between wealth and court appearances in New Haven and those of other towns.
    (D) There is little correlation between occupations and court appearances in New Haven and those of other towns.
    (E) There is a direct relationship between land ownership in New Haven and that in ten surrounding towns.

6. Which of the following is most likely to be the author of the passage?

   (A) a sociologist
   (B) a genealogist
   (C) a heraldrist
   (D) an anthropologist
   (E) a legal historian

7. The passage suggests that all of the following would be advantages of using court records and performance as a means of determining social status EXCEPT

   (A) court records can be reconstructed over long periods of time
   (B) court appearances change with status within the society
   (C) court records are generally preserved in most jurisdictions
   (D) court appearances can be treated collectively to reveal status
   (E) court procedures remain the same over long periods of time

PASSAGES PRETEST 15-4

Much advertising is patently uninformative; rational consumers should not care what sort of breakfast cereal is eaten by famous baseball players. Nonetheless, advertisers spend large sums of money on these sorts of
(5) messages as well as on many others of equal value as information. Rational consumers should not be influenced by such messages, and rational advertisers should not spend money on messages without influence.

There are two types of goods: search goods and
(10) experience goods. A search good is one whose salient characteristics can be ascertained by pre-sale inspection (e.g., the comfort of a pair of shoes); experience goods are those which must be consumed to be evaluated (e.g., the taste of a candy bar). The role of advertising differs
(15) depending on which type of good is involved. In the case of search goods, where consumers can and will easily determine for themselves whether the goods are what they want, advertisers have little incentive to misrepresent the quality of their goods. Thus, advertisers simply urge the
(20) consumer to make the inspection, and their message should be largely informative and truthful. In the case of the experience good, the consumer can determine quality only by purchasing and using the good. The function of advertising, therefore, is to get the consumer to try the
(25) product. Here, advertisers might have an incentive to mislead and make false claims.

With respect to advertising, then, the characteristics of goods and services form a continuum, from those in which it is very easy to detect the truth or falsity of
(30) advertising claims (search goods: the truth of the claim can be ascertained before purchase) through experience goods (where the truth of the claim can be detected only after purchase and use) through credence goods (where the validity of advertisements may never be determined).
(35) As we move along this continuum from search to credence characteristics, misrepresentation becomes relatively more profitable, since detection by consumers becomes more expensive. Nonetheless, it is in the case of credence characteristics that self-protection becomes most
(40) difficult and in which some legal remedy would seem most important.

For any one purchase where credence qualities are involved, consumers cannot be sure that they are getting a desirable good; i.e., there is a low probability of finding
(45) out whether claims about any one good are true or false. However, if the consumer buys many goods from the same source, the probability of ascertaining that claims about one of those goods are false would be increased. In this situation, claims about individual goods have
(50) credence characteristics; but the reputation of the seller of all the goods is an experience characteristic. It may be that consumer trust in the reputation of the intermediary is misplaced in the situation of mail-order advertisements carried by magazines. Although the consumer may rely on
(55) the publisher of the magazine to police its advertisers, Consumers Union claims that in fact such policing is minimal or nonexistent.

1. Which of the following best states the primary objective of the passage?
   (A) to point out that advertising reliability varies by type of good
   (B) to contrast advertising purposes for three types of goods
   (C) to differentiate between advertising for two types of goods
   (D) to discuss the role of advertising as information
   (E) to question the trustworthiness of magazine mail-order advertising

2. According to the passage, the consumer can determine the quality of experience goods by which of the following?
   I. advertising
   II. inspection
   III. consumption
   (A) I only
   (B) II only
   (C) III only
   (D) I and III only
   (E) II and III only

3. According to the passage, each of the following is true EXCEPT
   (A) search goods advertising is likely to be informative and truthful
   (B) mail-order advertising in magazines is not likely to be truthful
   (C) experience goods advertisers have incentive to mislead
   (D) credence goods advertisements may never be determined to be valid
   (E) advertisers spend large sums of money on informative messages

4. Which of the following articles is the most likely source of the passage?
   (A) The Economics of Advertising
   (B) The Law of False Advertising
   (C) Advertising by Type of Good
   (D) Analysis of the Function of Advertising
   (E) Advertising and the Quality of Goods

5. It can be inferred from the passage that which of the following are credence goods?
   I. auto transmission oil
   II. vitamin pills
   III. plant fertilizer
   (A) I only
   (B) II only
   (C) III only
   (D) I and II only
   (E) I, II, and III

6. Which of the following best describes the author's attitude toward advertising?
   (A) Many advertisers and consumers do not act rationally.
   (B) Many advertisers spend too much money on ads.
   (C) Many consumers are influenced by advertising.
   (D) Many advertisers are not interested in informing consumers.
   (E) Many consumers use advertising to determine the quality of goods.

7. The author implies which of the following in the passage?
   (A) Search goods consumers are easily misled by advertising.
   (B) Experience goods consumers purchase by mail order.
   (C) Credence goods consumers require statutory protection.
   (D) Experience goods consumers ascertain value by inspection.
   (E) Credence goods consumers depend on seller credibility.

PASSAGES PRETEST 15-5

It is not easy to describe the present position of legal opinion on advertising and free speech. Only a poet can capture the essence of chaos. Nor is it easy to foresee how things will develop. Lacking any rationale for the First
(5) Amendment, with the courts depending on time-honored slogans to sustain conclusions, there is no obvious resting-place, from the moment the slogans cease to work their magic. At the present time, the courts are tending to bring a greater proportion of advertising within the
(10) protection of the First Amendment. And cases now proceeding through the courts, such as the litigation concerning what egg producers can say about heart disease and cholesterol or what can be said about margarine in advertisements, will undoubtedly continue
(15) the process. Where will it end?
Some legal writers have sought to treat First Amendment rights as being, in some sense, absolute and have objected to what is termed the "balancing" by the courts of these rights against others. But such "balancing"
(20) is inevitable if judges must direct their attention to the general welfare. Freedom to speak and write is bound to be restricted when exercise of these freedoms prevents the carrying out of other activities that people value. Thus it is reasonable that First Amendment freedoms should be
(25) curtailed when they impair the enjoyment of life (privacy), inflict great damage on others (slander and libel), are disturbing (loudness), destroy incentives to carry out useful work (copyright), create dangers for society (sedition and national security), or are offensive
(30) and corrupting (obscenity). The determination of the boundaries to which a doctrine can be applied is not likely to come about in a very conscious or even consistent way. But it is through recognition of the fact that rights should be assigned to those to whom they are most valuable that
(35) such boundaries come to be set. It is only in recent years that there has been any serious consideration of the relation of advertising to freedom of speech and of writing. Now that the value of advertising in providing information has been accepted, it seems improbable that it
(40) will long be thought that this is true only for price advertising. And the action of the Federal Trade Commission in treating prohibitions by professional associations of advertising by their members as anticompetitive will bring greater awareness of the
(45) informational role of advertising. Similarly, the many studies of the failures of government regulatory agencies that have been made in recent years are bound to make the courts somewhat reluctant to expand and more willing to take advantage of opportunities to contract the regulation
(50) of advertising. Where will it end? It seems likely that the law will be interpreted to allow the Federal Trade Commission to continue to regulate false and deceptive advertising, but with greater freedom for what can be said in advertising than now exists, and with somewhat
(55) diminished powers for the various government agencies that regulate advertising.

1. Which of the following best describes the point of the passage?
   (A) The First Amendment is primarily an assemblage of slogans.
   (B) All advertising is protected by the right of free speech.
   (C) Courts must balance the right of free speech with others.
   (D) Advertising regulation has been a failure of the government.
   (E) More advertising will be protected by the First Amendment.

2. According to the passage, which of the following may be limited by restrictions on the freedom of speech?
   I. advertising claims
   II. obscene films
   III. amplified music in a public park
   (A) I only
   (B) II only
   (C) III only
   (D) I and II only
   (E) I, II, and III

3. According to the passage, which of the following is true?
   (A) The Federal Trade Commission is losing its power to regulate false advertising.
   (B) Price advertising is protected by the First Amendment.
   (C) The First Amendment right of freedom to speak and write is absolute.
   (D) Rationales for First Amendment rights are time-honored.
   (E) Boundaries on First Amendment freedoms are consciously determined by the courts.

4. The author refers to "chaos" in line 3 to indicate which of the following?
   (A) that the passage is written by a poet
   (B) that the state of the law of free speech is disorganized
   (C) that advertising and free speech are intermingled
   (D) that it is difficult to describe the confusion in the law related to advertising and free speech
   (E) that the essence of free speech applies to advertising

5. The passage suggests all of the following EXCEPT
   (A) government regulation of advertising is losing power
   (B) advertising is procompetitive
   (C) government regulation of advertising will continue
   (D) advertising is protected by the First Amendment
   (E) government regulation of advertising is anticompetitive

6. According to the passage, limitations on free speech are permitted in order to protect
   I. the general welfare
   II. individual damages
   III. the national government
   (A) I only
   (B) II only
   (C) III only
   (D) I and II only
   (E) I, II, and III

7. According to the passage, all of the following are factors in the changing relationship of advertising to freedom of speech EXCEPT
   (A) failures of government agencies
   (B) providing information to the public
   (C) balancing of various rights
   (D) assigning rights to those for whom they are most valuable
   (E) the absolute nature of the freedom of speech

PASSAGES PRETEST 15-6

There is a certain elemental appeal to the policy. People generally tend to think that if they pay money to have something made for them, they "own" it and should be able to do with it as they please. Government people
(5) frequently express this kind of sentiment toward the spending of government money and seem not to understand why private firms might object to the policy. They perceive the government policy to be fair, and any private firm that doesn't agree is, to put it bluntly, being
(10) greedy. The private firms, of course, tend to think that the government is trying to get something for nothing. The truth is that when it comes to their rights as against those of their employees, private firms very well understand this principle of getting all the rights and benefits when one
(15) pays for something. Within a firm, ownership of intellectual property and the profits resulting from the value of the intellectual property do not belong to the creative employee but to the shareholders of the firm.

Yet government people do understand—even if they
(20) don't much like it—that private firms seem to lack incentives to develop and deliver their best products to the government when the firms have no reasonable expectation of receiving a continuing stream of income from the product, so that, as a result, the government isn't
(25) getting a lot of the best technology.

Some government people might think, "But, hey, a private firm has incentive to deliver the best technology to us (even though we have unlimited rights) because it's OK with us if they take the thing to the commercial
(30) market." There are a couple of problems with this theory. One is that, since the government claims an unlimited right to disclose the technology developed at public expense to anyone for any purpose, the government has the power at any time to pull the rug out from under the
(35) commercial market (for in today's market, it is the valuable secrets embodied in the technology that seem to determine its commercial value). Secondly, the government tends to want to "give away" valuable technology in which it has unlimited rights to other
(40) private firms whom the technology's developer may see as its primary commercial market. Both of these can undermine the potential incentives that government people tend to think the private firm has retained.

It is worth pointing out that Congress has enacted a
(45) law to encourage small firms to develop and deliver to the government the highest quality, most innovative products, namely the Small Business Innovation Development Act. This law gives participating small firms the right to retain ownership rights in patents developed at public expense,
(50) with a license back to the government to use the patent for governmental purpose. In trying to decide whether to retain its broad unlimited rights policy, the government should think about whether it really needs "unlimited rights" in technology. It should ask itself why it needs
(55) more than government purpose rights. It also should understand that one of the costs of the unlimited rights policy is that the government is likely to get delivery of less-than-high-quality products.

1. The primary purpose of the passage is to
   (A) advocate an expansion of the Small Business Innovation Development Act
   (B) explain the inability of the government to secure the best available technology
   (C) propose a method to ensure business a continuing stream of income from technological products
   (D) contrast the perspectives of government and industry people concerning technology
   (E) encourage the government to surrender its unlimited rights policy as to technology

2. The passage uses the term "greedy" in line 10 to
   (A) indicate the attitude of government workers toward private firms that sell technology to the government
   (B) describe the attitude of private firms toward government procurement policy
   (C) highlight the conflict between private and government views of technology purchased by the public
   (D) contrast the sentiment of government people with that of private firms
   (E) express the author's view of government policy toward technology acquisition

3. "Governmental purpose" in line 51 describes which of the following?
   (A) a restriction on the governmental use of technology
   (B) an enlightened policy for private-firm technology development
   (C) a license for the governmental use of technology
   (D) the retention of ownership of technology by private firms
   (E) a law to encourage the development of technology by private firms

4. Which of the following may be inferred from the passage?
   (A) Private firms dislike dealing with the government.
   (B) The government could get better technology that it does.
   (C) The commercial value of technology is difficult to exploit.
   (D) Intellectual property is owned by those who create it.
   (E) People do not own property that they have paid for.

5. The author's attitude toward the "unlimited rights" policy of the federal government is best described as
   (A) approving
   (B) understanding
   (C) questioning
   (D) hostile
   (E) neutral

6. Which of the following, if true, would most strengthen the author's argument?
   (A) Technology is a small part of government acquisitions.
   (B) The government acquires its most advanced technology on the open market.
   (C) There is limited competition among technology companies.
   (D) Less that 1 percent of government technology acquisitions are provided by small firms.
   (E) Private firms seldom exploit the technology they develop for the government.

7. The government policy concerning the ownership of technology acquired from private firms is the same as
   (A) that of private firms toward their creative employees
   (B) that of shareholders toward the government
   (C) that of employees toward their employers
   (D) that of government employees toward private firms
   (E) that of private firms toward government employees

TRAINING SESSION 16

The Writing Sample

There is one Writing Sample on the LSAT. It may be administered before the multiple-choice section-tests or after. It is important to understand the various objectives and uses of the Writing Sample, as well as the mechanics of completing it successfully.

What are the test-maker's objectives for the Writing Sample?

The test-maker declares four objectives for the Writing Sample. The first is to elicit a clear expression of your position on the assigned topic. The second is to determine the care with which you support your position. The third is to secure information about your skills in organization, vocabulary, and grammar. The last is to determine how well you write.

This is a heavy burden for a 30-minute Writing Sample to bear, especially since test-takers have no information about the topic in advance. As a practical matter, a 30-minute Writing Sample cannot achieve the formidable objectives set for it. But this does not mean that these objectives can be ignored. A realistic plan for the Writing Sample must take the objectives into account.

How do law schools use your Writing Sample?

A photocopy of your Writing Sample accompanies each report of your LSAT score. Law schools use this in various ways. The vast majority of them file the Writing Sample and make no other use of it. Some use a deficient Writing Sample to disqualify applicants. A few use it to identify students who might benefit from writing instruction in the law school context. Infrequently the Writing Sample is used to differentiate between applicants who present otherwise indistinguishable admission credentials.

✓ THERE IS NO EVIDENCE THAT LAW SCHOOLS USE THE WRITING SAMPLE TO IDENTIFY APPLICANTS WITH GREAT POTENTIAL AS LAW STUDENTS OR LEGAL WRITERS.

What are your objectives for the Writing Sample?

Both the nature and use of the Writing Sample dictate your single objective: to ensure that it cannot be used to disqualify you for admission.

Given its limitations, the Writing Sample certainly gives you no opportunity to impress anyone with your writing skill. What it does give you is the opportunity to demonstrate one or more failings, such as illegible handwriting, not addressing the assigned topic, not following directions, not producing a cogent sample, and using inappropriate vocabulary or grammar.

✓ A GOOD PLAN IS CRUCIAL TO PRODUCING A WRITING SAMPLE THAT WILL NOT DISQUALIFY YOUR LAW SCHOOL APPLICATION.

You will develop a plan for reaching your objective that takes into account organization, vocabulary, and the mechanical aspects of writing. It will include the preparation of an outline on scratch paper provided at the test center exclusively for use on the Writing Sample.

What is your task on the Writing Sample?

As with other aspects of the LSAT, the Writing Sample is not what it seems. As we have seen, it cannot meet fully the objectives set for it, nor does it meet the expectations raised by your academic conditioning. The Writing Sample is no term paper or exam essay. It does not require journalistic or creative writing. The type of writing required resembles the completion of forms more than anything else.

✓ THE REAL TASK IS TO GIVE A ONE–SENTENCE RESPONSE TO EACH OF THE DEMANDS OF THE WRITING SAMPLE.

It is most important that you avoid the temptation to extemporize or be inventive. This can best be ensured by sticking to the directions.

What are the elements of the Writing Sample?

THE DIRECTIONS

The Writing Sample directions tell you that how well you write is more important than how much you write. Law schools are mainly interested in how clearly you express the position you take on the topic, how carefully you support that position, and your organization, vocabulary, and writing mechanics.

You are told to write on the assigned topic only. Under no circumstances should you write on a topic of your choosing. Why prepare a writing sample in advance on your own topic when you can use the test-maker's topic and satisfy the expectations exactly? No special knowledge about the topic is expected or required, but you *are* expected to write on the topic assigned.

You are also advised that there is no right or wrong answer to the topic. The test-maker does not evaluate the position you take, nor are the law schools provided with model answers or model Writing Samples. As with all LSAT questions, the test-maker uses the Writing Sample topic to elicit a response. There is no interest in your knowledge of the topic.

Time is short. You are told that you have 30 minutes to plan, organize, and write your sample. This places a premium on your plan for completing the Writing Sample. Remember coloring books and being told to color inside the lines? The Writing Sample is like that: only the writing on the lined area in the booklet is reproduced and sent to the law schools. The space provided is more than enough to accommodate your sample, provided you follow your plan. Just be sure that you limit your writing to a reasonable size that fits easily between the lines. Use the black pen provided by the test-maker so that your Writing Sample will reproduce clearly.

Legible handwriting is an imperative. If your writing is not entirely legible, print. If your printing is not entirely legible, draw.

✓ AVOID PRODUCING A WRITING SAMPLE THAT IS HARD TO READ.

If you need to be convinced, imagine a law professor on the admission committee who is faced with a choice between reading your illegible exam papers for three or four years or your competitor's perfectly legible ones.

The directions provide you with an advantage. You are told exactly how to produce your Writing Sample. Follow the directions, and you will satisfy the test-maker's expectations and complete a Writing Sample that cannot be used to disqualify your law school application.

THE TOPIC

All Writing Sample topics have a similar, predictable layout. They are made up of three components—**positions**, **conditions**, and **evidence**. In the following example, the components are spelled out. These headings do not appear on the LSAT, but the components are obvious and cannot be confused.

There are two positions and two conditions in each topic. The positions are stated first, the conditions follow, and then comes the evidence.

POSITIONS

As a trustee of Whistler College, you will soon vote on how a recent donation of $1-million will be used. Write an argument in support of applying the donation to the development of either the Art Department or the Economics Department. Two considerations guide your decision:

CONDITIONS
- Enrollments at Whistler have been decreasing in the last few years.
- Disharmony between faculty and students has been increasing in the last few years.

EVIDENCE

For years, the Art Department has had an inadequate staff and limited course offerings, and what has been offered has not been of good quality. This gift would enable the college to hire four excellent people, including an artist-in-residence. One or two could round out the course offerings in art history, and others could do something about the lack of courses in studio art. That should change the department's image. It should also attract some new art majors or at least keep students from leaving. Quite a few potential art majors have been lost in recent years because of the poor quality of the department. The best that could be expected from the improvement is a decent Art Department.

In contrast, the money could make the already strong Economics Department more than excellent. Its expansion would result in its being the best in Whistler's part of the country. But such an expansion presents some risk. The Economics Department is already causing problems. The economists think one way politically; the majority of the student body thinks another way. Healthy disagreement in an academic setting is acceptable, but out-and-out rebellion is very problematic. Whistler is a small, tightly knit community, and it is important that harmony be maintained.

✓ PREPARATION OF THE WRITING SAMPLE OUTLINE IS COMPLETED IN 5 TO 7 MINUTES.

How do you develop your Writing Sample outline?

Even before you read the topic, you should take the first step in your Writing Sample plan. Write down the following outline on the scratch paper provided.

I. Positions
II. Condition 1
   A. Evidence item 1
   B. Evidence item 2
III. Condition 2
   A. Evidence item 3
   B. Evidence item 4
IV. Summary

As you read the Writing Sample topic, extract the information called for by the outline and place it in the appropriate place in the outline format. All of the information you need is provided in the topic. The outline uses the information and organization of the topic to establish the structure of the Writing Sample. An example based on the preceding topic follows.

> I. Positions
>   Trustee
>   Vote to use million for Art Dept.

Under the positions heading, two points are noted. The first is the position or perspective from which you will write. In this instance, the topic is to be viewed from the perspective of a college trustee. The test-maker will always indicate this perspective. It is there for you to use.

The second point is the position that you will advocate. It makes no difference which position you choose, as long as you choose. Any ambivalence, however, *will* make a difference—it wastes time and introduces confusion. To avoid ambivalence, select the position you will advocate *before* you go to the test center to take the LSAT. In fact, *decide right now!* Determine whether you will always advocate position one or position two for any Writing Sample topic. Then, be disciplined enough to consistently advocate the position you selected.

> II. Condition 1
>   Decreasing enrollment over years
>   A. Evidence item 1
>   Poor quality of Art Dept. overcome by:
>   studio art program addition
>   art history curriculum expansion
>   B. Evidence item 2
>   Strong Economics Dept. will get all students it normally would without getting donation

Decreasing enrollments is the first condition to be addressed. The first item of evidence is drawn directly from the topic as presented; the second is not drawn directly from the topic but is consistent with it.

> III. Condition 2
>   Disharmony between faculty and students over years
>   A. Evidence item 3
>   Add four art faculty members with views compatible with students' views
>   B. Evidence item 4
>   Using donation to expand economics faculty will exacerbate existing disharmony, because faculty members will choose more like themselves

Faculty-student disharmony is the second condition to be addressed. Evidence item 3 is drawn directly from the topic, while item 4 is an extension of material given in the topic.

> IV. Summary
>   Using donations for Art Dept. will increase enrollment and improve faculty-student harmony

The summary statement reiterates how the conditions will be answered by the position selected.

How do you produce your Writing Sample?

You will organize your Writing Sample in much the same way that a lawyer makes a jury presentation. Advocate the position you selected, writing positively and confidently in support of it. Avoid weighing the pros and cons of the competing positions, and steer clear of improvisations, inspirations, and uncertainties.

✓   SPEND ABOUT 15 MINUTES COMPLETING YOUR WRITING SAMPLE.

The necessary steps can be summarized as follows:

1. State your position and what you will *prove*.
2. Select and support your position with available *proof*.
3. Summarize what you have *proved*.

Based upon the outline, your Writing Sample should be structured into four paragraphs. In paragraph one, you use one sentence to state your position and a second sentence to state what you will establish.

> As a trustee, I will vote to use the million-dollar donation for the development of the Art Department at Whistler College. Using the donation to expand the art faculty and hire an artist-in-residence will result in an increase in enrollment at the college and a reduction in the disharmony between faculty and students.

In paragraph two, use one or two sentences to present an item of evidence that meets the first condition, using the topic material. Then use a second sentence or two to support the position you chose or oppose the position you did not choose. If you opt for the latter, be sure to explain the position you oppose.

Responding to the first condition by supporting your position with two items of evidence is sufficient for the second paragraph. Some test-takers feel compelled to write more in paragraph two. If you must, use another sentence or two to support the position you chose or oppose the position you did not choose.

> Recently, many students left Whistler or chose not to enroll at the college because of the poor quality of the Art Department. By using the donation to develop a studio art program and to support the expansion of the art history curriculum, the Art Department will become attractive to students who previously left or did not consider Whistler, and enrollment at the college will increase. Conversely, using the donation to improve the Economics Department will not lead to an increase in enrollment at Whistler, because the strength of the economics faculty already attracts all of the economics students who consider going to college here.

Paragraph three has the same structure as paragraph two. Use one or two sentences to present an item of evidence that meets the second condition, using the topic material. Then write a sentence or two to support the position you chose or oppose the position you did not choose. Again, support of your position on the second condition with two items of evidence is sufficient to complete the third paragraph, though, if you must write more, it is all right to use another sentence or two to support the position you chose or oppose the position you did not choose.

> The disharmony between faculty and students will be reduced by using the donation to add four faculty members to the Art Department. Selecting new faculty members whose political views are more compatible with those of the students will result in an improved balance between the political views of faculty and students. Were the donation used to expand the economics faculty, the present faculty members would choose new members whose political views were the same as their own, and the existing disharmony between faculty and students would be increased.

In paragraph four, summarize how the position you selected will satisfy the topic conditions. This paragraph should be brief—no more than two sentences.

> In conclusion, by using the million-dollar donation to improve the Art Department at Whistler College, the trustees will have acted to ensure that student enrollment increases and that harmony between faculty and students is enhanced.

Upon completion of the Writing Sample, proofread your work and correct the vocabulary, grammar, punctuation, and spelling.

✓ MAKE SURE YOU LEAVE 5 MINUTES TO PROOFREAD YOUR WRITING SAMPLE.

Do not vary this structure. It applies to every Writing Sample.

Suppose that you selected the second position. As noted earlier, the position you choose makes no difference with respect to the Writing Sample. You would follow the same plan and produce a similar Writing Sample.

As a trustee, I will vote to use the million-dollar donation for the development of the Economics Department at Whistler College. Using the donation to improve the economics faculty will result in an increase in enrollment at the college and a reduction in the disharmony between faculty and students.

Recently, enrollment at Whistler has declined. By using the donation to turn the already strong Economics Department into the best in the region, we will attract students who presently choose to go elsewhere. The student body will grow on a foundation of excellence. Conversely, using the donation to improve the Art Department will result, at best, in a decent program that will not be good enough to attract any more students than now attend Whistler.

The disharmony between faculty and students will be reduced by using the donation to add faculty members to the Economics Department. New faculty members will be chosen whose political views are more compatible with those of the students, and this will result in a balance of views within the Economics Department. Thus, there will be greater harmony between the students and the economics faculty because there will be less difference between their views. Were the donation used to expand the art faculty, the disharmony between the economics faculty and the students would not be reduced and would continue to cause problems for Whistler.

In conclusion, by using the million-dollar donation to improve the Economics Department at Whistler College, the trustees will have acted to ensure that student enrollment increases and that harmony between faculty and students is improved and maintained.

✓ BY STRICT ADHERENCE TO YOUR PLAN, YOU WILL BE ABLE TO PRODUCE WITH EFFICIENCY A WRITING SAMPLE THAT SATISFIES THE TEST–MAKER'S OBJECTIVES AND YOURS.

What principles of vocabulary, grammar, punctuation, and mechanics are important to your Writing Sample performance?

For the same reason that the test-maker uses the same-language disguise on the LSAT, you should use the same language as is used in the topic. Not only does this sound convincing, but it helps you avoid misusing words. Misuse will not be a problem if you use only words that are familiar and have clear meaning for you.

Avoid clichés or idiomatic expressions: they invariably offend someone. Never use a pronoun other than "I." "It," "they," and the like often have unclear referents. Avoid legalese in any form.

You should already be familiar with the rules of grammar required to produce a Writing Sample. The following alerts are reminders of a few matters of particular importance: sentences must be complete; adjectives modify nouns, and adverbs modify verbs or adjectives; parallel construction is required; and double negatives should be avoided.

Use only two forms of punctuation on your Writing Sample—the period and the comma. Avoid the need to use any other form of punctuation. Keep it simple, correct, and safe from mistake.

There are three mechanical items that are of concern. Paragraphs should be indented. The passive voice should be avoided; it is difficult to use properly, especially under pressure. And last, avoid contractions. They make a less powerful presentation.

TRAINING SESSION 17

Writing Sample Pretests

The Writing Sample pretest session will differ from those involving Relationships, Arguments, and Passages. The 9-12-18 planning system is not applicable to the Writing Sample, in which there is no need to balance speed and accuracy. The need is to complete the Writing Sample with a cogent argument that responds clearly to the assigned topic by taking one of the given positions and satisfying the stated conditions.

What is your Writing Sample plan?

The techniques you worked through in Session 16 provide the basis for your plan, which is designed to take advantage of the predictability of the Writing Sample. Except for the specific words, you should have the structure and all the structural details of your Writing Sample fixed in advance of the test.

As with all sections of the LSAT, time is a critical factor. The plan permits you to take maximum advantage of the 30 minutes available for the Writing Sample. Your objective is to use the 30 minutes to connect your predetermined structure to the test topic and complete the required writing. First you fill in the outline, which is used to structure the components of your Writing Sample, and then you write the actual sample.

How do you use the Passages pretests?

There are four Writing Sample pretests at the end of this session. They are to be used to familiarize yourself with the process you will follow in completing the actual LSAT Writing Sample. After you have completed working through all of the techniques in Session 16, complete one of the pretests. Take no more than 30 minutes.

Upon completion of the pretest, go through and criticize your performance sentence by sentence. Be certain that you have executed all aspects of your plan. If you have, you will have produced a legible and cogent writing sample. If you can identify a weakness or omission, review all of the techniques in Session 16. Only after this review, complete another pretest, and repeat your critique.

How many pretests should you complete?

Once your Writing Sample satisfies your plan, there is no improvement to be realized by completing additional pretests. You can use any remaining pretests to maintain your familiarity with the Writing Sample techniques.

While there is little reason to seek out further Writing Samples, the disclosed tests offered by Law School Admission Services include a Writing Sample topic. Some LSAT preparation books also provide topics, but if you use such preparation books, you must make certain that the topics are constructed to the same specifications as those of the LSAT.

What are the directions for the Writing Sample pretests?

The general directions for the Writing Sample, which were discussed in Session 16, apply to the pretests as well. You are to complete a short writing exercise on the assigned topic. You have only 30 minutes to plan, organize, and write the sample. *You must write only on the topic specified.*

There is no right or wrong answer to the topic. No special knowledge is expected or required. Law schools are interested in how clearly you express the position you take on the topic and how carefully you support that position. They are interested in organization, vocabulary, and writing mechanics. How well you write is more important than the amount you write. The schools understand that you will be writing under pressure and are limited to a short time in which to produce the finished sample.

Your writing should be confined to the lined area in the booklet, since only this area will be reproduced for the law schools. You will have enough space in the booklet if you plan carefully, write on every line, avoid margins, and limit your writing to a reasonable size. Be certain that you write legibly.

WRITING SAMPLE PRETEST 1

The First Church of Newhope, having outgrown its 150-year-old building, has moved into a new facility and is trying to decide what to do with the old building. As a member of the committee charged with making the decision, you must write an article in support of selling the old building to Newhope University or renting it to the Lutheran Church. Two considerations guide your decision:
- There is a high risk of vandalism in the area where the old church building is located.
- First Church income has been steadily declining in the past three years.

The real-estate market is depressed at the present time, and the University's offer to buy the church for $200,000 is 40 percent greater than any other offer received. The University will use the building as a student rathskeller, selling beer and snacks as well as holding dances and parties. The University needs an immediate answer, because it is committed to opening a rathskeller within six months to overcome student and community concerns about the problems caused by the lack of such a facility. Many church members object to the use planned by the University, and some residents of the neighborhood in which the church is located are very upset about the noise and traffic that would result from the University's purchase.

The Lutherans are remodeling their Sunday school and want to rent the old church for about a year. They can only pay rent of $400 per month, and minimal upkeep on the building is $5,000 a year. The use by a church satisfies those who object to the use planned by the University, but others are concerned because the building will only be occupied on Sunday. Some church members feel that the real-estate market will be stronger in a year and there will be more options then, while others feel that property in the area is depreciating in value and the church will have to find another tenant, which will be very difficult.

WRITING SAMPLE PRETEST 2

As the director of the Atreeta State Park, you must write in support of one of two staff recommendations to the state Parks Department on how to alleviate the crowded conditions in and damage to the natural character of Atreeta that has resulted from a recent increase in wilderness hiking and camping. One recommendation is to reduce the number of trails and designated camping areas and install a booking system to limit the number of visitors using the park at any one time. The other recommendation is to increase the number of trails and designated camping areas and charge a fee for the use of the park. Two Parks Department policies guide your decision.
- Encouraging more people to enjoy wilderness backpacking and camping.
- Preserving the natural wilderness environment for public enjoyment.

By decreasing the number of trails and campsites, damage would be confined to specific small areas of the park, and the enforcement of rules designed to prevent damage would be made easier. The reservation system would eliminate overcrowding and, by designating trails and campsites, ensure that hikers and campers enjoy the solitude of the wilderness. But, by confining park users and requiring reservations, the park objectives of spontaneity and freedom to enjoy the natural environment would be destroyed.

By increasing the number of trails and campsites in the park, more people would be able to hike and camp comfortably, while damage would be less concentrated and easier to repair. The fee would provide funds to make any needed repairs. But the fee would tend to reduce the number of people using the park, and more trails and campsites would make it more difficult to enforce park rules.

WRITING SAMPLE PRETEST 3

As the conductor of the Ventara Symphony Orchestra, you must give your decision on whether to try to offset a serious operating deficit for the coming year by increasing ticket prices or by lengthening the concert schedule and including a greater number of more popular programs in the schedule. Two considerations guide your decision:
- Most of the orchestra's grant support depends upon its maintaining its very strong artistic reputation.
- For the past three years, orchestra ticket sales have averaged only 70 percent of capacity.

Increasing ticket prices by 35 percent would produce sufficient revenue to meet the projected operating deficit, provided that ticket sales increased to 85 percent of capacity. Some advisers have indicated that higher ticket prices would result in reduced attendance, and that there is some risk that a price increase would alienate some of those who now provide grants to the orchestra.

The orchestra's income should increase with the presentation of more concerts, but the musicians' contract does not permit more concerts, and, despite the financial problems, the musicians are likely to demand increased salaries for additional work. Also, while scheduling more popular concerts should increase attendance, such concerts do not enhance the orchestra's reputation and, in the eyes of many, detract from it.

WRITING SAMPLE PRETEST 4

As the director of the Carthage University Press, Inc., you must recommend to the board of managers a long-range plan to counteract the financial decline of the Press. You must choose between making a merger with a high-quality publisher and changing your publishing policy in a way that should greatly increase income. Two considerations guide your decision:
- The plan must provide a relatively permanent solution to the financial problems of the Press.
- The Press must maintain its tradition of publishing only work of the highest quality using only the best paper, printing, and binding.

By merging with Lisle & Fish, Ltd., savings would result from combined sales, advertising, management, and printing and ensure a strong financial future. Lisle & Fish has an impeccable reputation in the industry, and their taste is fastidious. If the companies were merged, Carthage would lose its autonomy, and Lisle & Fish policies would control, including the use of somewhat lower-quality paper, printing, and binding.

By changing the Carthage publishing policy and introducing a series of annotated works of Shakespeare for use in high school and college courses, a permanently enlarged market would result. Professor Barth, the series author, produces popular and effective material but is not a highly respected scholar. And the Shakespeare series would require Carthage to publish in paperback form, which Carthage has refused to do for decades because it felt its reputation would suffer.

TRAINING SESSION 18

The Finishing Touches

In this final session, you will put the finishing touches on your LSAT training techniques. The first part of the session briefly reviews the critical test performance factors you have been concentrating on. If you are uncertain about any of the test-taking techniques as you work through the review, stop and go back to the session that deals with the subject. Work through the techniques until your uncertainty is put to rest.

The second part of the session alerts you to a variety of minor factors that also influence your test performance and discusses quick-and-easy techniques for controlling them.

What are the critical test performance factors?

ANXIETY

Preparation anxiety and test anxiety influence your performance. Control is the key to managing them. You gain control by choosing to take the test, familiarizing yourself with it, thinking positively, and worrying constructively. You choose to accept the LSAT challenge and all of the baggage that travels with it. You make yourself familiar with the test and its use in every practical detail. You develop techniques that allow you to have a positive response to every aspect of the LSAT. You recognize worry as the sign of a loss of control, which triggers a response that will work to regain that control.

CONDITIONING

Conditioning is even more important to your test performance than anxiety. Nearly all of your former academic and test-taking conditioning is potentially detrimental to your LSAT performance. You have neither the time nor reason to alter it. Your strategy is to avoid your conditioning and, as a consequence, minimize its influence on your performance. Learning specific techniques for handling every aspect of the test renders your conditioning irrelevant to the LSAT.

THE BASIC REASONING TASK

The basic reasoning task, which is required by every LSAT question, can be characterized as conditional reasoning. Each of the three types of LSAT question presents the conditional reasoning task in a different format, but every one asks you to determine which evidence or conclusion satisfies the conditions presented in the statement and question. More specifically, you are asked to determine the evidence or conclusion that **must**, **could**, or **cannot** satisfy the given conditions.

THE TECHNIQUES

Good techniques yield optimal LSAT performance. The right techniques ensure that you perform the basic reasoning task effectively and consistently. They neutralize the test-maker's strategy of obfuscation. The test-maker uses unfamiliar contexts, varied structures, ambiguities, illusions, distractions, complexities, and multiple formats to obfuscate the basic reasoning task. Various disguises—**same language, too-little-too-much, true but,** and **false assertion**—are also used. Your techniques consistently and expeditiously guide you through the jungle of obfuscation directly to the familiar reasoning task.

DISCIPLINE

Discipline is required for you to develop your section-test plan. Maintaining the discipline of working through the LSAT by question sets is the keystone of your performance. The discipline of completing the pretest question sets provides you with the information upon which you base your plan for optimum performance (highest score). Having the discipline to consistently execute the techniques within the context of your plan maximizes your performance.

What should you do when the test is imminent?

THE DATE

You choose the date on which you will take the LSAT. The most important factor to consider when making the choice is readiness. Use the fact that the LSAT is administered four times a year to your advantage. Unlike performance on many other standardized tests, LSAT performance does not improve clearly with educational level. Aside from specific test preparation, there seems to be no significant improvement in test performance after the completion of two years of college. So you have many test dates from which to choose. After you are ready, choose the test date that makes you most comfortable. For example, June may be most comfortable for students, teachers, or people in the ski-resort business.

THE SITE

Register to take the test at a site that gives you an advantage. For many the "home court advantage" is a major performance plus. Others trade familiarity for small size. A huge test site with central check-in, room assignments, and other complexities can trash a large reserve of control in short order, whereas a small center sometimes provides the advantages of informality and low tension. Find out about the location and size of test centers from Law School Admission Services if you think that either might give you an advantage.

Wherever you choose to take the LSAT, familiarize yourself with the site in advance. Know exactly how you will travel there and what you will do with your car when you arrive. Many a person has lost test-taker control to campus parking, rearranged for a homecoming football game. If you cannot visit the site before the test date, get there early and check it out. Then leave the test area and return just before test time.

Locate the rest room at the test site and the most direct route to it from the test room. This is important since, if you have to use the rest room during the test, it is on your time. There is usually a 15-minute break between the second and third section-tests.

Light is also a matter of concern. Trying to concentrate on the LSAT when you are sitting in a dark corner of an auditorium or staring into the sun is not advantageous. If the light at your assigned seat is inadequate, seek out the proctor and insist, politely but firmly, that you be moved.

Avoid distractions. If you are easily distracted, you should not sit at the back of a room of 200 people, each of whom will provide you with at least one distraction in the course of the test. For you, it's "down in front."

What should you do when the test is tomorrow?

THE TOOLS

You will need some obvious and not-so-obvious tools to take the LSAT. Get them together early on the day before the test. The No. 2 pencil is tool number one, as answer sheets must be completed in pencil. Prepare and take four pencils to the test—they should have full erasers and not be needle sharp. (Needle-sharp pencils lacerate answer sheets, and their points splinter. Slightly blunted points are best.) The Writing Sample must be completed in pen, and pens are provided at the test. Though it is not explicitly sanctioned, many test-takers prefer to use their own pens. They should have black ink and be erasable, which eliminates the need for crossing out. The resulting neat look is a plus in ensuring that your Writing Sample does not disqualify you. If you wish to use a highlighter for marking Passages or Arguments problems, bring at least two in the flavors of your choice.

A reliable watch or equivalent time-minder is essential to your performance. Before you begin to work through a section-test, calculate and write at the starting point of each question set within it the exact time you have planned to be at that point. This makes your time checks easy to perform as you track your pace through each question set.

The test-maker discourages the ingestion of food at the test center, but the test is long, and administrative procedures at some centers make the testing time even longer. How does a conscientious test-taker reconcile a desire not to transgress by eating with the equally strong desire not to have a growling stomach disturb the test center. Those who have resolved this dilemma successfully strongly advise against the crunchy, the smelly, and the gooey. Pretzels, potato chips, or celery sticks crunch noisily when eaten. Worse still are beef jerky, pepperoni, and cheese. Their capacity for olfactory offense is nearly limitless. Avoid fudge, toffee, nougat, and the like, since they are sticky and endanger neat paperwork. Otherwise, it is the test-taker's choice—cookies and candy work well. During cool weather, jacket pockets are good for holding food. The marsupial sweatshirt with the pouch in the front carries a lot, is comfortable, and gives convenient access to your food. Make sure you snack between, not during, question sets.

If you take medication, be sure that you have a supply with you. Aspirin or some alternative form of medicine may prevent a distracting headache. Smoking is not permitted at LSAT test centers. If it will help, get your nicotine gum prescription filled before the test. The test is not a good time to go cold turkey.

THE RUN-UP

Two basic strategies are advocated for the time just before the test. Advocates of the Jell-O strategy believe that it is best to sit back and let your plan and techniques gel during this period. Ben-Gay advocates claim that a little warm-up working one last set of questions is the best way to spend it. Studies have shown that neither strategy has a greater impact than the other on performance.

What is significant is that you avoid either "zoom" or "doom and gloom." Extremes of emotion and activity can have a negative impact on your performance. Maintaining emotional equilibrium and your typical level of activity will ensure that you are in the best position to concentrate during the test. Follow a regimen that encourages a sense of relaxation. If a good party the night before is a shortcut to relaxation for you, try to avoid relaxing too far. There is no evidence that a roaring hangover leads to poor test performance, but the LSAT is hard enough without helping it along.

Adjust your personal schedule to the hour of the test. If you are not a morning person and are scheduled to take the LSAT in the morning, set your alarm to give you sufficient time to come out of your morning fog before the test starts.

What should you do when the test is today?

THE ROUTINES

On the day of the test, proceed as normally as possible, especially with respect to your schedule, level of activity, and intake of food and liquid. Staying as close as possible to your regular schedule supports you in carrying out your planned response to the predictability of the LSAT. Changing all of your routines in honor of test day is counterproductive, since it disrupts your plan. Eating a lumberjack's breakfast on the morning of the test in order to avoid the risk of midmorning burnout is more likely to give you indigestion, and drinking twelve cups of coffee to make sure you stay awake will probably make you hyperactive in more ways than one. Stick with the familiar.

THE TEST ADMINISTRATION

Travel to the test site on a schedule that leaves you feeling unhurried. Make sure you have built in enough flexibility to allow for unexpected holdups. Once you reach the test center, find a place where you can stay relaxed until the time for check-in. Milling about the test center with other test-takers for an hour or two before the exam is not constructive.

After check-in, make certain that there is no problem with your seat assignment—check that you have the light and work space that you require. Then be prepared for a full dose of "hurry up and wait."

After all test-takers are seated, the supervisor will read the test instructions. Listen carefully. You will be told exactly how to mark your answer sheet, the amount of warning you will be given before the end of each section-test (usually 5 minutes), the timing of the break (usually 15 minutes between the second and third sections), and what the "housekeeping" arrangements are.

The test may begin with the 30-minute Writing Sample, or this may appear at the end. Upon its completion, you will work though two of the 35-minute section-tests. The order of the section-tests is scrambled, so not all test-takers are working through the same section-tests at the same time. Next comes a break, and, after that, the last three section-tests are administered. As you begin each section-test, remember to mark at the start of each question set the time at which your plan calls for you to start that set.

Work your way through the question sets, identifying and dumping as many wrong answer options as you can. Use comparison and contrast to analyze the answer options that remain. If all fails, and you have not been able to identify some of the wrong answer options, guess. Believe it or not, statistics gathered over the years favor answer options other than A and E as the best selections, so, when guessing, avoid these two options. In fact, it is a good practice to always guess the *same* answer option—B, C, or D. Do not try to hit the test-maker's choice; let the test-maker hit yours.

Plan on the unexpected when you take the LSAT. Babies have been born, bands have played outside the test-room window, people have walked out and passed out, blizzards have blown, power has failed, plumbing has broken, supervisors have mistimed, fire alarms have sounded, and mysterious smells have wafted across the room. Anticipate the unexpected, and stay relaxed during a crisis. It will pass, and, when order is restored and the test resumes, you do not want to be too distracted to perform at your best.

To be perfectly realistic, you will be distracted from time to time during the many-hour test. You will lose your concentration. When you do, take a short break. Then take three deep breaths, exhaling slowly after each one. Your concentration will be restored, and you will return to maximum performance power.

If you lose all control and panic, freeze, choke, or go blank, stop. Get up and ask permission to leave the test room. Get a drink of water, take a number of deep breaths, and give yourself a chance to regroup outside of the test room. Most people quickly regain their composure, return to the test, and complete it without further bother. If you do not regain yours, cancel your score and go. (The cancellation process is described later in this session.) Avoid sitting through the test, waiting for a picture to come onto your screen. If there is no signal from the tower, there can be no picture on the screen. Try again another day.

There is one overarching rule for test-takers: *conform*—just for a few hours. Do not fight the process, your plan, your techniques, the questions, or the answer options. Forget tricks, quibbles, creativity, or proving the test-maker wrong.

Avoid leaving stray marks and incomplete erasures on your answer sheet. Always mark every correct answer in the test book, and write your name on it. If your answer sheet were to be lost, having every answer marked in a test book with your name on it could save you from having to retake the test. Are answer sheets lost?—yes. Often?—rarely.

ASSORTED ALERTS

As your work in previous sessions has shown you, the techniques designed to neutralize the test-maker's obfuscation patterns and strategies simultaneously facilitate wrong-answer identification and superior test performance. There are also a number of patterns and strategies that the test-maker uses episodically with all LSAT question types. Being alert to these further patterns and strategies while applying the other test-taking techniques you have learned will enhance your identification of wrong answers and your test performance.

The first alert relates to the test-maker's use of absolutes and qualifiers—always, never, some, few, all, none, every, many, and similar terms usually flag a pivotal or decisive condition. When you encounter an absolute or a qualifier in a statement or answer option, focus your full attention on its implications within the question context. It is not coincidental—the use of an absolute or qualifier is intentional and significant.

The test-maker's use of negatives and exceptions is frequently an obfuscation strategy. Be alert to NOT, EXCEPT, and their progeny and relatives (they are usually capitalized, as shown here). The rate of best-answer selection falls substantially for many test-takers when negatives and exceptions are involved. Because the large majority of LSAT statements, questions, and answer options involve positives, you anticipate a positive and often overlook a negative. So, when you first see a negative or an exception in a statement, question, or answer option, note it boldly to keep yourself alert to the point as you work through the question.

When a double negative appears—a NOT in the statement and a CANNOT in the question, or a CANNOT in the question and a NOT in an answer option—a double alert is called for. A similar double alert applies to the combination of a negative and an exception. For example, such questions as "All of the following are not true EXCEPT. . . ." require redoubled concentration from you.

The mismatched answer-option structure also deserves an alert. When you encounter an answer-option set in which four of the options present a similar word pattern and the fifth is totally different, your eye is drawn to the different one as a possible best answer. It usually is not.

Be alert to questions and answer options that appear later in a series based on a single statement. You may often be attracted to an answer because your thinking has been influenced by the preceding questions and answer options. If you find yourself falling prey to this phenomenon, try considering questions and answer options out of the sequence in which they appear. Work through the last first or the middle last.

Be especially alert to the multiple-option format. Recall that it appears to be more difficult because more than one of the Roman numeral options can satisfy the required conditions. For most test-takers, performance suffers on questions employing this format.

How do you make post-test decisions?

DEBRIEFING

Immediately upon completion of the test and before you leave the test center, take a few minutes to note particulars of the test and the administration that you are able to remember. For future reference, record the order of the section-tests, the number of question sets you completed, special difficulties encountered, surprises, uncertainties, and the like. At some point during the next 24 hours, review these notes. It is desirable to conduct this debriefing with someone else—preferably someone familiar with the LSAT.

The objectives of this debriefing are to ascertain any significant discrepancies between your test plan and your actual performance and to identify any factors that had a negative impact on your performance. If you deviated significantly from your test plan or encountered a problem that you are convinced means you did not perform well on the test, the possibility of canceling your test score arises.

CANCELLATION

Once the test administration has begun, your options with respect to the test score are to do nothing or to cancel your score. If you do nothing, your answer sheet is scored and the score reported. If you cancel your score, it is not reported, but the fact that the score was canceled is reported. Thus, you cancel your score only when the debriefing produces solid information that an informed person other than yourself interprets as a significant deviation from your test plan or a serious problem. A mere sense of unease about your performance or a feeling that you did not perform as well as you might have does not constitute a clear and convincing reason to cancel your score.

You have five working days to cancel your test score. There is no reason to rush to cancel with less than full information and an informed perspective to guide your decision. If you do decide to cancel, you must do so *in writing* to LSAS, Box 2000-T, Newtown, PA 18940. A mailgram, telegram, or letter requesting that your score be canceled is sufficient. (At the time of this writing, a request by fax does not meet the stated requirements of LSAS.) You do not need to explain your decision, so don't.

In addition to your name and your Social Security (USA), Social Insurance (Canada), or LSAS identification number, your request to cancel must also include the test date, test center, and test center code of the administration involved. The score you would have received is not reported to you or to the law schools.

POSTMORTEMS

Reviewing test questions, answer selections, and the like with fellow test-takers seldom provides any reliable information about your performance. In fact, the typical LSAT postmortem tends to confound post-test decision making. The prospect of getting any benefit from a postmortem is so slight that you should make every effort to avoid such after-test comparisons. Stick with the debriefing as the most effective way of making informed post-test decisions.

RETAKES

There is no restriction on the number of times you may take the LSAT. Of course, totally different questions are used at each administration of the test. And the average of an applicant's test scores is reported to law schools in addition to the scores themselves.

Studies done over a period of many years show that most—but certainly not all—people who retake the LSAT *do* score higher on the retake. The same studies show that the increase is small for the majority, and the score increase appears to be even smaller when averaged. For example, a score improvement of four points on a retake results in an averaged score increase of only two points.

Only when your pretest data indicate that a large score improvement could be realized is a retake recommended. From the perspective of most admission committees, the reflection of a very small or nonexistent score increase seems to cast a shadow rather than a glow on an applicant.

What about test results?

THE WAIT

The wait for test results is relatively long. It generally takes between four and six weeks for results to be reported. The test-maker waits for nearly all answer sheets to be received, processed, and checked before issuing scores. There is no way to hurry the process along.

THE CHECK

Your test score is issued on an LSAT Candidate Report form. The report is accompanied by a photocopy of your answer sheet and a copy of all scored test questions.

Your LSAT answer sheet is scored by a machine that "reads" the blackened bubbles and produces a score report reflecting what was "seen." The score report also includes your answer selection and the best selection for each question on the test. When the two failed to match, your perfect score was reduced by one. *Check every answer on your score report against your answer sheet.*

What the scoring machine "sees" is what you get. The machine can mistakenly interpret a stray mark, incomplete erasure, or similar phenomenon and not give you proper credit. If you have misplaced a series of answers, the machine does not know. By checking your answer sheet for any discrepancies, you can identify problems.

The most direct way to resolve a problem of this nature is the hand-scoring process. Upon your request and the payment of a fee, your answer sheet will be scored by hand, but this will take place only after machine scoring and score reporting are completed. Write to LSAS at Box 2000-T, Newtown, PA 18940, and describe the problem fully. Include exhibits with your description. If, for example, you misplaced a series of responses on your answer sheet, specify where the misplacement started and stopped, and indicate the misplacement on a photocopy of the photocopy of your answer sheet. Any verifiable problem will be resolved and a revised score report issued.

It is *very important* that you complete this checking process immediately upon receipt of your score report.

THE RESPONSE

Your test results ought to reflect your test plan. If there is a substantial difference between the expected and actual results, carefully review your performance, and determine the nature and extent of the differences. Based upon your review, decide whether a retake of the test is warranted.

Your test results will provide you with options and choices. Law school admission is not quite as predictable as the LSAT, but with some well-guided research and counseling, realistic options and choices can be defined clearly and quickly acted upon. Just as you balanced your speed and accuracy to achieve optimal performance on the LSAT section-tests, you should balance your prospects and objectives for admission to develop an optimal list of law schools to which you should apply. Based upon this list, complete your plan by applying to the law schools that suit you.

Are there any last words of advice?

Now that you have reached this point, you know that there *is* a better way to prepare for the LSAT. If you consistently apply the techniques acquired through the eighteen training sessions in this book and assiduously avoid the reflexes developed through your many years of academic conditioning, you will put the LSAT in its place—*working for you.*

May you take advantage of the LSAT in every way on your test day!

Law School Admission Test Simulation

On the following pages is an example of what a real LSAT is like. According to the test-taking strategies you have developed during the course of your training, you may use this test in one of two ways.

First, you could work only on those sections of the test that you feel require additional practice. Use the individual section-tests of this simulation as if they were four pretests, employing the 9-12-18 system to sharpen your test-taking techniques. Review the sessions on the particular question type before beginning, and be sure to follow the instructions for each section-test carefully.

The second way to approach this simulated test is to treat it as if you were taking an actual LSAT. In this case, you would spend 30 minutes on the Writing Sample and 35 minutes on each of the five section-tests (remember the experimental section?), in effect putting the 9-12-18 system through a dry run in preparation for this 2-hour-and-55-minute test. Work only on one section during the 35 minutes allowed, and do not work on or review other sections. Take a 15-minute break between Sections III and IV of the test.

Whichever method of working through the questions you choose, mark the best answers in the book and, when you have finished a question set, transfer your choices to the answer sheet (on the facing page). For ease of use, you might want to photocopy the answer sheet before working on the questions.

Answers to the LSAT simulation are on page 168.

LSAT WRITING SAMPLE TOPIC

Directions: Complete the short writing exercise on the topic that follows. You have only 30 minutes to plan, organize, and write your sample. WRITE ONLY ON THE TOPIC SPECIFIED.

Alice Anderson is a senior at John Paul Jones University. She has been offered two positions as a result of her outstanding record in her major, Television and Radio Broadcasting. As her counselor, you are to write an argument favoring one of the two offers. Two considerations guide your decision:
- Alice has a large student loan debt that she has to begin to repay immediately upon graduation.
- Alice has as her career goal a position as a network news anchorperson.

WAND is the only television station serving a large area located some 250 miles north of the capital of the state. The station has offered Alice a job as a reporter whose principal assignments would be to cover the activities of local governments, politics, and business. In addition to her assigned stories, Alice would have the opportunity to independently prepare stories for possible broadcast. Because the station is small, has a very stable staff, and has limited growth prospects, Alice's chances for advancement are not good. WAND's owner is a former network executive who purchased the station in order to get away from the pressures of broadcasting in major markets. Alice would get only a modest salary at WAND, and she would have to supplement her income with outside work.

KBSC is one of three television stations located in the state capital. The station has offered Alice a job as a production assistant in the news department. She would primarily do background research and check facts and sources for the producers and reporters. Production assistants who work hard are promoted to positions as special assignment reporters in about two years. There are many special assignment reporters competing for assignments, most of which involve covering minor events such as political dinners, award ceremonies, and concerts and writing human-interest stories. Most special assignment reporters spend at least five years covering minor events before moving into a position as a general reporter-anchorperson. KBSC would pay Alice a salary in excess of the amount she would need to live comfortably in the city.

SECTION I
Time—35 minutes
24 Questions

Directions: The questions in this section are based on a set of conditions. A diagram may be helpful in the answer selection process. Select the best answer to each question, and mark the corresponding space on the answer sheet.

Questions 1-6

A student is preparing a report on statehood. The source material is incomplete, but the following is known.

Wyoming became a state before Ohio.
Kansas became a state before Wyoming.
Ohio became a state after Maine.

1. Which of the following CANNOT be true?
   (A) Kansas was a state before Maine.
   (B) Maine was a state before Wyoming.
   (C) Ohio was a state before Kansas.
   (D) Wyoming was a state before Maine.
   (E) Kansas was a state before Ohio.

2. Which of the following must be true?
   (A) Kansas was a state before Maine.
   (B) Wyoming was a state before Kansas.
   (C) Maine was a state before Kansas.
   (D) Ohio was a state before Maine.
   (E) Kansas was a state before Ohio.

3. If Texas was a state before Maine, which of the following must be true?
   (A) Texas was a state first.
   (B) Texas was a state before Kansas.
   (C) Wyoming was a state before Texas.
   (D) Texas was a state before Ohio.
   (E) Maine was a state before Texas.

4. If Kansas became a state before Maine, Wyoming became a state after Maine, and Vermont was last to become a state, which of the following must be the order of statehood, first to last?
   (A) Vermont, Wyoming, Maine, Ohio, Kansas
   (B) Wyoming, Ohio, Kansas, Vermont, Maine
   (C) Maine, Kansas, Ohio, Vermont, Wyoming
   (D) Kansas, Maine, Wyoming, Ohio, Vermont
   (E) Ohio, Wyoming, Vermont, Kansas, Maine

5. If Utah became a state before Ohio, and Florida became a state after Wyoming, which of the following CANNOT be true if Maine became a state after Utah and before Florida?
   (A) Utah was a state before Wyoming.
   (B) Florida was a state before Ohio.
   (C) Florida was a state before Kansas.
   (D) Maine was a state before Ohio.
   (E) Wyoming was a state before Florida.

6. If Alaska became a state after Iowa and Wyoming, which of the following must be true?
   (A) Alaska was a state before Maine.
   (B) Iowa was a state before Wyoming.
   (C) Iowa was a state before Ohio.
   (D) Alaska was a state before Ohio.
   (E) Kansas was a state before Alaska.

GO ON TO THE NEXT PAGE.

142 Inside the LSAT

Questions 7–12

T lives in a smaller house than her brother.
T lives in a larger house than her parents.
T's children live with T.
T has no other relatives.

7. If four females and two males live in smaller houses than T's brother, how many of T's children are boys and girls, respectively?

    (A) 1, 0
    (B) 0, 1
    (C) 2, 1
    (D) 1, 2
    (E) 2, 0

8. If T's relative U lives in a larger house than her relative S, and both U and S are the same sex, what relationship could U be to S?

    (A) father to son
    (B) mother to daughter
    (C) daughter to mother
    (D) grandfather to grandson
    (E) son to father

9. If T's relative U lives in a larger house than T's relative S, all of the following may be true EXCEPT

    (A) S is U's son.
    (B) S is U's mother.
    (C) U is younger than S.
    (D) S is younger than U.
    (E) U and S are both female.

10. If T's relative U is not as old as T, who is not as old as her relative V, what relationship can U NOT be to V?

    (A) grandson
    (B) uncle
    (C) nephew
    (D) son
    (E) granddaughter

11. If, of all T's relatives who could possibly be either older or younger than T, none are the same age or older, how many of T's relatives must be younger than T?

    (A) less than 2
    (B) 2
    (C) 2 or 3
    (D) 3
    (E) more than 3

12. If the number of males related to T equals the number of females related to T, which of the following can be true?

    I. T has exactly two children.
    II. T has exactly three children.
    III. T has exactly four children.

    (A) I only
    (B) II only
    (C) III only
    (D) I and III only
    (E) I, II, and III

GO ON TO THE NEXT PAGE.

Questions 13-18

Buses 1, 2, and 3 make one trip each day, and they are the only ones that riders A, B, C, D, E, F, and G take to work.

Neither E nor G takes bus 1 on a day when B does.
G does not take bus 2 on a day when D does.
When A and F take the same bus, it is always bus 3.
C always takes bus 3.

13. Which of the following groups consists of riders who could take the same bus to work?
   I. A, C, F
   II. B, D, E
   III. C, D, G
   (A) I only
   (B) II only
   (C) III only
   (D) I and III only
   (E) I, II, and III

14. Traveling together to work, B, C, and G could take which of the same buses on a given day?
   (A) 1 only
   (B) 2 only
   (C) 3 only
   (D) 2 and 3 only
   (E) 1, 2, and 3

15. The maximum number of riders who could take bus 2 to work on a given day must be
   (A) 3
   (B) 4
   (C) 5
   (D) 6
   (E) 7

16. Traveling together to work, B, D, E, F, and G could take which of the same buses on a given day?
   (A) 1 only
   (B) 2 only
   (C) 3 only
   (D) 1 and 3 only
   (E) 2 and 3 only

17. On a day when each of the riders takes one of the three buses to work, exactly how many riders CANNOT take other than bus 2?
   (A) 0
   (B) 1
   (C) 2
   (D) 3
   (E) 4

18. Which of the following could be a group of riders that takes bus 1 to work on a given day?
   (A) A, C, E, G
   (B) A, D, E, G
   (C) A, E, F, G
   (D) B, D, E, F
   (E) B, D, E, G

GO ON TO THE NEXT PAGE.

Questions 19-24

Angela, Bruce, Cora, Dora, and Elmer live at different points along a straight east-west highway.

Angela lives 5 miles away from Bruce.
Cora lives 7 miles away from Dora.
Elmer lives 2 miles away from Cora.
Bruce lives 3 miles away from Cora.
The distance between houses is measured by straight line only.

19. Which of the following could be true?
    I. Dora lives 9 miles from Elmer.
    II. Dora lives 2 miles from Bruce.
    III. Angela lives 5 miles from Cora.
    (A) I only
    (B) II only
    (C) III only
    (D) I and II only
    (E) I and III only

20. Which of the following must be true?
    (A) The distance between Elmer's and Bruce's houses is greater than the distance between Cora's and Angela's houses.
    (B) The distance between Bruce's and Elmer's houses is shorter than the distance between Cora's and Dora's houses.
    (C) Of the group, Dora lives farthest from Cora.
    (D) Cora lives closer to Dora than she does to Angela.
    (E) Elmer lives closer to Cora than Angela does.

21. Which of the following statements must be FALSE?
    (A) Angela and Cora live 12 miles apart.
    (B) Angela and Dora live 5 miles apart.
    (C) Bruce and Dora live 10 miles apart.
    (D) Elmer and Dora live 9 miles apart.
    (E) Elmer and Bruce live 5 miles apart.

22. If Bruce and Dora live east of Cora, which of the following must be the distance between Bruce's and Dora's houses?
    (A) 10 miles
    (B) 8 miles
    (C) 5 miles
    (D) 4 miles
    (E) 2 miles

23. If Bruce and Elmer live east of Cora, and Dora lives west of Cora, which of the following must be true?
    (A) Dora lives closer to Elmer than Cora does to Bruce.
    (B) Cora lives closer to Dora than Elmer does to Bruce.
    (C) Elmer lives closer to Cora than Bruce does to Elmer.
    (D) Bruce lives closer to Elmer than Cora does to Dora.
    (E) Angela lives closer to Bruce than Cora does to Elmer.

24. If Cora, starting from her house, visits Dora, Bruce, and Elmer in that order and then returns home, what is the smallest number of miles she walks?
    (A) 14
    (B) 15
    (C) 16
    (D) 17
    (E) 18

END OF SECTION I

SECTION II
Time—35 minutes
24 Questions

Directions: Evaluate the reasoning contained in the brief statements, and select the best answer. Do not make implausible, superfluous, or incompatible assumptions. Select the best answer to each question, and mark the corresponding space on the answer sheet.

1. Well-designed clothing was once described as the hallmark of a stylish person. We agree, and our clothing is designed for stylish people. Their life-styles are well-defined. They do everything in good taste. And they search out well-designed clothing as the guarantee of good workmanship.

   This advertisement is intended to suggest which of the following conclusions?

   I. The clothing is characterized by good workmanship.
   II. Well-designed clothing defines a life-style.
   III. Purchasers of this brand of clothing will be stylish.

   (A) I only
   (B) II only
   (C) III only
   (D) I and III only
   (E) I, II, and III

2. Native American tribes seeking monetary reparations from the government are often told, "There is neither wealth nor wisdom enough in the world to compensate in money for all the wrongs in history."

   Which of the following most weakens the above argument?

   (A) Prior wrongs should not be permitted as a justification for present wrongs.
   (B) Even though all wrongs cannot be compensated for, some wrongs can be.
   (C) Since most people committed wrongs, the government should compensate for wrongs with money.
   (D) Monetary reparations upset social order less than other forms of reparation.
   (E) Since money is the basic cause of the wrongs, should it not be the cure?

3. A mother told her daughter, "You lie too much. You cannot be believed. When you start telling me the truth I will start believing you."

   Which of the following is assumed by the mother's statement?

   (A) The mother has explained what is wrong about lying.
   (B) The mother has determined that her daughter knows what a lie is.
   (C) The mother knows when the daughter has been truthful.
   (D) The mother is routinely truthful with her daughter.
   (E) The mother believes her daughter ultimately will tell the truth.

4. Manufacturing products using glass made from sand rather than materials made from other natural resources can save energy, despite the fact that the initial cost is high.

   Which of the following, if true, does NOT support the above argument?

   (A) Manufacturing wood and metal products requires energy that could have been more efficiently used to make glass.
   (B) Unlike metal and wood products, those made from glass must be discarded rather than repaired when they break.
   (C) Aluminum products require much more energy to produce than do those made of glass.
   (D) Fiberglass insulation is much more energy efficient than insulation made with other materials.
   (E) Glass cookware transfers heat more efficiently than that made from metal.

5. The United States gets 5 percent of its oil from Mexico. If Mexico raises the price of its oil by 20 percent, that will result in an increase of 1 percent (5 percent times 20 percent) in the price of oil products in the United States.

   Which of the following is an assumption upon which the above argument depends?

   (A) Oil prices in the United States are not affected by inflation in Mexico.
   (B) Other countries will not increase oil exports to the United States.
   (C) The price increase will not result in a decrease in the sales of Mexican oil products.
   (D) People will not substitute other products for those made from Mexican oil.
   (E) A 1 percent price increase in oil products will not be recognized by the buying public.

GO ON TO THE NEXT PAGE.

6. Historians by trade describe events that are confused as to motive and significance. Therefore, historians, however well-intentioned, primarily traffic in half-truths and lies. But novelists are free from such burdens. Even though they relate many things that are untrue, their characterizations are not offered as true and, therefore, are not half-truths or lies.

   Which of the following, if true, would be an extension of the argument above?

   I. Journalists report on motives and the significance of events and, like historians, traffic primarily in half-truths and lies.
   II. Poets, like novelists, do not offer their writing as true and, thus, do not deal in half-truths and lies.
   III. Historians and novelists by trade characterize events and, therefore, are required to deal in half-truths and lies.

   (A) I only
   (B) III only
   (C) I and II only
   (D) I and III only
   (E) II and III only

7. The policy of equal pay for women continues to erode the importance of the mother's role in society.

   The above argument can be criticized for which of the following reasons?

   I. It contains a contradiction.
   II. Equal pay for women is unrelated to motherhood.
   III. It is based upon unsupported assumptions.

   (A) I only
   (B) II only
   (C) III only
   (D) II and III only
   (E) I, II, and III

8. The earth receives energy in the form of heat from the sun and discharges heat energy into space by its own emissions. The heat energy received undergoes many transformations. But in the long run, no significant amount of heat energy is stored on the earth, and there is no continuing trend toward higher or lower temperatures.

   Which of the following sentences provides the most logical continuation of this paragraph?

   (A) It is obvious, therefore, that much of the heat energy that reaches the earth is transformed by some means not yet understood.
   (B) Thus, it is imperative that we develop a way to use solar energy before it is dissipated into outer space.
   (C) As a result, the amount of heat energy lost by the earth must closely approximate the amount gained from the sun.
   (D) The earth would become as hot as the sun without the many transformations of heat energy.
   (E) The earth's slow but persistent recession from the sun prevents it from overheating.

Questions 9-10

Lecturer: On average, the majority of Americans enjoy the highest standard of living of any people in the world.
Critic: There are thousands of Americans who have annual incomes of less than $3,000 per year.

9. Which of the following best describes the critic's response?
   (A) It is not inconsistent with the lecturer's statement.
   (B) It cites data confirming the lecturer's statement.
   (C) It fails to distinguish between cause and effect.
   (D) It generalizes from too small a number of cases.
   (E) It resorts to emotional language.

10. A logical criticism of the lecturer's statement would focus on the existence of
    (A) a country in which the majority of people enjoy a higher standard of living than that of the American people
    (B) a country with a higher level of employment than America
    (C) poor Americans who receive federal aid
    (D) a higher level of inflation in America than in other countries
    (E) many poor American families that are so isolated that they are not included in statistical surveys

Questions 11-12

The position that the prohibition of morally offensive works is wrong in principle is hardly tenable. There certainly are circumstances in which censorship could be desirable. If it were shown that all or most people of a certain type who saw a film and thereafter committed a burglary or murder that they would not otherwise have committed, no one would deny that public exhibition of the film should be prohibited. To admit this is to admit that censorship is not wrong in principle. But to approve the principle of censorship on these grounds does not, of course, commit one to approve censorship in every form.

11. Which of the following can be inferred from the paragraph above?
    (A) No film affects any two individuals in the same way.
    (B) The causal connection between specific acts and exposure to specific films is not established.
    (C) We cannot anticipate the abuses to which censorship may lead.
    (D) People not exposed to morally offensive works will commit socially offensive acts.
    (E) There can be no relationship between a general principle and specific practices.

12. The paragraph questions the position that censorship is wrong in principle by
    (A) pointing out the ambiguity of a key term
    (B) rehearsing facts that are not generally known
    (C) questioning the truth of a factual generalization
    (D) exposing a logical inconsistency
    (E) presenting a hypothetical case

GO ON TO THE NEXT PAGE.

13. No Vikings carried watches. Some Vikings were explorers. Therefore, some explorers did not carry watches.

    Which of the following is logically most similar to the argument above?

    (A) Everyone who eats too much candy will be sick. I do not eat too much candy and will therefore probably avoid sickness.
    (B) All dogs are excluded from this motel, but many dogs are friendly. Therefore, some friendly animals are kept out of this motel.
    (C) People who want to avoid the pain of dental work will see the dentist twice a year. My children refuse to have their cavities filled. Therefore, my children like pain.
    (D) Some who are athletic are young people, and all young people can run. Therefore, everyone who can run is young.
    (E) Hawaii is a beautiful place. Some Hawaiians emigrate to California. Therefore, California is a beautiful place.

14. Many people confuse reasons and causes. Any justification for performing an action is a reason. Anything that makes performing an action necessary is a cause—for example, a strong urge, hunger, an intense desire, social pressure, or some brain disorder. Those people who believe that the same thing may be both a reason for performing an action and its cause are clearly mistaken.

    Which of the above examples of a cause that makes an action necessary best fits the description of the cause of an action rather than the reason or justification for it?

    (A) "hunger"
    (B) "some brain disorder"
    (C) "social pressure"
    (D) "a strong urge"
    (E) "an intense desire"

15. One form of reasoning holds that, by eliminating all possible explanations until only one remains, that one should be accepted. Critics argue that the flaw in this form of reasoning is that one cannot know about all possible explanations.

    Which of the following examples best supports this criticism?

    (A) the possible causes of heart disease
    (B) the possible results of rolling dice
    (C) the possible family members who left the house unlocked
    (D) the possible candidates running for mayor of Atlanta, Georgia
    (E) the possible countries with nuclear weapons

16. Doctor: The law of genetics holds that if both parents have brown eyes, then they can have only brown-eyed children.
    Patient: That is not true; my mother has blue eyes, and I have brown eyes.

    The patient has misinterpreted the doctor's statement to mean that

    (A) only brown-eyed people can have blue-eyed children
    (B) brown-eyed people cannot have blue-eyed children
    (C) people with blue eyes invariably have blue-eyed children
    (D) parents with the same eye color have children with a different eye color
    (E) children have the same eye color as their parents

17. Certain similarities between prehistoric art and the art of children has led some people to the mistaken conclusion that either early humans had the mentality of children or that they were as unskilled as children.

    These conclusions assume which of the following?

    (A) Art that is considered sophisticated today must always have been considered sophisticated.
    (B) What is easy for humans today must always have been easy.
    (C) The significance of art is consistent over time.
    (D) Prehistoric humans painted in the same way that children now paint.
    (E) Modern humans have learned from prehistoric man.

18. During the cultural revolution in China under Chairman Mao, thousands of "enemies of the republic" were killed. When Mao's critics accused him of confusing his personal enemies with enemies of the republic, he responded, "I deny the accusation, and the proof is that you are still alive."

    Which of the following assumptions was Mao making?

    I. All the enemies of the republic are dead.
    II. His critics are his personal enemies.
    III. Some personal enemies are also enemies of the republic.

    (A) I only
    (B) II only
    (C) III only
    (D) I and II only
    (E) I, II, and III

GO ON TO THE NEXT PAGE.

19. Today neither scientists nor the pharmaceutical companies for which they work are willing to run the risk of being wrong. In the past these scientists were encouraged to experiment with imaginative hypotheses that had a high probability of failure. If this situation continues, the country's drug development work will come to a standstill.

    The point of the argument above is that
    (A) scientists are too concerned about failure
    (B) scientists are not concerned about the outcome of experimentation
    (C) risk should be an issue in experimental research
    (D) scientific advances repay extensive experimentation
    (E) support for drug research is vanishing

20. In his latest book, John does some clever writing, but even he might have been encouraged to use more everyday language.

    Which of the following has a logical structure most like that of the above statement?
    (A) The fertilizer serves some valuable purposes, but the smell of it when it is used is offensive.
    (B) The latest sermon was effective as inspirational writing, but it did not offer the path to realize the objectives it outlined.
    (C) The star's last movie contained the usual bit of impressive acting, but her director should have advised her to act more like an average person.
    (D) The chef at the resort makes wonderful desserts, but the manager should explain how to apportion them more reasonably.
    (E) Cage was a brilliant composer, but only a few people are able to understand his music.

21. The end of overcrowding at colleges and universities provides them with the opportunity to improve the quality of the educational services that they offer. As enrollment declines, services and campus facilities should better serve student needs.

    If true, which of the following statements most weakens the above conclusion?
    (A) The quality of educational services does not depend on the variety of services offered.
    (B) Fees paid by students are the major source of funding for educational services.
    (C) Educational services are a critical factor in a student's choice of school.
    (D) As campus facilities grow older, their maintenance becomes more expensive.
    (E) Student needs are different than they were when colleges and universities were overcrowded.

22. When pregnant laboratory rats are given caffeine equivalent to the amount a human would consume by drinking six cups of coffee per day, an increase in the incidence of birth defects results. When asked if the government would require warning labels on products containing caffeine, a spokesperson stated that it would not, because "if the finding of these studies were to be refuted in the future, the government would lose credibility."

    Which of the following is most strongly suggested by the government's statement above?
    (A) A warning that applies to a small population is inappropriate.
    (B) Very few people drink as many as six cups of coffee a day.
    (C) There are doubts about the conclusive nature of studies on animals.
    (D) Studies on rats provide little data about human birth defects.
    (E) The seriousness of birth defects involving caffeine is not clear.

23. The Mercers are avid sailors. They have a child who will never be able to accompany them sailing because he is afraid of water.

    Upon which of the following assumptions does the conclusion above depend?
    I. The Mercers' child will never want to sail.
    II. The Mercer's child will never overcome his fear of water.
    III. Sailors cannot be afraid of water.
    (A) II only
    (B) III only
    (C) I and III only
    (D) II and III only
    (E) I, II, and III

GO ON TO THE NEXT PAGE.

24. Sam: Olive oil can help prevent heart attacks, according to physicians.
    Betty: It cannot. My mother cooked with olive oil her entire life, and she died of a heart attack last year.

Betty's statement can best be countered by pointing out that

(A) Betty's mother was an exception
(B) other factors could have nullified the influence of the olive oil
(C) Betty does not know that her mother always cooked with olive oil
(D) it has never been scientifically proven that olive oil causes heart attacks
(E) Betty's mother might have used olive oil irregularly

END OF SECTION II

SECTION III
Time—35 minutes
24 Questions

Directions: The questions in this section are based on a set of conditions. A diagram may be helpful in the answer selection process. Select the best answer to each question, and mark the corresponding space on the answer sheet.

Questions 1-6

A restaurant franchise has several locations in Ames County that are designated by the letters A, B, C, D, etc. The restaurants have the following relationships to the Central Office and one another:

  A is northwest of the Central Office.
  B is northeast of the Central Office.
  C is northeast of the Central Office, but C is located farther east than B.
  D is south (but not necessarily due south) of the Central Office.
  E is southwest of the Central Office.
  A is farther north than C and farther west than D.
  E is farther west than A.
  G is southeast of the Central Office and farther east than B.

1. If a delivery truck travels in a straight line from E to the Central Office and continues in exactly the same direction, it could pass directly by which of the following?
   (A) the northwest corner of D
   (B) the southeast corner of G
   (C) the northwest corner of A
   (D) the west side of A
   (E) the east side of G

2. If F is located due north of the Central Office, which of the following could be true?
   I. F is located due west of C.
   II. F is located due north of G.
   III. F is located due west of B.
   (A) I only
   (B) II only
   (C) I and II only
   (D) I and III only
   (E) I, II, and III

3. A restaurant located precisely midway between C and G must be
   I. north of the Central Office
   II. farther east than B
   III. farther south than B
   (A) II only
   (B) III only
   (C) I and III only
   (D) II and III only
   (E) I, II, and III

4. Which of the following CANNOT be the location of D?
   (A) southwest of A
   (B) northeast of C
   (C) southeast of E
   (D) southeast of G
   (E) northwest of G

5. Which of the following CANNOT be true?
   (A) B is precisely midway between E and G.
   (B) B is precisely midway between C and D.
   (C) B is precisely midway between C and E.
   (D) G is precisely midway between C and E.
   (E) D is precisely midway between C and E.

6. If G is southeast of D, and D is farther east than B, which of the following must be true?
   (A) The Central Office is closer to D than to G.
   (B) E is located closer to D than to G.
   (C) E is closer to G than to D.
   (D) E is closer to the Central Office than to G.
   (E) C is closer to D than to G.

GO ON TO THE NEXT PAGE.

Questions 7-12

Six college officers—H, I, J, K, L, and M—are seated at equal distances around a circular table according to a list of personal preferences submitted by each officer.

> The Secretary and the Treasurer have no preference as to where they sit.
> The President must be seated directly opposite the Vice President.
> The two Trustees may not sit together.
> H must sit next to either J or K.
> While it is unclear who occupies which office, M is neither the President nor a Trustee.
> The Vice President is either L or J.
> Either H or I or both are Trustees.

7. If, in satisfying all of the above conditions, the officers are seated around the table in the order K, I, J, H, L, and M, all of the following may be true EXCEPT
   (A) J is the Vice President
   (B) H is a Trustee
   (C) I is the President
   (D) K is the Treasurer
   (E) M is the Secretary

8. If H is seated between K and L, and M is seated opposite H, what is a complete and accurate listing of every officer who could be sitting next to M?
   (A) President, Vice President
   (B) President, Vice President, Secretary
   (C) President, Vice President, Trustee, Secretary, Treasurer
   (D) Trustee, Secretary, Treasurer
   (E) Vice President, Trustee, Secretary, Treasurer

9. If J, the Secretary, must sit across from one of the Trustees, how might the officers be arranged clockwise in order to satisfy all conditions?
   (A) L, M, I, K, J, H
   (B) K, M, J, L, H, I
   (C) J, K, L, H, M, I
   (D) K, I, H, J, M, L
   (E) I, J, K, M, H, L

10. If the President has M to her right and H to her left, which is NOT an acceptable arrangement for the other three officers, assuming that their order starts with H and goes around the table clockwise?
    (A) J, K, L
    (B) I, J, L
    (C) K, J, I
    (D) K, L, I
    (E) L, J, K

11. If the officers are seated around the table clockwise in the order J, H, I, K, M, and L, and I is the Treasurer, who are the two Trustees?
    (A) I and K
    (B) H and J
    (C) H and K
    (D) I and J
    (E) H and L

12. If the officers are seated around the table clockwise in the order H, J, K, L, M, and I, all of the following must be true EXCEPT
    (A) M is the Secretary
    (B) H is not the Treasurer
    (C) J is not the Vice President
    (D) I is a Trustee
    (E) either J or K is a Trustee

GO ON TO THE NEXT PAGE.

Questions 13-18

Holly Hauling has six vehicles. The Kenworth, Mack, and White are trucks; the Chevrolet, Dodge, and Ford are vans.

Holly always fuels and washes the trucks before the vans.
Within the respective groups, Holly fuels the vehicles that hold comparatively more fuel before he fuels those that hold comparatively less.
Holly washes the vehicles in their respective groups in the opposite order of their fueling.
The White holds more fuel than the Chevrolet, and no vehicle holds both more than the Chevrolet and less than the White.
The Dodge holds more than the Mack, and no vehicle holds both less than the Dodge and more than the Mack.
Only the Ford and the Kenworth hold the same amount of fuel.

13. If the Kenworth is fueled first and the White third, which of the following must be true?
    (A) The Ford is fueled fifth.
    (B) The Ford is fueled last.
    (C) The Chevrolet is fueled fifth.
    (D) The Chevrolet is fueled last.
    (E) The Dodge is fueled fourth.

14. If the White is washed first, which of the following could NOT be possible?
    (A) The Kenworth is fueled before the White.
    (B) The Mack is fueled before the Kenworth.
    (C) The Chevrolet is fueled before the Ford.
    (D) The Dodge is fueled after the Ford.
    (E) The Ford is fueled before the Chevrolet.

15. If the Mack is fueled first and the White third, which of the following must be true?
    (A) The Ford is washed first.
    (B) The Dodge is washed second.
    (C) The Kenworth is washed second.
    (D) The White is washed third.
    (E) The Chevrolet is washed third.

16. Which of the following is NOT a possible order in which the vehicles are washed?
    (A) Kenworth, White, Mack, Ford, Chevrolet, Dodge
    (B) Mack, Kenworth, White, Dodge, Ford, Chevrolet
    (C) Mack, White, Kenworth, Dodge, Chevrolet, Ford
    (D) White, Kenworth, Mack, Chevrolet, Ford, Dodge
    (E) White, Mack, Kenworth, Ford, Dodge, Chevrolet

17. Suppose Holly does not wash the trucks first but alternates by washing a van and then a truck. If the Mack is fueled first, it would NOT be possible for which pair of vehicles to be washed sequentially?
    (A) the Kenworth immediately before the Chevrolet
    (B) the Chevrolet immediately before the White
    (C) the White immediately before the Ford
    (D) the Dodge immediately before the Mack
    (E) the Ford immediately before the Dodge

18. If Holly fuels the trucks after the vans on a day the White is washed second and the Dodge is washed fourth, the order of fueling must be
    (A) Chevrolet, Dodge, Ford, White, Mack, Kenworth
    (B) Chevrolet, Ford, Dodge, White, Kenworth, Mack
    (C) Ford, Chevrolet, Dodge, Kenworth, White, Mack
    (D) Ford, Dodge, Chevrolet, Kenworth, Mack, White
    (E) Dodge, Chevrolet, Ford, Mack, White, Kenworth

GO ON TO THE NEXT PAGE.

Questions 19-24

There are six distinct building groups in a large office complex. From smallest to largest, respectively, the groups are constructed of aluminum, brick, concrete, glass, stone, and wood. The building groups are designated Groups 1 through 6.

Group 1, which is not stone, is larger than Group 3.
Group 2 is larger than Group 5 and Group 6.
Group 2 is smaller than Group 4.
Group 3 is larger than Group 6.

19. What material must Group 6 be made of if Group 3 is smaller than Group 5?
    (A) aluminum
    (B) brick
    (C) concrete
    (D) glass
    (E) stone

20. From smallest to largest, which of the following is a possible arrangement of the groups?
    (A) 5, 3, 6, 1, 2, 4
    (B) 6, 3, 1, 5, 2, 4
    (C) 6, 3, 1, 2, 5, 4
    (D) 6, 3, 5, 2, 1, 4
    (E) 6, 5, 3, 2, 1, 4

21. If Group 1 is concrete, Group 3 must be which of the following?
    (A) aluminum
    (B) brick
    (C) glass
    (D) stone
    (E) wood

22. Which of the following CANNOT be a possible arrangement of the groups from smallest to largest?
    (A) 5, 6, 3, 1, 2, 4
    (B) 5, 6, 3, 2, 4, 1
    (C) 6, 5, 2, 4, 3, 1
    (D) 6, 5, 3, 1, 2, 4
    (E) 6, 5, 4, 3, 2, 1

23. If Group 5 is glass, Group 2 could be made of which of the following materials?
    I. concrete
    II. stone
    III. wood
    (A) I only
    (B) II only
    (C) I and II only
    (D) II and III only
    (E) I, II, and III

24. If Group 4 is stone, Group 2 could be made of which of the following materials?
    I. brick
    II. concrete
    III. glass
    (A) I only
    (B) II only
    (C) III only
    (D) I and II only
    (E) II and III only

END OF SECTION III

SECTION IV
Time—35 minutes
28 Questions

Directions: The questions in this section are based on what is stated or implied in the passage. Select the best answer to each question, and mark the corresponding space on the answer sheet.

A. L. Macfie makes the distinction between what he calls the Scottish method, characteristic of Adam Smith's approach to problems of social policy, and the scientific or analytical method, which is more familiar to
(5) modern social scientists. In the former, the center of attention lay in the society as observed rather than in the idealized version of the society considered as an abstraction. Smith did have an underlying model or paradigm for social interaction; he could scarcely have
(10) discussed reforms without one. But his interest was in making the existing social structure "work better," in terms of the norms that he laid down, rather than in evaluating the possible limitations of the structure as it might work ideally if organized on specific principles.
(15) Frank Knight suggested that critics of the free-enterprise system are seldom clear as to whether they object to the system because it does not work in accordance with its idealized principles or because it does, in fact, work in some approximation to these
(20) principles. There is no such uncertainty with respect to Adam Smith. He was critical of the economic order of his time because it did not work in accordance with the principles of natural liberty. He was not, and need not have been, overly concerned with some ultimate
(25) evaluation of an idealized structure.
Smith's methodology has been turned on its head by many modern scientists. The post-Pigovian theory of welfare economics has largely, if not entirely, consisted in a search for conceptual flaws in the working of an
(30) idealized competitive economic order, conceived independently of the flawed and imperfect order that may be observed to exist. Partial correctives are offered in both the theory of the second-best and in the still-emerging theory of public choice, but the
(35) perfect-competition paradigm continues to dominate applied economic policy discussions.
This methodological distinction is important in our examination of Smith's conception of justice. In one sense, John Rawls's efforts in defining and delineating
(40) "a theory of justice" are akin to those of the neoclassical economists who first described the idealized competitive economy. By contrast, Adam Smith saw no need for defining in great detail the idealized operation of a market system and for evaluating this system in terms of
(45) strict efficiency criteria. Similarly, he would have seen no need for elaborating in detail a complete "theory of justice" for defining those principles that must be operative in a society that would be adjudged to be "just." In comparing Smith with Rawls, therefore, we
(50) must somehow bridge the contrasting methodologies. We can make an attempt to infer from Smith's applied discussion of real problems what his idealized principles of justice might have embodied. Or we can infer from John Rawls's treatment of idealized principles what his
(55) particular application of these might be in an institutional context.

1. Which of the following best describes the passage's objective?
   (A) distinguishing between the Scottish and Pigovian theories of justice
   (B) supporting Adam Smith's concept of justice
   (C) comparing Smith's and Rawls's views of a just society
   (D) supporting John Rawls's theory of justice
   (E) analyzing the contrasting methodologies of Smith and Rawls

2. According to the passage, all of the following are methods used to explain social policy EXCEPT
   (A) the Scottish method
   (B) the theory of welfare economics
   (C) the perfect-competition paradigm
   (D) the scientific method
   (E) the principles of natural liberty

3. According to the passage, John Rawls's "theory of justice" is similar to which of the following?
   (A) the description of the free-enterprise system
   (B) the description of the efficiency of the market system
   (C) the description of the idealized structure of natural liberty
   (D) the description of the idealized competitive economy
   (E) the description of the society considered as an abstraction

4. It can be inferred from the passage that Adam Smith was
   (A) not interested in achieving a just society
   (B) concerned with improving the operation of society
   (C) not worried about efficiency in the operation of society
   (D) indifferent to the economic operation of society
   (E) anxious to achieve an idealized operation of society

5. The author of the passage is presenting which of the following?
   (A) a recitation of methods of approaching social problems
   (B) an analysis of various economic systems
   (C) a comparison of the theories of Knight, Rawls, and Smith
   (D) an exposition of various theories of justice
   (E) an argument supporting idealized versions of social order

GO ON TO THE NEXT PAGE.

6. Which of the following is most likely to be the next sentence of the passage?
   (A) Since Smith planned a book on jurisprudence, there is a reason to develop his theory of justice.
   (B) The practical application of theories of what is "just" is guided by principles of natural justice.
   (C) In what follows, both of these routes will be explored.
   (D) Neither Rawls nor Smith was successful in dealing with real problems.
   (E) Rawls's "theory of justice" is difficult to apply to questions of natural liberty.

7. The author's purpose in finding a bridge between the Rawls and Smith methodologies (line 50) is to
   (A) facilitate understanding of their philosophies
   (B) identify principles that each feels are just
   (C) explore their views toward an idealized market system
   (D) permit comparison of their concepts of justice
   (E) support their attempts to reform society

GO ON TO THE NEXT PAGE.

Many, perhaps most, well-disposed, practical people would, if they had to designate a philosophy that comes closest to expressing their unstated principles, pick utilitarianism. The philosophy that proclaims as its sovereign criterion the procuring of the greatest good of the greatest number has indeed served as a powerful engine of legal reform and rationalization. And it is a crucial feature of utilitarianism that it is consequences that count. Now it is interesting that some judgments that are actually made in the law and elsewhere do not appear to accord with this thoroughgoing consequentialism. For instance, both in law and morals there are many instances of a distinction being made between direct and indirect intention—i.e., the distinction between on the one hand the doing of evil as an end in itself or on the other hand bringing about the same evil result as a consequence of one's direct ends or means. So also the distinction is drawn between the consequences that we bring about by our actions and consequences that come about through our failures to act. Also, when bad consequences ensue from our actions and what was done was in the exercise of a right or privilege, the law is less likely to lay those bad consequences at our doorstep. And, finally, if the only way to prevent some great harm would be by inflicting a lesser harm on ourself or on others, then too the law is inclined to absolve us of responsibility for that avoidable greater harm. It is as if the net value of the consequences were not crucial, at least where net benefit is procured by the intentional infliction of harm.

Not only are these distinctions drawn in some moral systems, but there are numerous places in the law where they are made regularly. Since in utilitarianism and consequentialism in general the ultimate questions must always be whether and to what extent the valued end-state (be it happiness or possession of true knowledge) obtains at a particular moment, it is inevitable that the judgments on the human agencies that may affect this end-state must be wholly instrumental: human actions can be judged only by their tendency to produce the relevant end-states.

Indeed it may well be that even the point and contents of normative judgments—whether legal or moral—are concerned not just with particular end-states of the world but also with how end-states are brought about. These kinds of substantive judgments take the form: there are some things one should just never do—kill an innocent person, falsely accuse a defendant in a criminal proceeding, engage in sex for pay. These are to be contrasted to judgments that this or that is an unfortunate, perhaps terrible, result that (other things being equal) one would want to avoid. The former are—very generally—judgments of right and wrong. It is wrong to do this or that, even if the balance of advantages favors it; a person is right to do some particular thing (help a friend, protect his client's interests) even though more good will come if he does not.

8. The author's point in the passage is primarily that
   (A) law and utilitarianism are not always compatible
   (B) utilitarianism is the operating philosophy of most people
   (C) consequentialism is the basis for legal reform
   (D) direct and indirect intentions lead to different end-states
   (E) judgments about human actions can be made only by the resulting end-states

9. Which of the following is NOT a feature of utilitarianism?
   (A) Results are considered important.
   (B) Consequences are considered important.
   (C) The valued end-state is considered important.
   (D) The means of achieving results are considered important.
   (E) The net value of consequences is considered important.

10. Which of the following are examples of judgments that may conflict with the utilitarian philosophy?
    I. It is legally acceptable to avoid a small harm to oneself, even if the result is a great harm to another.
    II. It is legally acceptable for bad consequences to flow from the exercise of an individual's right or privilege.
    III. It is legally acceptable for human actions that produce more harm than good to be punished.
    (A) I only
    (B) II only
    (C) III only
    (D) I and II only
    (E) I and III only

11. The point of the last paragraph is to
    (A) explain the differences between utilitarianism and consequentialism
    (B) contrast judgments of right and wrong with other types of judgments
    (C) discuss the role of intention in both law and words
    (D) distinguish between the results of actions and inaction
    (E) develop a rationale upon which to judge human actions

12. It can be inferred from the passage that the author is concerned with which of the following?
    I. the results of human action
    II. the means used to produce results
    III. the aspirations producing human action
    (A) I only
    (B) II only
    (C) III only
    (D) I and II only
    (E) I and III only

GO ON TO THE NEXT PAGE.

13. The passage suggests that utilitarianism
    (A) explains all legal and moral judgments
    (B) explains only judgments of right and wrong
    (C) explains some judgments in law and morals
    (D) explains judgments of direct and indirect intentions
    (E) explains judgments of right and privilege

14. The author's attitude about utilitarianism as a philosophy is best described as
    (A) somewhat critical
    (B) generally supportive
    (C) mostly accepting
    (D) totally convinced
    (E) nearly convinced

GO ON TO THE NEXT PAGE.

Although lawyers frequently reason in terms of models, they tend to reason, in Henry Steiner's terms, in *prose* models. I think there are some real advantages of the symbolic logic type of reasoning in the law.

(5) Although lawyers pride themselves on their method of argumentation and on being logicians, actually a lot of their arguments are very flabby. One way of teasing them is to say, "Well let's write this problem down in formal terms and abstract systems, let's agree on a
(10) rigorous abstract definition of this concept or behavioral principle and derive its logical implications." And then you allege that two situations they consider as absolutely distinct are really formally identical. That is what the model says. And if they are not formally identical, what
(15) really is the distinction? How has the model been misspecified? You ask them whether they may be making a distinction without a difference.

I think that the benefit of formal logic is that it sets out very nakedly, with all of its warts and pimples
(20) exposed, whatever difficulties there are in the argumentation. By using prose, a lot of that is swept under the carpet. Lawyers invoke the forces of "equity" and "fairness" on both sides of precisely the same set of facts. Two arguments produce equity and fairness
(25) "clearly or obviously," as they put it, while pointing in different directions.

Formal models can be built assuming that all people act in accord with the Kantian categorical imperative—or pick any principle you want. The
(30) desirable thing is to write it down, to define your terms as well as you can, say what you mean, and then argue about it.

Those of us who have been making models for a long time realize that all models are bad, but some models are
(35) worse than others. Part of the seduction of mathematical models is that they look much more rigorous than they are. They are always abstractions; there is always something wrong with them, something left out of consideration. But I think that this is no less true in the
(40) physical sciences, where the models are supposed to be very good. My chemist friends tell me that the fundamental laws of chemistry are contradicted every day in the laboratory. In the last analysis, I think the way one ought to look at this is as a method of
(45) argumentation. I feel that, for a lot of uses in the law, it will demonstrate to you problems you did not think existed, inconsistencies and incidences of illogic. Although we are never going to get all of the answers from formal models, we would be foolish not to take
(50) them for what they are worth.

And, if the Landes and Posner thesis stimulated this argument, that is precisely what "writing it down" is supposed to accomplish.

15. The passage can best be summarized as
    (A) an analysis of law as a social science
    (B) a comparison of formal and flabby models
    (C) an argument for the use of formal models by lawyers
    (D) a criticism of the method of argumentation of lawyers
    (E) a challenge to the value of models in the sciences

16. According to the passage, which of the following applies to both prose models and formal models?
    I. a method of argumentation
    II. appear to be more rigorous than they are
    III. demonstrably useful in the law
    (A) I only
    (B) II only
    (C) III only
    (D) I and II only
    (E) I and III only

17. The author contends that all of the following are benefits of using formal models EXCEPT
    (A) determining that an argument is making a distinction without a difference
    (B) locating something left out of consideration
    (C) demonstrating inconsistencies in an argument
    (D) setting out difficulties with the form of argumentation
    (E) assisting in the derivation of the logical implications of an argument

18. The author means that a "flabby" argument (line 7) is one that
    (A) is not internally contradicted
    (B) is presented in prose
    (C) is too abstract
    (D) is not logically rigorous
    (E) is formally identical to another

19. According to the passage, the primary purpose of "writing it down" is to
    (A) avoid contradictions in arguments
    (B) pick the principle for the model
    (C) provide the basis for argumentation
    (D) determine the worth of an argument
    (E) identify distinctions without differences

GO ON TO THE NEXT PAGE.

20. The passage indicates that models are used as all of the following EXCEPT
    (A) as a method of argumentation
    (B) as a source of answers to problems
    (C) as a form of reasoning used by lawyers
    (D) as a method to identify problems with logic
    (E) as a technique to ensure equity

21. Which of the following, if true, most weakens the author's argument about formal models?
    (A) Abstract symbols are the same as words.
    (B) Behavioral principles are hard to reduce to abstract symbols.
    (C) Models are regularly contradicted by facts.
    (D) Formal models are as illogical as prose models.
    (E) Prose models are routinely used by scientists.

22. Which of the following is implied by the author of the passage?
    (A) Symbols are inefficient expressions of behavioral principles.
    (B) A lawyer should not use an argument on both sides of a set of facts.
    (C) Prose is not a useful form of argumentation.
    (D) Omissions are a problem with formal models.
    (E) Mathematical inconsistencies are a problem with formal models.

GO ON TO THE NEXT PAGE.

Applying communications theory to legal discourse has foundered on a lack of clear conception of what the theory means in the context of law and can tell attorneys about the legal process. Communications theory is not a
(5) unified body of thought. It has three quite distinct branches. The first, "syntactics," is concerned with the logical arrangement, transmission, and receipt of signals or signs. The second is "semantics," which is concerned with the meaning of signals to people. The third is
(10) "pragmatics," which is the study of the impact of signal transmission on human behavior.

The key concepts of syntactics are "information," "redundancy," and "feedback," of which the first two are best discussed together. For the telegraphic engineer,
(15) information is the content of the signal that could not have been predicted by the receiver; it is a probability concept. The more probable the transmission of a given sign, the less information its actual transmission conveys. "Redundancy" is the opposite of information. It
(20) is the introduction of repetition or pattern into the message. If the telegrapher sends each message twice, his second sending is redundant and contains less information than his first.

The ideal transmission, then, in terms of pure
(25) "information," would contain no repetition and no pattern. The engineer finds it wise, however, to introduce redundancy at the cost of reducing the information content of the message, because otherwise any loss of information due to malfunctions in the
(30) transmission system would be undetectable and irremediable. It is only when we can predict, at least partially, what message we are going to receive that we can spot an erroneous transmission or substitution in the message and call for its correction. The ideal message,
(35) then, will contain the highest proportion of information and the lowest proportion of redundancy necessary to identify and correct errors in transmission.

Thus it will be seen that redundancy and information, in syntactic terms, are reciprocals of each other. But the
(40) situation is more complicated when we consider the semantic dimension of communication, for both information and redundancy convey meaning. And the line is even more blurred when we consider the pragmatics of communication. Weakland has said,
(45) "There is no redundancy," his point being, of course, that repetitions and patterns in messages do have significance to participants in the communication process. Such redundancies carry a freight of meaning, knowledge, and stimuli to the receiver and in this
(50) important sense are not redundant.

In the law, the strongest argument that an attorney can make is that the current case is "on all fours" with many previous cases, all of which were decided by repeatedly applying the same legal principle. So it is
(55) that, in terms of communications theory, the rules of legal discourse seem to require attorneys to suppress as much information and transmit as much redundancy as possible.

23. The passage can best be characterized as
 (A) an explanation of the principles of communications theory
 (B) a description of conflict between information and redundancy
 (C) an interpretation of syntactics applied to aspects of legal discourse
 (D) an exposition of redundancy
 (E) a review of the branches of thought in communications theory

24. According to the passage, which of the following describes an ideal transmission in terms of pure information?
  I. A, 2, #, +, §, ?, ©, ¶, %, $
  II. A, C, A, E, A, G, A, I, A, K
  III. 1, 2, 3, 4, 5, 6, 5, 4, 3, 2, 1
 (A) I only
 (B) II only
 (C) III only
 (D) II and III only
 (E) I, II, and III

25. According to the passage, which of the following is an unambiguous example of syntactic redundancy?
 (A) the transmission of the dash in dot-dot-dash
 (B) the transmission of the dash in dot-dot-dash when two dots are always followed by a dash
 (C) the transmission of a dot in dot-dot-dash
 (D) the transmission of a dot when two dashes are never followed by a dot
 (E) the transmission of the dash in dot-dot-dash when two dots are never followed by a dash

26. In the context of the passage, "on all fours" (line 52) most likely refers to
 (A) a type of information in terms of communications theory
 (B) a legal principle that is applied to many different cases
 (C) the most recent example in a series of cases
 (D) a type of argument lawyers use to distinguish one case from another
 (E) a case that is exactly the same as previous cases

GO ON TO THE NEXT PAGE.

27. According to the passage, which of the following is NOT true?
    I. Redundancy in a message reduces the information transmitted.
    II. Information in a message can be predicted by a telegraphic engineer.
    III. Meaning in a message is transmitted by both redundancy and information.
    (A) I only
    (B) II only
    (C) III only
    (D) I and III only
    (E) I, II, and III

28. Which of the following best reflects the author's view about the application of communications theory to legal discourse?
    (A) Syntactics tells lawyers very little about the legal process.
    (B) Redundancy accounts for the difference between strong and weak legal arguments.
    (C) Engineering, not law, has been the profession making use of communications theory.
    (D) Communications theory is too difficult for lawyers to understand clearly.
    (E) Legal discourse is dominated by the attempt to present pure information.

END OF SECTION IV

SECTION V
Time—35 minutes
24 Questions

Directions: Evaluate the reasoning contained in the brief statements, and select the best answer. Do not make implausible, superfluous, or incompatible assumptions. Select the best answer to each question, and mark the corresponding space on the answer sheet.

1. There are no great writers in Largo because freedom of expression does not exist there.
   The conclusion above depends upon which of the following assumptions?
   I. In the absence of freedom of expression, great writers do not develop.
   II. If there is freedom of expression, there will be many great writers.
   III. Where there is no freedom of expression, great writers turn to politics.
   (A) I only
   (B) III only
   (C) I and II only
   (D) I and III only
   (E) I, II, and III

2. Archaeologists have determined that the bison was the primary source of meat for the cave-dwellers, but their caves also contain the bones of birds, snakes, and fish, which indicates that they also liked to eat these animals.
   Which of the following, if true, would weaken the conclusion reached in the statement above?
   I. Birds, snakes, and fish were used by cave-dwellers in religious ceremonies.
   II. Cave-dwellers were not always able to eat what they liked.
   III. Birds rather than cave-dwellers may have brought snakes and fish to the caves to eat.
   (A) I only
   (B) II only
   (C) I and III only
   (D) II and III only
   (E) I, II, and III

3. Some psychologists believe that humans, like porpoises, are, by nature, benevolent creatures. These psychologists assume that human nature is essentially disposed to benevolent conduct. To account for social evils, psychologists have to blame institutions that corrupt the native disposition of humans.
   The psychologists' argument described above would be most strengthened if it were to explain how
   (A) a way of life consistent with benevolent ideals is possible in the modern world
   (B) people can be persuaded to abandon technology, urbanization, and mass production
   (C) benevolent conduct can result from humans living in accordance with their natural dispositions
   (D) benevolent dispositions give rise to evil institutions
   (E) corrupt institutions can be eliminated or reformed

4. Whenever the sky is cloudy and rain is falling, Bob wears his slicker. Whenever the sky is cloudy and rain is not falling, Bob ties his slicker around his waist. Sometimes rain falls when the sky is not cloudy.
   If the statements above are true, and it is true that Bob is not wearing his slicker, which of the following must also be true?
   (A) Bob has tied his slicker around his waist.
   (B) The sky is not overcast.
   (C) The sky is not cloudy, and rain is not falling.
   (D) The sky is cloudy, and/or rain is not falling.
   (E) The sky is not cloudy, and/or rain is not falling.

5. Only excellent musicians can be professors at Juilliard. No insensitive people are great lovers of poetry. No one who is not sensitive can be a lover. There are no excellent musicians who are not great lovers of poetry. Therefore, all Juilliard professors are lovers.
   Which of the following inferences leading to the conclusion above is NOT valid?
   (A) All Juilliard professors are excellent musicians.
   (B) Juilliard professors are sensitive people.
   (C) Sensitive people are lovers.
   (D) Great lovers of poetry are sensitive people.
   (E) Excellent musicians are great lovers of poetry.

6. Since plaznium evaporates in air, and this cube did not evaporate when it was exposed to air, it is not plaznium.
   Which of the following is most like the argument above?
   (A) Since no cats have hooves, and Fifi is a cat, Fifi does not have hooves.
   (B) Since owls feed only at night, the bird feeding in daylight is not an owl.
   (C) Since this box is made of brass, and boxes not made of brass are better than brass boxes, this brass box is not as good as a box not made of brass.
   (D) Since chicks are never furry, and this animal is not furry, it is not a chick.
   (E) Since every Canarbik dog is black or white, and Fido is a Canarbik, Fido cannot be gray.

GO ON TO THE NEXT PAGE.

7. Some ocean-liner captains are alcoholics. Ocean-liner captains who are alcoholics are dangerous. Every captain of an ocean liner is responsible for the care of the passengers.
   The above leads to which of the following conclusions?
   (A) All ocean-liner passengers are in the care of an alcoholic.
   (B) Some ocean-liner passengers are dangerous when they drink.
   (C) Some ocean-liner passengers are in the care of a dangerous person.
   (D) All ocean-liner captains are dangerous when they drink.
   (E) Some ocean-liner captains are dangerous when they drink.

8. Because coal is a nonrenewable resource, states that produce coal will experience problems that will never be faced by lumber-producing states.
   Which of the following, if true, most weakens this argument?
   (A) The resources required to log forests cannot be replenished.
   (B) States with economies dominated by coal are trying to develop forest products.
   (C) Lumber-producing states must secure much of the food they require from other states.
   (D) Renewable resources are an insignificant part of the economies of coal-producing states.
   (E) Coal-producing states depend on money from coal sales to buy lumber.

9. A criminal-justice study has found that 82 percent of people presented with eyewitness testimony of a crime were willing to convict the accused. However, only 58 percent of the same people were willing to convict the accused when presented with lie-detector, fingerprint, and handwriting evidence from experts.
   Which of the following conclusions is most reasonably supported by the above?
   (A) Most crimes do not involve eyewitness and expert testimony.
   (B) An accused can only be convicted by evidence that eliminates all reasonable doubt.
   (C) Most people do not understand expert evidence.
   (D) Prosecutors can ensure conviction by presenting both eyewitness and expert testimony.
   (E) Jurors think eyewitness testimony leaves less room for doubt than does expert testimony.

10. By 1995 the number of 18-year-olds will be dramatically lower than it was in 1961, when population growth in the United States reached its highest point. This decline in the number of potential college students will result in large enrollment decreases at colleges in the United States.
    If true, which of the following would most weaken the conclusion of the above argument?
    (A) Colleges prospered in the 1950s with lower enrollments than there are today.
    (B) By 1995 there will be more colleges than there are today.
    (C) Colleges will compete more aggressively for students when the number of 18-year-olds declines sharply.
    (D) In the future, more older students will enter college than ever before.
    (E) College enrollments in the 1960s were inflated by students avoiding the draft.

11. The contemporary film is a form of mass entertainment rather than an important art form. It fascinates, amuses, and distracts but fails to elevate the human spirit and deepen awareness. Film can be ignored if one is looking for art rather than escape.
    Which of the following is NOT implied by the above?
    I. In the past, film was an important art form.
    II. Art is a form of escape.
    III. When looking for art, film can be ignored.
    (A) I only
    (B) II only
    (C) III only
    (D) I and II only
    (E) I and III only

GO ON TO THE NEXT PAGE.

Questions 12-13

Critics who claim that the sale of U.S. military equipment to other countries is destabilizing and leads to war take a narrow view of history. War occurs when one country gains a military advantage over another. By selling arms, the United States can ensure that the military balance among countries is maintained and war avoided.

12. The above argument depends on which of the following assumptions?
    (A) Arms sales by the United States do not lead to wars between countries.
    (B) Critics do not understand military history.
    (C) Countries can accurately determine one another's military strength.
    (D) Arms imbalances stimulate conflict between countries.
    (E) Critics misunderstand the principle of military balance between countries.

13. Which of the following, if true, most weakens the above argument?
    (A) Military equipment is usually used to intimidate rather than to actually conduct war.
    (B) A country's military strength depends on military equipment rather than on the expertise of military commanders.
    (C) The sale and delivery of military equipment is usually known only by the two countries involved.
    (D) The military advantages of all countries are well-known by the United States.
    (E) Military equipment sold by the United States to other countries is less sophisticated than the equipment it produces for itself.

14. A study by the motor vehicle bureau shows that only 3 percent of all cars fail the annual safety inspection because of defective lights. Consequently, the bureau has decided to discontinue inspecting lights, because the benefit is not worth the expense involved.

    Which of the following, if true, is the greatest weakness in the decision of the bureau?
    (A) Studies in other states show that a larger percentage of cars have defective lights.
    (B) Cars with defective lights often have safety problems that are not part of the inspection.
    (C) Lights are maintained in good working order because of the inspection requirement.
    (D) Most cars fail inspection for more than one defect.
    (E) Inspecting for defective lights costs less than 2 percent of the annual budget of the motor vehicle bureau.

Questions 15-16

The public's right to know is an inadequate justification for exposing people's private lives to public scrutiny. Only when the public welfare is involved does the public have a right to know information about a person's private life.

15. Which of the following, if true, most weakens the position taken in the above argument?
    (A) The public seldom knows which activities promote its welfare.
    (B) The public seldom wants much of the information exposed to it.
    (C) It is seldom possible to discover the most intimate details of someone's personal life.
    (D) The public seldom understands the implications of the information exposed to it.
    (E) It is seldom possible to determine which information involves the public welfare.

16. Which of the following best expresses the underlying point of the above argument?
    (A) Public welfare is the greatest good.
    (B) A justification is not a reason.
    (C) Personal privacy is an important right.
    (D) The common good is an insufficient justification.
    (E) Public rights supersede individual privacy.

17. A study shows that there is a strong positive relationship between voting and political involvement.
    Which of the following can be inferred from this finding?
    I. Political involvement and voting appear to be interrelated.
    II. People who are not involved in politics are less likely to vote than those who are involved.
    III. After people become involved in politics, they vote more frequently than before.
    (A) I only
    (B) I and III only
    (C) I and II only
    (D) II and III only
    (E) I, II, and III

GO ON TO THE NEXT PAGE.

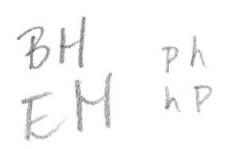

Questions 18-19

A survey of students concludes that some students prefer physics to history; all students prefer history to geometry; no students prefer history to economics; and all students prefer biology to history.

18. Based on the survey results, which of the following must represent students' preference?
    (A) Some students prefer geometry to physics.
    (B) Some students prefer physics to geometry.
    (C) Some students prefer biology to economics.
    (D) Some students prefer geometry to economics.
    (E) Some students prefer physics to economics.

19. Based on the survey results, which of the following CANNOT represent students' preference?
    (A) Some students prefer geometry to physics.
    (B) Some students prefer physics to geometry.
    (C) Some students prefer biology to economics.
    (D) Some students prefer economics to biology.
    (E) Some students prefer physics to economics.

20. Voters who complain about a trusted politician's betrayal remind me of the tale of the man who nursed a starving snake back to health. Afterward the snake bit the man, who then complained about the snake's ingratitude. The snake responded to the complaint by saying, "You knew I was a snake when you saved me."

    Which of the following can be derived from the above?
    (A) Don't cut off your nose to spite your face.
    (B) Things are not always what they seem.
    (C) Chickens always come home to roost.
    (D) Nature cannot be changed.
    (E) Take the bitter with the sweet.

21. Representatives of daily producers say that government subsidies are needed to ensure that milk processors produce sufficient amounts for children. If there are no milk price subsidies, processors will attempt to meet the demand for cheese and butter before producing milk.

    Which of the following can be inferred from the above argument?
    (A) The demand for milk is volatile, often leading to underproduction and shortage.
    (B) Processors have produced sufficient milk in the past because they understood the needs of hungry children.
    (C) Cheese and butter produce greater profits for processors than does milk.
    (D) Representatives of dairies have a lobby that is powerful enough to ensure the passage of favorable subsidies.
    (E) Dairy representatives are trying to avoid a surplus of cheese and butter.

22. The sculpture of the woman was carved during the early Greek period. The shape of the fingers, the style of hair, and the design of her sandals indicate the early period. The tilt of the chin and the closed eyes are frequently found in early Greek sculpture.

    Which of the following is an assumption upon which this argument is based?
    (A) The period of a work of art can be established with certainty.
    (B) Certain attributes of works of art are typical of specific periods.
    (C) Tilted chins and closed eyes always appear together in Greek sculpture.
    (D) Sculptures of women first appeared in the early Greek period.
    (E) Closed eyes are characteristics of early art.

23. The village is overrun by poisonous snakes. The mayor argues that paying a $10 bounty for each dead snake turned in by a villager will result in ridding the village of snakes.

    Which of the following does NOT weaken the mayor's argument?
    (A) The bounty ensures that breeding the snakes is in the economic interest of the villagers.
    (B) Village taxes will triple if the mayor's proposal is implemented.
    (C) The villagers do not trust the mayor.
    (D) The snakes control the rat population, so the villagers will not kill the snakes.
    (E) A drug company pays villagers $15 for each live snake delivered to it.

24. Spring Lake does not appear to be good for sailing. I have gone to the lake many times this year, and each time the water was too rough for sailing.

    Which of the following most closely parallels the above argument?
    (A) It appears that we will move to Spring Lake this year. The city is simply too rough for safe living.
    (B) Economy-grade gasoline apparently does not prevent my car from running rough. It appears that a good grade of fuel is required.
    (C) It appears that the cost of housing at Spring Lake is prohibitive. I looked at a number of houses last month, and they cost much more than I could afford.
    (D) I am withdrawing from Spring Lake College. Two months at school was sufficient to prove that college was too rough for me.
    (E) It appears that I will never play the clarinet. I began lessons many times, but each time I quit.

END OF SECTION V

Answers to Pretests and LSAT Simulation

Pretest 6-1 Answer Key

Relationships		Arguments		Passages	
Question	Answer	Question	Answer	Question	Answer
1.	B	1.	B	1.	A
2.	D	2.	B	2.	B
3.	E	3.	B	3.	E
4.	B	4.	D	4.	B
5.	A	5.	C	5.	E
6.	C	6.	E	6.	B
		7.	A	7.	A

Relationships Pretest Answer Key

Pretest 10-1		Pretest 10-2		Pretest 10-3	
Question	Answer	Question	Answer	Question	Answer
1.	A	1.	A	1.	E
2.	C	2.	A	2.	E
3.	A	3.	D	3.	E
4.	D	4.	A	4.	A
5.	B	5.	E	5.	C
6.	E	6.	C	6.	E

Pretest 10-4		Pretest 10-5		Pretest 10-6	
Question	Answer	Question	Answer	Question	Answer
1.	E	1.	D	1.	B
2.	E	2.	E	2.	E
3.	D	3.	B	3.	C
4.	B	4.	C	4.	C
5.	C	5.	E	5.	A
6.	D	6.	E	6.	B

Arguments Pretest Answer Key

Pretest 13-1
Question	Answer
1.	B
2.	A
3.	B
4.	C
5.	C
6.	B

Pretest 13-2
Question	Answer
1.	D
2.	C
3.	A
4.	D
5.	B
6.	C

Pretest 13-3
Question	Answer
1.	B
2.	E
3.	A
4.	E
5.	D
6.	D

Pretest 13-4
Question	Answer
1.	E
2.	C
3.	D
4.	E
5.	A
6.	D

Pretest 13-5
Question	Answer
1.	B
2.	E
3.	C
4.	A
5.	C
6.	D

Pretest 13-6
Question	Answer
1.	C
2.	D
3.	A
4.	A
5.	C
6.	D

Passages Pretest Answer Key

Pretest 15-1
Question	Answer
1.	C
2.	D
3.	A
4.	D
5.	A
6.	C
7.	C

Pretest 15-2
Question	Answer
1.	D
2.	C
3.	E
4.	B
5.	B
6.	D
7.	C

Pretest 15-3
Question	Answer
1.	D
2.	B
3.	D
4.	A
5.	B
6.	E
7.	E

Pretest 15-4
Question	Answer
1.	A
2.	C
3.	E
4.	D
5.	A
6.	A
7.	C

Pretest 15-5
Question	Answer
1.	E
2.	E
3.	B
4.	D
5.	E
6.	A
7.	E

Pretest 15-6
Question	Answer
1.	E
2.	A
3.	C
4.	B
5.	C
6.	B
7.	A

LSAT Simulation Answer Key

Section I		Section II		Section III		Section IV		Section V	
Question	Answer	Question	Answer	Question	Answer	Question	Answer	Question	Answer
1.	C	1.	D	1.	A	1.	C	1.	A
2.	E	2.	B	2.	D	2.	B	2.	C
3.	D	3.	C	3.	A	3.	D	3.	B
4.	D	4.	B	4.	B	4.	B	4.	C
5.	C	5.	C	5.	A	5.	A	5.	C
6.	E	6.	C	6.	A	6.	C	6.	B
7.	D	7.	C	7.	A	7.	D	7.	C
8.	E	8.	C	8.	C	8.	E	8.	A
9.	A	9.	A	9.	D	9.	E	9.	E
10.	B	10.	A	10.	A	10.	D	10.	D
11.	D	11.	E	11.	B	11.	B	11.	D
12.	B	12.	E	12.	A	12.	D	12.	C
13.	E	13.	B	13.	C	13.	C	13.	C
14.	C	14.	C	14.	C	14.	A	14.	C
15.	B	15.	A	15.	C	15.	C	15.	E
16.	C	16.	C	16.	E	16.	E	16.	C
17.	A	17.	C	17.	E	17.	B	17.	E
18.	B	18.	A	18.	C	18.	D	18.	B
19.	A	19.	A	19.	A	19.	C	19.	A
20.	B	20.	C	20.	B	20.	E	20.	D
21.	A	21.	B	21.	B	21.	D	21.	C
22.	D	22.	C	22.	E	22.	D	22.	B
23.	D	23.	D	23.	B	23.	C	23.	C
24.	A	24.	B	24.	E	24.	A	24.	C
						25.	B		
						26.	E		
						27.	D		
						28.	B		

About the Author

Thomas O. White developed his special knowledge of the LSAT from the inside. After more than a decade on the faculty of the University of Pittsburgh, where he was professor of law and associate dean of the School of Law, he joined Educational Testing Service, the noted testing organization. As vice president, he was responsible for the Multistate Bar Examination and the Law School Admission Test, which was at that time administered by ETS. When U.S. law schools established Law School Admission Services to administer the LSAT and provide other evaluation and information services, White was its founding president. During his tenure there, he also worked with the University of Cambridge Examinations Syndicate, the leading testing organization in the British Commonwealth.

MORE OUTSTANDING TITLES FROM PETERSON'S

FULL DISCLOSURE
Do You *Really* Want to Be a Lawyer?

The Young Lawyers Division of the American Bar Association

Compiled by Susan J. Bell

This candid and entertaining book gives would-be lawyers an authoritative inside account of what really goes on in law school and law practice. The result is a thought-provoking compendium of everything today's lawyers wish they had known before entering law school.

Full Disclosure shares the wisdom and experience of some two dozen top legal professionals—addressing such issues as:

- A Talent for Torts: Is Law for You?
- The Tunnel at the End of the Light: Taking the Bar Exam
- Eve, Esq.: Women in Law
- I Have a Dream: Minorities in the Profession

$11.95 paperback

PETERSON'S GUIDE TO PROGRAMS IN BUSINESS, EDUCATION, HEALTH, AND LAW

If you are considering a career in law, this book is *the* resource for choosing the *right* program. It provides comprehensive information on:

- Programs and degrees offered
- Requirements for entrance
- Tuition, fees, and financial aid
- Accreditation of schools

You won't want to conduct your law school search without the help of this invaluable guide.

$21.95 paperback

PARALEGAL
An Insider's Guide to the Fastest-Growing Occupation of the 1990s

Barbara Bernardo

Career seekers and career changers alike will want to explore the many opportunities this burgeoning profession offers. *Paralegal* gives the first insider's look at what it's like to be a paralegal, as well as advice on how to enter the profession and succeed in it. *Paralegal* touches all the key issues you will want to know about:

- The what, where, and how of paralegal work
- Finding a job as a paralegal
- Earning potential and opportunities for advancement

The author: Having worked as a paralegal and legal administrator, Barbara Bernardo currently heads her own paralegal services company.

$10.95 paperback

Look for these and other Peterson's titles in your local bookstore